"Eccentric and [...]   Review

"The vivid food writing captivates. . . . The luxuriant descriptions of family meals, and the obvious joy Machado takes in recounting them, make this memoir a tasty read."   —*Publishers Weekly*

"For non-Cubans, Machado's memoir will bring to life a world lost in time and offer recipes that are authentic, easy to follow and delicious. For Cuban Americans, it is too close to the bone to be read without emotion or strong opinion."   —*The Miami Herald*

"Captivating."   —*Seattle Post-Intelligencer*

"As I have regrettably never traveled to my father's birthplace, Eduardo's vivid memories and specific writer's eye details made his life come alive for me. Maybe it's genetic. Because I share his love of family and the preparation of their meals that is so important in a Cuban household."
                              — Lucie Arnaz

"Eduardo Machado's and Michael Domitrovich's touching, evocative memoir not only makes the mouth water with its deliciously descriptive accounts of Cuban cuisine, but fills the tear ducts with longing for a culture and a people denied us for half a century by the regretful policies of the U.S. government."   —Ed Harris and Amy Madigan

"Extraordinary, moving, a great read whether you come from Cuba or Greece."   —Olympia Dukakis

"[A] feast for the senses and the soul. We bask in the earthly paradise of a boy's Cuban childhood, and when he is sent to the U.S. at age eight, we suffer. From then on we're in thrall to the drama (painful, funny, bitter, sweet) of his search for a new life. What better metaphor than food? We all crave recipes for survival. We hunt down the ingredients that will nourish our hopes and memories. Machado has filled his book with richly drawn characters. The richest of them all may be that neighbor whose complexities we have refused to accept or understand for so long: Cuba."   —Margo Jefferson, critic and Pulitzer Prize winner

"*Tastes like Cuba* is a wonderful multilayered addition to the ongoing and ever-expanding tapestry of exile history. . . . It also has a lot to say about the artistic life and, in particular, what it is like to be a Latino playwright in this country. That alone makes the book unique and worthy of a wide readership."
—Oscar Hijuelos

CONNIE RAMIREZ

Eduardo Machado was born in Cuba in 1953 and came to the United States on the Peter Pan flights in 1961. In a career spanning more than twenty-five years, Machado has captivated audiences with over forty plays, including *The Cook, Havana Is Waiting,* and *The Floating Island Plays*. He has been produced off-Broadway and at regional theaters in the United States, Europe, and Latin America. For sixteen years he taught in Columbia University's Graduate Playwriting Program, serving as head of the program for the last ten. He is the visiting arts professor in the Goldberg Department of Dramatic Writing at New York University and the artistic director of INTAR, a Latino theater in New York that has been producing plays for nearly four decades.

Michael Domitrovich was born and raised in a family of restaurateurs and has worked with food all his life. As a playwright his work has been produced off-Broadway and off-off-Broadway. His play *Artfuckers* premiered to sold-out houses in 2007 and opened off-Broadway in early 2008. He was commissioned to write the book of a musical about the record industry called *Breach,* with music by David Nehls (*The Great American Trailer Park Musical*), to open in 2008. He is currently writing a play about young New York City chefs, as well as a novel (with recipes) about the waitstaff at a seasonal restaurant on Martha's Vineyard. He holds a BFA in Cinema Studies from NYU. Both authors live in Manhattan.

Tastes Like Cuba

AN EXILE'S HUNGER FOR HOME

Eduardo Machado

and

Michael Domitrovich

GOTHAM BOOKS

GOTHAM BOOKS
Published by Penguin Group (USA) Inc.
375 Hudson Street, New York, New York 10014, U.S.A.

Penguin Group (Canada), 90 Eglinton Avenue East, Suite 700, Toronto, Ontario M4P 2Y3, Canada (a division of Pearson Penguin Canada Inc.); Penguin Books Ltd, 80 Strand, London WC2R 0RL, England; Penguin Ireland, 25 St Stephen's Green, Dublin 2, Ireland (a division of Penguin Books Ltd); Penguin Group (Australia), 250 Camberwell Road, Camberwell, Victoria 3124, Australia (a division of Pearson Australia Group Pty Ltd); Penguin Books India Pvt Ltd, 11 Community Centre, Panchsheel Park, New Delhi – 110 017, India; Penguin Group (NZ), 67 Apollo Drive, Rosedale, North Shore 0632, New Zealand (a division of Pearson New Zealand Ltd); Penguin Books (South Africa) (Pty) Ltd, 24 Sturdee Avenue, Rosebank, Johannesburg 2196, South Africa

Penguin Books Ltd, Registered Offices: 80 Strand, London WC2R 0RL, England

Published by Gotham Books, a member of Penguin Group (USA) Inc.

Previously published as a Gotham Books hardcover edition

First trade paperback printing, October 2008

1   3   5   7   9   10   8   6   4   2

Gotham Books and the skyscraper logo are trademarks of Penguin Group (USA) Inc.

Copyright © 2007 by Eduardo Machado and Michael Domitrovich
All rights reserved

Photograph credits appear on page 358.

The Library of Congress has catalogued the hardcover edition of this book as follows:

Machado, Eduardo, 1953–
Tastes like Cuba: an exile's hunger for home / Eduardo Machado, Michael Domitrovich.
p.   cm.
ISBN 978-1-592-40321-9 (hardcover)   ISBN 978-1-592-40405-6 (paperback)
1. Cookery, Cuban.   2. Food habits—Cuba.   3. Cuba—Social life and customs.   4. Machado,
Eduardo, 1953–   I. Domitrovich, Michael.   II. Title.
TX716.C8M335 2007
641.597291—dc22   2007032864

Printed in the United States of America
Set in Perpetua • Designed by Elke Sigal

While the author has made every effort to provide accurate telephone numbers and Internet addresses at the time of publication, neither the publisher nor the author assumes any responsibility for errors, or for changes that occur after publication. Further, the publisher does not have any control over and does not assume any responsibility for author or third-party Web sites or their content.

For my little brother, Othin

Contents

Tastes Like Cuba

My parents, Gilda and Othon, on their honeymoon in Key West, 1952

One

Cojimar, 1958

I awoke to the smell of boiling milk. Not 1% or 2% or soy milk or rice milk. This milk had never touched a cardboard box. It had been freshly drawn, hours before, delivered at dawn from my grandmother's small farm just outside town. Every morning in our house was scented with the aroma of raw milk boiling with a little bit of salt.

If it were in my apartment now it would be contraband, a smuggled delicacy, but then, the foamy, silky, still-warm sweetness was a familiar part of every day. Once boiled, the cream would be ladled out and pressed into butter by our cook, Conchita, but at this early hour there was another priority. My grandmother Concepcion, along with Conchita, would be responsible for bringing life to a houseful of people, preparing the *café con leche* for at least fourteen.

It was the summer of 1958, and the Revolution was raging on. There was fighting in the Sierra Maestra and the surrounding provinces, far enough from our home for us to feel safe. But every night when Concepcion sat in the back of the house listening to the pirate radio frequency that Fidel Castro broadcast from, our sense of urgency and danger grew. There was an occasional bomb in Havana, and when I went to the city to go shopping with my mother, I would scan the storefronts and alleyways, making note of suspicious characters who could be the next martyrs for our cause. I sometimes feared that my father would go to work one morning and never return.

A quiet tension resulted. We were protected by the house, and we felt safe in our own little world. Still, I knew something was going on, but only because I listened. To the deliverymen who brought bright yellow bananas and pineapples. To the baker from town with his fresh bread and pastries. To the fishermen selling their early catches. And most of all to my grandmother Concepcion, whom we called Cuca, sharing the highlights of last night's broadcast with Conchita as the milk bubbled away.

"He said last night that he would stop the gambling casinos. Wouldn't that be something?" Cuca would say.

"Get rid of all those mobsters. That's why there's so much violence," whispered Conchita.

"Let's pray he gets here soon."

Cuca was always the first one up. She took pride in her café, preparing it how everyone liked it, but always starting with the strong dark base of freshly brewed Cuban coffee. With all the fuss over the machinery we use to make the so-called perfect brew today, I wonder why we don't just keep it simple. Cuca did without automatic drips, heatproof presses, or grind 'n brew options. Instead she relied on her minimalist, functional gadget, her *teta*, nothing but a piece of cloth stitched around a metal hoop with a wooden handle. She would fill the *teta* with a few spoonfuls of coffee, then pour recently boiled water over the top. The freshness of the coffee was important, so it was best when served immediately, but Cuca had to contend with fourteen people waking at different times. She'd brew large batches of coffee to make sure there was enough, and if it cooled even slightly she'd just freshen it up by adding piping hot milk to each cup.

It was the milk boiling, the coffee brewing, and the quiet whispers that woke me up every morning. I would leave my room, go down the hall and into the kitchen to sit at an expansive counter with twelve stools. My grandmother poured my coffee, topped it off with boiled milk, and added one, two, three teaspoons of Cuban sugar. Somehow she knew I was coming before I ever arrived, and timed it so that as I took my first sip of café, she would pop a piece of perfectly crisp, browned toast out of the toaster. She'd smear it with rich golden butter, then hand it to me on a little plate.

Café con leche with buttered toast is a true delicacy. It is so simple yet provides so much joy. Cuban bread has a thin crust, and though it may resemble a baguette, it gives sooner to an airy inside. Its melting richness owes to its key ingredient: lard, which it is most often made with. When you dunk the toast, the bread takes on a spongy texture, accentuating the nuttiness of fine coffee. The milk is warming, soothing, and nutritive, the coffee gently invigorating. To feel truly decadent one only needs to admire the droplets of shiny butter swimming on the surface of the cup.

I was only five years old, but I knew one thing for sure. All I had to do was dunk the bread into the cup. Chew, sip, and heaven in the morning was possible.

The rest of the house would take longer to wake up. One by one or in pairs, the kitchen would be visited by my aunts and uncles. They would emerge from their rooms, fully made up, perfumed and pomaded in silk pajamas or negligees with lace cutouts. My father and his brothers Fernando and Oscar would most often collect their café and return to their rooms with cups for their wives. While our parents woke up in private, my cousins Lupe, Maria Elena, Fernandito, and Oscarito sat with me in the kitchen. Sometimes our single uncles Pipo and Benito would join us, or they would meet up with their sister Maria in the French-style rose garden adjoining the house.

You might think living with so many people would be chaotic, but if anything it was more like a perfectly planned and executed garden party, every morning, day after day. Sometimes I wonder why I tend toward living casually as an adult: I am barefoot whenever possible and refuse to touch an iron. I used to think it was a California thing—absorbed from twenty years of West Coast living—but more and more it seems like a form of rebellion against a childhood where formality was always present, even at eight in the morning.

Still, beneath all the composure lay a tumult of conflict. Four different families living under one roof makes for a dangerous cocktail of competition and emotion. My father's sisters-in-law, who had been poor growing up in Guanabacoa, now had to vie for Cuca and Fernando's attention and money. They did their best to remain poised while scraping and scrambling for a compliment or a handout from the heads of the family, but it's not easy to hide desperation. My mother always felt superior, proud that neither she nor her son would have to beg for anything from her husband's parents. We had her parents, Oscar and Manuela, and they were always just a few steps away.

Manuela and me at
her house, Cojimar, 1953

Before breakfast was over, Cuca would already be peeling root vegetables. By eleven A.M. at the latest, you could hear the sound of her knife chopping up the *malanga*, *yuca*, and pumpkin for a staple of her kitchen, Newspaper Soup. The preparation of this tropical vegetable potage ushered in a different set of sounds, another group of familiar smells that could only mean one thing: lunch.

In my family, you didn't rush in to or out of anything having to do with food. Especially when it was lunch. Our whole family was on a different schedule, and the midday meal was our opportunity to be together. We'd have our leisurely morning, then as the men went off to work and we children went to school, the women went and did what they did— start preparing lunch. Lunch was really a three-hour break during the hottest part of the day. If we had been served a plate of rice and nothing else, I'm sure we would have taken just as much time to enjoy the break. But the thing I liked the most about lunch was that it was the meal when the most choices were available. What to eat depended first on where it would be eaten. Would I dine at the table of my puritanical grandmother or down the hall with her wild-eyed husband? Perhaps

I'd take the less dramatic option and cross the street to the home of my other grandparents.

In my grandparents' house on my father's side there was a civil war of culinary ideology. The house was large enough to have two dining rooms, and each one was presided over by a different grandparent. Though they had been married for thirty years, Cuca's and Fernando's personal tastes could not have been further apart. The distance between their separate dining rooms enforced this idea, as did the fact that neither one dined in the other's space.

The middle dining room was Cuca's domain. To understand her particular taste, you must understand something else about her. She was thin, even by today's standards. And then, in 1958, in comparison to the other voluptuous women of Havana, she was like Twiggy. On a diet. And what about this Newspaper Soup? The story goes that it was from a recipe printed in the newspaper in the 1930s. When Cuca ripped the recipe from the paper, she missed the topmost portion that contained the actual name of the soup. So, adapting accordingly, the soup was christened.

And what a soup it was. I am sure that if a health guru tasted it today it would quickly be declared the newest fountain of youth. Rich in fiber and nutrients, Newspaper Soup walked the line between the delectable and the medicinal, making me dread it and crave it all at once. The flavors of the roots were both blended and distinct. The waxy starch of *malanga*, the nutty thickness of *yuca*, and the sweetness and color of pumpkin all combined to produce a complex heartiness, not unlike the best chicken stocks or veal broths. What was so great about the soup, though, was its adaptability. There was always a pot bubbling away, which meant that an array of garnishes to accompany were not far off. Chopped ham, hard-boiled eggs, and crispy croutons added accents of texture and overtones of saltiness that further emphasized the strength and depth of the thick soup.

Beyond this nutritive starter, the other familiar presence at Cuca's lunch table was, of course, beans and rice. But Cuca's beans were different. I guess she had a thing about pureeing because her bean dish was more the texture of the Newspaper Soup, thick enough to coat a spoon, without a bean in sight. The dish was hearty but not heavy, with a mild smokiness and sweetness. Cuca's smooth puree, served over bowls of flaky white rice, managed to elevate a staple to a culinary treasure.

The rest of the menu wouldn't be health conscious by today's standards. Most of it was fried. *Bistec Empanizado*, or breaded steaks, was a favorite of mine. Like the Cuban version of Veal Milanese, it is made from the top round or *palomilla* portion of the cow. The steaks are portioned and pounded thin, dipped in egg and crushed Cuban crackers, or *galletas*, then fried in lard or oil. Cuca also liked to use this method when preparing fish.

No matter the protein Cuca made, it was always served with rice, pureed beans, Newspaper Soup, and sweet plantains. And that was it. Every day. The same thing. If we were very lucky, we might get a little sliced avocado with lime or (heaven be praised) homemade *croquetas* with chicken or ham.

How did Cuca stay so thin? For her, everything was portioned out in relation to the size of the dish. While the rest of us got big plates with hearty servings, Cuca herself dined only on demitasse plates. One ounce of steak, one piece of banana, a tablespoon of rice, and a teaspoon of beans. Every day, with lots of coffee and boiled milk. Looking back, I can see that maybe she was just ahead of her time. How many ladies who lunch finish everything on their plates? Cuca simply took what she needed, although I'm sure she could have done with a little more. Still, she practiced this self-restraint every time, even though she wasn't all willpower. In fact, Cuca had a dark little secret, one that is shared by well-heeled women the world over: She was saving herself. For dessert.

It is the sweetness that I remember when I dream of Cuca's table. More than the Newspaper Soup. More than the *Bistec Empanizado*. Meringues float before my eyes, baked gently in the oven until dry and crisp. They were brown, which I marveled at, not white like the ones at the bakery in front of the convent where my mother went to school. Those were sacred meringues, made by nuns, pure and clean. Cuca's meringues had something of the earth in them, but the simple sweetness was still the same. Cuban sugar and fluffy egg whites, holding the shape she gave them, only to dissolve on my tongue and become more a part of me than I ever thought possible. Truly, that is the sweetness I remember.

Sweet was never the word to come to mind when talking about my grandfather. Fernando was stubborn, stylish, or witty, maybe, but nothing so helpless as sweet. Lunch with him was never subtle, and compared to Newspaper Soup, his staples would have turned any saint to sinning. The spread in his kitchen, and on plates in his dining room, was more like a nightclub than a convent. Exotic imports from Spain like *Serrano* ham, *manchego* cheese, and big juicy olives were piled lasciviously on top of one another. There was always cigar smoke, wine, and Pedro Varga or Nat King Cole on the record player. It was never guaranteed that he would actually cook and serve lunch in his dining room. Sometimes he would eat whatever Conchita made him—hearty Eastern European fare like Chicken Kiev or Beef Stroganoff—but never, ever would he eat my grandmother's cooking. If he were to write a review of the food in Cuca's dining room, he might have used words like *bland*, *tame*, or *frigid*. But then he probably would have written the same review for his marriage. Divorce was never an option. They had to act out in other ways, so neither one ever ate what the other cooked.

I remember the first time I decided to eat with Fernando. Cuca asked, "Don't you want Newspaper Soup?"

"No," I said, "I want lobster and shrimp and a little taste of brandy." I walked toward the smell of the sea, and I was never hers again.

For, where Cuca was divine, like a vestal virgin tending the hearth, Fernando was like a demon, tempting with delicacies impossible to refuse. He was an official at the docks in Havana and he made a habit of visiting the cook on every ship that came to port. He would make the rounds and come home with armloads full of the finest delicacies. In addition to the ham and olives from Spain, there were fine French cheeses, apples (which were rarely seen in Cuba at the time), and, best of all, bittersweet dark chocolate from Switzerland. It was because of Fernando that, long before I ever came to New York, I got to try my first taste of a truly American treat. Bagels. With lox and a schmear. Although then it was still called *crema de queso*—cream cheese.

On the days Fernando decided he felt like putting on an apron, the choice of where I would dine was clear. When Fernando cooked, his tastes were less exotic but by no means boring. Though he appreciated the treats from his foreign ambassadors, he preferred the essential flavors of the sea. He loved lobster cocktail and fried shrimp; anything with shellfish really. He had two specialties; the first was *Camarones Enchilados* (Shrimp in Spicy Tomato Sauce) served over white rice. He would make it with special care, chopping the ingredients with precision and consistency. And when he seasoned the dish, it was like a wizard tending his cauldron. The flavors he produced were sweet, salty, and tangy, with the brine of shrimp freshly caught the same day. The savory aroma was perfectly calibrated to satisfy your hunger and leave you wanting more. But no matter how good his *camarones* were, nothing and no one could beat his *Arroz con Pollo* (Chicken with Rice).

Fernando's *Arroz con Pollo* is legendary in my family. Everyone's personal recipe is some small variation on his, and at family gatherings to this day, great arguments arise over what exactly should go in, when, and in what quantities. I think every family has a recipe like this, and if they don't, they should. The tricky thing about *Arroz con Pollo* is the texture. How do you make it creamy but not heavy? Soupy, but not watery? Firm but not crunchy? And how do you cook the chicken so it's moist? So the skin isn't gummy? So the whole thing just works? I have my opinions, of course, but I don't pretend to know. Wise chefs might forget everything they've been told and just start over from scratch. But for me, no matter how backward, making *Arroz con Pollo* will always start with Fernando's recipe.

There was one more choice for lunch. It was a place filled with excitement and the comings and goings of all sorts of people, like a café, or a truckstop diner. Only it was closer to home; just across the street in fact. Even better, the owners of this fine establishment were my mother's parents, my grandparents Oscar and Manuela.

Oscar was a hard-working Cuban. He started his professional life selling fruit on the streets of Guanabacoa when he was just eight years old. With hard work (not to mention the pinching of a few pennies), he rose to a position of power, working first as a cab driver, then investing in several small businesses before eventually starting a bus company that covered all the routes between Cojimar and Havana.

In both size and style the house reflected his social standing. It was like a Frank Lloyd Wright knockoff, all one floor, and bracingly modern compared to the homes around it. There was room enough for my mother's whole family, which was sizable given that my grandmother Manuela had six brothers. Three of these brothers had lost their wives when their children were young, so in total there were six women living in the house. The motherless daughters, Yolanda, Rosa, Barbara, and Dulce, along with my mother, Gilda, and her sister Chichi, were all raised together by Manuela and my great grandmother Maria.

This many mothers and sisters under the same roof no doubt had its problems, but the presence of the women was a boon for me. It was given that the men in Manuela's house were forbidden to cook, and God help us all if they so much as picked up a plate. Even though there were maids, it was the girls in the house who had the business of running the kitchen to attend to, an operation with importance equal to the running of the bus company.

There was always something going on in the kitchen, usually involving seafood my grandfather had brought home from the pier in Cojimar. Bloody swordfish heads, translucent shrimp skins, or gutted snappers lay about, torn apart with surgical precision by the fairest and most delicate hands. The piles of discarded odds and ends were clues of what lay ahead at the lunch table.

And although I would take whatever I could get, I was most excited if I heard the clacking of claws from the direction of the sink. To see little beady eyes staring back at me was a guarantee that we would be dining on *Harina con Cangrejos*, or Crabs with Cornmeal. This middle-class dish had a first-class flavor. It began with a *sofrito*, a mixture of aromatic vegetables and tomatoes, then became a broth by adding water, along with crab bodies and claws, bay leaves, and oregano. Cornmeal was added, and the whole thing blended together to create an aromatic dish with a flavor similar to a traditional New Orleans crab boil. The corn gave it a porridgelike consistency, but the crab elevated the dish to an exercise in refinement, coasting along on waves of flavor like the sea.

The rest of the menu often came from the fertile grounds of the house. My great grandmother Maria loved to garden, and she was very proud of the roses she cultivated in the consistent heat and humidity. Leafy banana trees shaded the back, while the front was cooled by coconut palms. *Yuca* was planted next to *boniato* and *malanga*, and all of it was pulled from the ground immediately before cooking. Maria also kept chickens that roamed freely and left the yard dotted with white and brown eggs.

The pride of Maria's garden lay nearby: three enormous *guayaba* (guava) trees stretching high into the sky. Once the trees started dropping their tart and tannic fruit, Manuela would get everyone to help gather the goodies. The *guayaba* would then be boiled in syrup, slowly, until the insides turned to candy and the syrup became a rosy pink. The *cascos de guayaba*, as they are called, were to be eaten with cream cheese and crackers, like a very tropical marmalade. When the *guayabas* rained, they truly poured. We would have *cascos* for months, and I can remember many days when I would eat them until my lips and fingers were stained pink and my stomach was swollen with sweetness.

The food at Manuela's house was decidedly Basque in its flavors. This Spanish influence wasn't limited to the *tapas* of Serrano ham, *manchego* cheese, and juicy olives. There were exotic main dishes like roast lamb with rosemary and filet mignon with a garlicky sauce rich in olive oil. We had offal like liver, pan-fried with onion and green pepper, or brains, made into fritters and deep-fried. We ate tiny fish like smelts and sardines, lightly breaded and fried, served with lemon. Larger fish was at its best when smothered in fresh laurel leaves and olives. Saffron was used liberally, in main dishes as well as sides. It gave its yellow hue to roast potatoes or simple white rice. Other rice dishes were made, with chopped okra or squid ink added for texture and flavor.

Unlike at grandmother Cuca's table, Manuela didn't serve black beans, instead opting for lima beans, peas, or garbanzos, sautéed with onions and chorizo, or dressed simply in a salad with olive oil and minced red onion. She loved to make Spanish tortillas from the fresh eggs in the yard. She filled these fluffy, omelettelike discs with sliced boiled potatoes or leftover plantains. And for dessert, nothing could beat Manuela's *churros*, crispy fried donut sticks rolled in cinnamon and sugar.

Meals were always accompanied by wine, especially when seafood was served. This was, in its own way, a salute to our Spanish ancestry, honoring an old wives' tale that stomachaches would follow seafood unless wine was imbibed. The women of the household also claimed that swimming within three hours of dining was sure to be calamitous. Three hours? A bit much. But traditions don't hold up unless you believe in them, no matter how ridiculous. Anyhow, I wasn't one to complain about a little wine over lunch. It was tasty, a grown-up thing to do, and what's more, it made sleep come quicker for the nap we'd all have before returning to work or school.

Whichever house I dined at would influence my disposition for the rest of the day. Cuca's lunch left me feeling like I'd accomplished something, a duty of sorts. I was sated, nourished, and ready for the next challenge before me. After lunch with Fernando, I dreaded returning to school, preferring to be swept away by pirates on the open sea, or whatever fantasy was most appetizing to me on that day. After lunch with Manuela, all I could do was sleep. I'd leave her table stuffed to the breaking point, a little woozy but all the more joyful for it. I would find myself truly thankful for food, for home, for the ability to enjoy ...

everything, really. The one commonality between the two houses (and three dining rooms) is that almost every day during my nap I would be awoken by a vendor in the street.

"*Tamales*, fresh *tamales*!"

No matter what I had just eaten or how full I was, I would grab the closest quarter and run into the street to purchase the little pocket of goodness.

The vendor carried two tin pots filled with hot water attached to a stick that rested on his shoulders. When he lifted the lid and the steam poured out, my mouth would instantly begin to water. I'd take my booty into the yard and unwrap the corn husk under the shade of a *guayaba* tree. Piping hot cornmeal, the saltiness of pork, all heightened by the bits of fatback throughout. The skin gave texture while the fat delivered the taste of corn and the pork in swirls of steaming flavor. I loved *tamales*. So much that I ate one every day. So much that my cousin Hugo would tell me that my head was going to get bigger and bigger with each *tamal* I ate, and that eventually it would explode in a mess of corn and pork bits. I never shared my *tamales* with him.

With lunchtime (and the afternoon snack) all over with, I went back to school. My education had started at age three. I went to a kindergarten across the street from my father's house every day to learn how to read and write. I remember the pretty young women from the neighborhood who taught us there.

Once I entered the first grade, school became a different animal altogether. No longer was it a simple hop, skip, and jump across the street. I had to take the bus. And instead of pretty young neighbors, I was taught by the stone-faced men and women of the cloth. Because in first grade, I started Catholic school at Los Escolapios in the nearby town of Guanabacoa.

Guanabacoa should have been familiar enough; everyone in my family who wasn't in Cojimar was there, so I had already spent enough time in Guanabacoa to feel at home. Still, every day while passing through the school's iron gates hedged by forbidding, high stone walls, I'd catch the faint, sickly smell of incense leaking from the cracks in the schoolhouse and would be reminded: This was not Guanabacoa; it was another world entirely.

The footprint of Los Escolapios took up several blocks. Its walls were large chunks of stone, mortared together, so that no matter how hot it was in the sun, inside was cool and damp. There were two court-yards in the center, and all the classrooms faced inward toward the light.

It was an all-boys school, of course, and I would tell you what everyone was like, where they were from, and what their families did, but it is hard to say. The school taught students from first grade to the end of high school, so there were plenty of kids. Students came from all the towns and villages in and around Havana, and we all wore starched uniforms of the traditional Catholic homogenized kind. The younger boys had shorts, the older wore pants, and we all had white shirts and ties of one sort or another. So while the usual signs of class or locale were not easily distinguished by the way a boy looked or dressed, let's just say that very few kids arrived at school without the accompaniment of a uniformed driver and a very nice car.

There was a small cafeteria for those kids who didn't go home for lunch. Some of their parents were working; others, I'm sure, were perfectly happy to eat at school. I, on the other hand, was horrified at the thought of dining in the cafeteria. On the rare days I didn't lunch in one of my family dining rooms, I refused the school's food with the resolve of a protestor on hunger strike. It may seem dramatic, but I thought it perfectly practical at the time. For, you see, just a few doors down from the school's cafeteria was a museum of exotic taxidermy. Mounted on the wall and preserved in glass cases were stuffed lions and tigers and birds, mid-flight, or poised to pounce on some unsus-pecting prey. Their glass eyes held an equally fixed stare, as though they were trapped in their glass cases, frozen in time forever. In my wild imagination, I was convinced that the meat they served in the cafeteria came from the stuffed animals. Birds or bunnies or wild cats were bad enough, but there was no way I would take a chance on eating anything that may or may not have been a crocodile or, worse, a snake.

Fast-held opinions of this sort were not exactly encouraged by the priests who were our keepers. I remember all too well the corners where I knelt, the stinging of rulers on my hands, and the ache of my arms, having held them out like Jesus on the cross for what seemed like hours at a time. I'm still perplexed that these dealers of pain and punishment were supposed to be our role models of good Catholics. Something about being beaten by the men who taught us math, history, and French didn't quite sit right, especially when their teachings encouraged us to live by the lives of the saints. Now, some forty years later, I am happy to say that I don't remember a single one of their names or their faces.

For better or worse, I know it is their aura that keeps the early mysteries of Catholicism alive in me today. Some deep part of me still stirs at the memory of those quiet corridors filled with incense, the timid shuffling nuns visiting from out of town, the rumors of ghosts in the eaves and courtyards, and a church filled with relics like the woman in the glass coffin who had never decomposed.

Every day school let out around six, and I would return to the safety of the bus, where one of my great uncles was always either driving or collecting the fares. If I was lucky and my grandfather Oscar was there, I knew for sure I would get something sweet for a late-afternoon snack. After we finished the route together, he liked taking me to a Cuban bakery that specialized in French pastries. We shared a napoleon or an éclair, so silky and luscious, filled with custard or pastry cream. Sometimes we bought those pure white meringues from the convent. They were crisp and dry on the outside and chewy on the inside. I always marveled that they stayed so white.

Eventually we returned home, usually to my mother's house. By the time we arrived, my grandmother and great grandmother had already set into counting the money that the bus drivers would drop by in big sacks. Bags and bags filled with nickels, dimes, and quarters: my inheritance. One of my many cousins would be playing the radio, maybe rock and roll, maybe something Cuban. Café was made and snacks served in place of dinner. They'd serve *croquetas* or *empanadas*, sometimes sandwiches or little salads. Usually it was more Spanish imports, hams and olives and little hunks of cheese. At that point no one wanted a full meal, and the rich, salty offerings, while delicious, were really fuel for the fire, energy for those who did the counting and those who got paid afterward.

And so the evenings would unfold, my relatives sitting with our extended family of bus drivers, usually talking politics. There were stories of customers from that day, a good-looking woman on one driver's bus, a popular singer that another recognized, and always the whispered jokes, full of innuendo, prompting chuckles or clucks of disapproval from the elder women, buried in their counting.

I would sit nearby and drink a glass of water, always observing, admiring my grandmother Manuela and her mother, Maria. They were all strength and beauty and quiet confidence as they literally counted every nickel and dime. The men looked on, waiting for their decrees: How much had been earned and how much they would be paid. These older women seemed invincible, like steel drums, especially when compared with my own mother, young, frail, vulnerable, a porcelain vase filled with red carnations just before they bloom.

Sometimes my mother would come to me during the counting, as if such a coarse activity were too much for her fragile sensibilities. She'd take my hand and we would walk around the backyard with my baby brother Jesus. There we'd sit on the porch, swaying back and forth in the rocking chairs, and she'd tell us the stories of our birth.

My brother was born on Christmas day, and while he was supposed to be named Othon, like my father, there was a problem at City Hall when they tried to register his name. One

My father and me with baby Jesus (Othin) in front of Manuela's house, Cojimar, 1956

of Batista's officials informed him that the devoutly Catholic dictator had passed a new law saying that every newborn in Cuba had to be named after a saint. Since there was no saint Othon, my father spouted the most obvious choice, with no small amount of resentment. So Jesus it was. Still, we called him Othin, the diminutive of my father's unholy moniker.

"What about me, Mama?" I'd ask.

"When people said how hard childbirth was, I believed them. But you proved them wrong."

My mother and me at Cuca's house, Cojimar, 1956

I was born in a clinic run by nuns. They massaged my mother's belly as she prepared for the worst, but I came out, simple as can be, just a few hours later. When my relatives found out that I was a boy, my grandfathers descended on the room with all their friends, my father, and uncles, and I'm sure plenty of cousins.

The men started smoking their celebratory cigars. I imagine it must have annoyed my mother to have her birthing room turn into a barroom so quickly, but in those days Cuban babies were never separated from their mothers when they were born. So when the men started smoking their cigars, there was no one to stop them and no one to take me away. I thank God and the nuns for giving me my first taste of Cuban cigars on the day I was born.

My brother and I listened to these stories, again and again, on the back porch in the early evenings with my mother. Breezes carried the ocean salt mixed with the smell of night-blooming jasmine and earth that rose up from the slowly cooling ground. My mother, my brother, and I would be bathed in the rosy glow of the evening sun. If I listened closely, I could hear the Caribbean calling. One of the men inside would light a cigar, and I could once again smell my beginning. There we sat, waiting for night, and as the sun finally set, it seemed that there was nothing at all wrong in the world.

❚ Newspaper Soup ❚

This is my grandmother Cuca's infamous recipe. I remember eating it nearly every day in Cuba, although my mother claims I refused it on many occasions. There is an interesting chemistry at work here: The water from the pumpkin thins the soup out while the starch from the *malanga* thickens it up in the second cooking. This vegetarian soup is certainly healthy, but it's also quite tasty. The sunny color and hearty warmth make it perfect for lunch on a chilly day, but this comforting cure-all works its magic any time of year.

3 celery stalks
4 carrots, peeled
1 Spanish onion, peeled
1 green pepper, stem and seeds removed
2 pounds *malanga**
3 to 4 pounds *calabasa* pumpkin**
⅔ cup olive oil
4 garlic cloves, peeled and smashed
½ cup Goya tomato sauce (from one 8-ounce can)
¼ gram saffron (about 1 big pinch)
8 cups water
Up to 2 tablespoons salt
Up to ½ teaspoon ground black pepper

*Malanga is a starchy root vegetable with white flesh and a thick brown skin, related to the taro root. It can be found in most Latin supermarkets' produce sections, although it is sometimes called *yautia*.
**Calabasa pumpkin is a round, greenish-skinned tropical pumpkin. Its orange flesh is sweeter and faster cooking than a traditional pumpkin.

They are very big, so they are usually sold in smaller pieces. Should you not find *calabasas*, butternut squash makes a fine substitute.

1. Prepare the vegetables: Cut the celery stalks into 1-inch pieces. Cut the carrots into 1-inch chunks. Slice the onion in half, then cut each half into chunks about 1-inch square. Slice the green pepper in half, then cut each half into chunks about 1-inch square. Peel each *malanga* with a vegetable peeler, then slice in half. Cut crosswise into chunks about 1-inch thick. Peel the tough skin from the *calabasa* pumpkin by slicing close to the flesh with a sharp knife. Remove any seeds with a spoon and cut the pumpkin into chunks about 1 inch square.

2. In an 8-quart soup pot, heat the olive oil over medium-high heat until hot but not smoking. Sauté the celery, carrots, onion, and green pepper, stirring occasionally until softened and lightly browned, 10 minutes.

3. Add the *malanga*, pumpkin, garlic, tomato sauce, saffron, and water. Season with 1 tablespoon of the salt. Bring to a boil. Cover and reduce the heat to medium. Cook at a gentle boil until soft enough to puree, about 1 hour. Turn off the heat and cool slightly, 15 minutes.

4. Puree the soup using an immersion blender. If you don't have an immersion blender, puree in batches using a standing blender. Note: Make sure you don't overfill the blender, and that the lid is slightly ajar so any steam can escape, otherwise you'll end up with a hot mess all over the place.

5. Return the puree to the stove. Bring to a boil over medium heat and simmer, covered, for 30 minutes, stirring occasionally. Taste and adjust the seasoning using no more than 1 tablespoon salt and ½ teaspoon black pepper. The salt needed will depend on how starchy the vegetables are, as well as personal preference. Serve

with bread and butter, or a garnish of croutons, chopped ham, and sliced hard-boiled eggs.

Makes 1 big pot of soup, 8 to 10 servings

❙ *Black Beans* ❙ (*Two Ways*)

My recipes for black beans start the same every time. The difference in these variations is in the *sofrito*—or base of flavors—and here I've included the two versions familiar to me. First my grandfather Fernando's recipe, every bit as robust as he was, and the more rustic of the two, with extra bacon and spice. Next my grandmother Cuca's, more refined, like she was: pureed with lots of sherry and a little extra sugar, to make the souplike side dish milder. Which is better? After many years, I still can't make up my mind.

Prepare the beans:
1 pound dry black beans
2 quarts water
1 ham hock
1 green pepper, stem and seeds removed, cut into 1-inch squares
4 garlic cloves, peeled and smashed
1 tablespoon salt
2 bay leaves

1. In a fine-mesh colander, rinse the beans thoroughly, making sure to remove any stones.

2. Place the beans in a 4-quart soup pot, cover them with the water, and soak at least 8 hours or overnight.

3. Add the ham hock, green pepper, garlic, salt, and bay leaves to the pot with the beans. Bring to a boil over high heat. Reduce the heat

to medium-low and simmer, covered, 1 hour, or until the beans are tender, skimming off any scum that floats to the top during cooking.

Fernando's way:

¼ cup olive oil

4 pieces thick-cut bacon, sliced into ½-inch pieces

1 Spanish onion, peeled and cut into ¼-inch dice

½ green pepper, stem and seeds removed, cut into ¼-inch dice

6 garlic cloves, peeled and finely chopped

1 jalapeño pepper, stem removed, cut into ¼-inch dice*

1 teaspoon dried oregano

½ teaspoon ground cumin

2 teaspoons salt

½ teaspoon ground black pepper

3 tablespoons distilled white vinegar

1 tablespoon turbinado or brown sugar

* Don't forget to wash your hands after handling the pepper. If you want to reduce the spiciness of the jalapeño, remove the seeds and inner membrane (which contain all the heat), using only the green flesh. Also, you may omit the jalapeno entirely.

1. Heat the olive oil in a large skillet over medium-high heat. Add the bacon and cook, stirring occasionally, until the fat is rendered and the bacon begins to caramelize, 4 to 5 minutes. Add the onion and green pepper and cook, stirring, until softened slightly, 3 minutes. Add the garlic, jalapeño, oregano, cumin, salt, and black pepper. Cook, stirring, 1 minute more. Add the vinegar and stir, scraping any caramelized bits off the bottom of the pan with a wooden spoon. Turn off the heat and set aside.

2. Remove the ham hock from the bean pot. Set aside until cool enough to handle. Using a fork, pull off any meat you can, but try not to get any gristle. Add the meat to the bean pot.

3. Transfer 1 scant cup of beans to a small bowl. Using the back of a fork, mash the beans into a smooth paste. Add the paste to the pot, along with the reserved *sofrito* and the sugar. Stir to combine.

4. Return the beans to a boil over medium-high heat. Reduce the heat to medium-low and simmer, uncovered, until the sauce thickens to the consistency of a thin gravy, 20 minutes. Serve with white rice.

Cuca's way:
½ cup olive oil

1 Spanish onion, peeled and cut into ¼-inch dice

½ green pepper, stem and seeds removed, cut into ¼-inch dice

3 garlic cloves, peeled and finely chopped

½ teaspoon ground cumin

2 teaspoons salt

½ teaspoon ground black pepper

1 cup dry sherry

¼ cup turbinado or brown sugar

1. Heat the olive oil in a large skillet over medium-high heat. Add the onion and green pepper and cook, stirring, until softened slightly, 3 minutes. Add the garlic, cumin, salt, and black pepper. Cook, stirring, 1 minute more. Add the sherry and cook until the alcohol has evaporated, 3 minutes. Turn off the heat and set aside.

2. Remove the ham hock from the bean pot and discard. Add the *sofrito* to the beans along with the sugar. Stir to combine.

3. Return the beans to a boil over medium-high heat. Reduce the heat to medium-low and simmer, uncovered, until the flavors blend, 15 minutes. Turn off the heat and cool slightly, 15 minutes.

4. Puree the beans using an immersion blender, or in batches in a standing blender, until they are the consistency of a thick gravy.

Note: Make sure you don't overfill the blender, and that the lid is slightly ajar so any steam can escape, otherwise you'll end up with a hot mess all over the place.

5. Return the puree to the stove, bring to a boil over medium-high heat, and cook, 5 minutes, until warmed through. Serve over white rice or in a small bowl as a very elegant side dish.

Both recipes make 8 to 10 servings with leftovers

Two

Oscar

As the story goes, my grandfather Oscar Hernandez started off selling fruit and ended up with a bus company. I worry that over time my own understanding of his life has taken on a dramatically Dickensian slant. The truth is he was a hard worker and entirely self-made against all odds.

Oscar was only four when his mother died. Without a wife to take care of him, his father remarried quickly. There was no grand house for everyone to live in happily, as Oscar and his parents were dirt poor from the start. So between the cost and the space and the fact that Oscar was a reminder of his mother that neither his father nor his new wife wanted, he was sent to live with his godparents. Soon after, his father left town, and no one heard from him again.

Oscar had a few quiet years, but by the time he was eight his godparents could no longer afford to take care of him, so he was forced to find work selling fruit. From early in the morning to the late afternoon he roamed the streets of Guanabacoa selling mangoes, bananas, avocados, and whatever else was growing and fresh.

This was his job through adolescence, wandering, calling *"Frutas para vender!"* and scraping together whatever he could save to contribute to the only family he knew. There was no time for education, only work. Streets. Fruits. But this was all he needed to spark the business sense that would one day make him rich.

By the time he was twenty, Oscar wanted more. He decided he

would drive a taxi, but he didn't have the skills needed to conduct this simple business. It was time to learn. He befriended a priest in town who agreed to teach him how to read, write, and do simple math. The priest was happy to barter for his time, and he offered an irresistible deal: nightly lessons in exchange for beers and company at a local bar that also served as a classroom. Perhaps the environment made it easier for him to learn. But I think it was just another example of how he wanted to do things his way.

Oscar was fiercely proud that his fortune was made on his own terms, and this extended to his education. He had no grand elocution on the values of schooling, higher or otherwise. He always told me he made it because of his quickness and his willingness to take huge risks. He was also skilled at applying his learning. He didn't care for literature, pulp fiction, or even the Bible. But he devoured newspapers and was better at absorbing a contract than any paralegal. Ultimately, though, it was his desire to grow beyond the meager means of his childhood that drove him. That's the Dickens in him.

He started planning at age eight, selling fruit on the streets. Every day he'd acquire a little more; every penny would be another rung on the ladder. But he'd always be going up, always getting somewhere better. He'd tell me that a bed was better than the street, a house was better than a room, a taxi better than a fruit cart, but a bus? Heaven. "A bus is everything." That's what he told me.

Oscar started courting my grandmother Manuela around 1930. Manuela's first fiancé had died only a couple years earlier. It would have been almost impossible for her to find another husband in Cuba at that time, even though she was only twenty-

Oscar and a bus driver, Cojimar, 1930s

seven. She had been promised to one man, and now that he was gone, she was as good as secondhand. But she was just what Oscar was looking for: tough, ambitious, and a little bit used. He didn't have time for girlish naiveté, and as for a virginal young bride? It was more important that she knew how to work.

This was not a problem, as Manuela and her four brothers all worked in their family's butcher shop as soon as they were tall enough to see over the counter. Their father, Eurgenio, was the boss, but Manuela was especially hard working. In addition to getting her hands bloodied at the butcher shop, she also worked in a factory sewing European-style dress shirts. It was while she was working there that she met Oscar.

I am sure they connected through their desire to improve their circumstances. Because even though Manuela had a cast-iron work ethic, she, too, wanted more than to be the unmarried daughter of a butcher. And while she was not naive, she was also not unfeminine. She wanted comfort: massages, facials, and fancy dresses. She wanted her own home and the luxury of throwing parties. But she also wanted power: status, respect, and people working under her command. She and Oscar had a lot in common. And they adored each other. They were married within a year of their meeting.

Their relationship proved to be beneficial to more than just the two of them. Once Oscar decided to start a bus company, he set out to find investors, and after some deft maneuvering he convinced Manuela's father, Eurgenio, that his plan would pay off. It must have been a great sales pitch, because Eurgenio decided to sell the butcher shop to finance the purchase of the first two buses. Suddenly the family was no longer interested in meat. They became drivers, mechanics, and bookkeepers without skipping a beat. All the proceeds were divvied up among the growing family. The business was growing even faster, but not without a few hitches along the way.

Just a few years after selling his shop, Eurgenio was shot while in bed with his mistress. And while nothing was proven and no one was jailed, it was suspected that his murderer was the mistress's husband.

After Eurgenio's death, Oscar became the head of the bus company. He had a big vision, so when the opportunity to join a cooperative of five other bus companies presented itself, he took it. Although the group passed as a level-headed business collective, there was intense conflict between government and private ownership even then. In the early 1930s the group pooled its efforts into organized dissent against President Machado's corrupt regime. The era was full of charged conflict, and I'm sure that more than a few members of the collective carried guns to go along with their slightly more acceptable forms of rebellion. But ultimately it was this larger group that enabled Oscar to finance the purchase of more and more buses until he presided over all the routes between Havana and Guanabacoa, Cojimar, Casablanca, and Regla.

Oscar's aspirations had no limit. From time to time he would drive me through the Cuban countryside in his giant gray Buick, telling me stories of his rise to riches. He also took the opportunity to show me any new piece of land he may have bought. But this was not just sightseeing. He intended to build hotels on the land. He used to tell me that if he could convince Manuela's father to sell his butcher shop to invest in a bus company, then he could do anything, including becoming a hotelier. I believed he could do it. Everyone did.

By 1958 Oscar had become a very powerful man. Everyone I met seemed to admire my grandfather. Even Manuela's brothers, who now worked for him, showed love and admiration in a way they never did toward their own father. They were all so grateful, the way people feel when someone saves them. And save them he did—from their domineering father and decades of cutting steaks for impatient women in Guanabacoa.

Immediately after they married, Oscar and Manuela moved to Cojimar, where they lived in a big house a block away from the bay. When my mother was married, they moved up the hill to their Frank Lloyd Wright knockoff. They said they moved because they wanted to be closer to my mother, who was living with my father and his parents. The strange thing is the house on the bay was only fifteen minutes away by foot, just five by car. I guess that wasn't close enough. Maybe they didn't like having to trek up the hill. Or maybe they just wanted people to know that they could afford a brand new modernist house designed by a real architect (even if it wasn't Frank Lloyd Wright).

With their parents so close and so much a part of their lives, my mother and father were a bit like grown-up children themselves. My mother was twenty when she had me, my father just twenty-three. If they were like children, then I was their doll. Fortunately, my mother had plenty of time to play with me. My father had none. He was always busy with basketball games or dominos or having drinks with friends. Sometimes he would kiss me goodnight before going off to his separate life of youth and excitement, but most often he did not. He never really seemed to be interested in me, but it didn't matter because I had my grandfather Oscar.

Oscar loved me, no questions asked. Just love, reassuring and so needed, grounding and, above all, consistent. I was glad I was his first grandson, and that he had two daughters and no sons, so everything—from crisp dollar bills to miniature toy Ferraris—was given to me. My brother Othin was only three and still too young to appreciate it. There was a revolution going on all around us and I was a very nervous kid. But Oscar was always there. Always with me, leading me through his secret world of men, business, and exotic-looking females.

At least once a week Oscar would take me with him to check on all his businesses. He had several now, in addition to the bus company. He built fishing boats near the bay in Cojimar. He made cement and sold it to builders. He bottled water from natural springs on his property in the country. He even managed to sell dirt.

This world of commerce was so different from my patrician upbringing that I always waited anxiously to be invited on one of our road trips. We'd drive from place to place, talking to a long list of farmers, fishermen, mechanics, and bartenders.

I loved those trips spent meeting people. My grandfather knew and spoke to anyone, everyone. He was a street kid before he was anything else. Always a hello and a bill slipped from hand to hand to someone that looked like they needed a tip. Earned or unearned, if it was needed, it was given. Nothing but loyalty was required in return.

After a long day of managing, our favorite spot to relax (and eat) was La Terasa. The bar was a local hot spot right on the bay. As such it was always filled with fisherman. One of them had been Hemingway's model for Santiago in *The Old Man and the Sea*. I'm sure Mr. Hemingway had a fair share of inspirations in the place, because he was indeed a regular. I never noticed him, but then I probably thought he was just another drunken tourist.

La Terasa had a huge bar in front. The tables for dining were in the back, next to windows that opened onto the bay. The whole place had beautiful tile floors that could be cleaned quickly. Maybe not a priority everywhere, but this was a bar for fishermen. The huge double doors that were always open led straight to the docks where there was another open-air bar. This made it possible for the fishermen to dock their boats, sell their fish, and have a rum all at the same time.

The meals at La Terasa were an everyday miracle. They served lunch and dinner, and specialized in fresh seafood. Fried snapper and grilled dorado, raw oysters, or swordfish *escabeche*. If it had seafood in it, it was guaranteed a winner, but nothing was as good as the *paella*. The *paella* at La Terasa was made with chicken, fish, lobster, shrimp, and clams. The first thing I did every time I walked into the restaurant was stop and breathe deeply, searching for *paella*. The sweet smell of saffron could always be detected through the smell of water and fish guts.

The *paella* took thirty-five minutes when cooked to order, plenty of time for my grandfather to have a couple drinks at the bar. I watched and listened, and stole a sip of whatever he had whenever it was offered. By the time the wait was over, I was always twice as hungry as when I walked in. And the *paella* never disappointed. It was not dry, like some Spanish *paella*, but moist like it was swimming. I loved to see if the waiter would drip any gravy from the oval terra-cotta casserole as he carried it to the table. The *petit pois* and *pimientos* that garnished the dish were the first thing you'd notice, but it was the yellow liquor of the seafood and saffron that made my mouth water. Breaking through the top layer of rice released a cloud of aromatic steam, then I'd dip in, and wow! Like old Spain attacking my tongue.

La Terasa was like home to my grandfather and me. The delicacies they served from the sea were as familiar to me as peanut butter and jelly. The truly exotic delights, that I got only with him, were the treats I'd look forward to whenever we hit the road.

The countryside near Havana was filled with hills, streams, palm trees, cane fields, and mango groves. At every turn you'd see horses, cows, goats, and pigs grazing in the lazy sunshine. For me the true landmarks were the food stands every few miles. They were ramshackle huts made of wood with roofs of thatched coconut palms. Each stand had a coffee maker, a small bar, and signs advertising whatever the special was that day. There was only one sign I cared about though, *Pollo Frito*, or Cuban fried chicken. If I saw that sign, even if I was only slightly hungry, I begged Oscar to stop, and he usually obliged.

Cuban fried chicken is marinated in *naranjas ágrias* (sour oranges, sometimes called bitter oranges) and garlic, then covered in onions until the meat soaks up all the flavor. It has no doughy coating but is instead fried in lard until the chicken is perfectly crisp. I'd bite into a thigh, a drumstick, or a wing and the juices would run down my chin. I long for the days before the white meat monopoly, when nothing was better than a dark and juicy drumstick.

The chicken was almost always served with *Moros*, a mixture of white rice and leftover black beans. The dish is officially called *Moros y Cristianos* (Moors and Christians), in which the black beans represent the Moors and the white rice the Christians. It is certainly a Cuban dish, but its name comes from the Spaniards who occupied Cuba in the 1500s. Their reference dates to the Moorish occupation of the Iberian Peninsula between the eighth and fifteenth centuries. Occupations and conquests, racial and holy wars, all in one little dish. How could anyone eat knowing there was such conflict in leftover rice and beans? Well, I certainly didn't let it stop me.

At every stand, no matter what, there would be *guarapo*, a drink made by juicing sugar cane through an elaborate ancient juicer. The vendor would feed cut pieces of cane into a hole on top of the machine, then turn a series of cranks in order to squeeze the dense fiber to extract every last drop of juice. It took around three large stalks to make one glass of juice. I drank mine with ice cubes; my grandfather had his with a little rum.

The drink was like candy and honey made liquid and cold. The intense sweetness would numb my mouth slightly as I sipped it. The best part was the way the sugar went right to my head upon drinking, delivering a burst of raw energy. The juice supposedly has nutrients in it, too, but come on. It's just an excuse for a sugar rush. When I was little, though, I thought it was like a potion from Merlin. With its cloudy color, strong flavor, and mysterious properties . . . clearly it was magical.

While we ate and drank, we inevitably would attract a homeless dog or two. My grandfather would always feed them. Sometimes I think he saw himself as a child whenever he saw one of those dogs. But if they reminded him of his struggle, I think he saw his dreams when he looked at me. Me in my freshly ironed linen shirts and shorts, sparkling clean after attending to my chin, wiping it with a napkin held by hands baby soft from the comfort of money. The money he had worked so hard for.

It seems funny to me now that it was Oscar who opened the door for me into a world usually obscured by class lines. If it wasn't for him I never would have known about the rest of the world outside Cojimar. He drove me down the dirt roads, where we'd pass children, my age and younger, trying to sell us a tire, a piece of candy, mangoes, anything, everything. He brought me down from the clouds and showed me people like he used to be, who thought of nothing but trying to get ahead. The smiles of women whose only future was a husband going somewhere just a little bit higher in the class struggle. Their eyes, full of need, that saw every man they waited on as a possible candidate. The skin, of men who worked in the sun, tan like leather, aged by sweat and labor. The teeth, if there were any, of those who smoked nickel cigars, yellowing into black. Or the palms, callused and cracked so as to appear white, no matter the tone on top. These were the features of a Cuba I knew nothing about, showed to me by the man who worked his entire life to save me from them.

Once we stopped by a natural spring where my grandfather had set up his bottling business. There were trucks lined up, with workers loading bottles on board. Work was winding down, as it was almost the end of the day. Oscar honked his horn and called the foreman over, inviting him for a drink. He climbed aboard and we set off.

We eventually reached the narrow streets of Guanabacoa. The foreman spoke about how the business was going, freely telling us all about the workers, and eventually his own wife and children. My grandfather would respond politely, but never, ever revealed anything about himself or our family. They of course talked politics, Batista this, Batista that. Fidel was never mentioned. I may have dozed off for a moment, because before I knew it we were going up steeper hills, down winding roads, until suddenly we were in the middle of Regla, a small town across the bay from La Habana. I could hear the frightening sound of drums in the distance, and I knew it for sure. This was the center of *Santería*, the white magic-voodoo of the Caribbean. But what were we doing here in such a poor neighborhood? Where were we going?

I never liked Regla because my father used to drag me there to visit his godmother, who was poor and had a lot of kids. Her small house was a mess with clothes and junk everywhere. That was fine, though. The real reason I dreaded the trip was because whenever she heard that my father was coming, she would make barbecued goat. I hate goat. Dry and mealy, it's like eating chewy hair or shredded carpet.

I was terrified. "Are we going there? Please, I hope not."

We turned another corner and a curvy black woman in a red dress with polka dots was walking down the street. My grandfather followed her close, slow and quiet until finally he whistled. She looked over her shoulder and smiled as if she knew him. Did she? What strange and sensuous world was this?

Sensuality is everywhere in Cuba, and even at seven I could feel it all around me. My uncles with their mixture of sweat and cologne, the looks Oscar gave Manuela, watching my cousin Hugo gallop on his horse in front of the local teenage girls; I was attuned to all of it, and it was strangely familiar. But this, Regla, the woman in polka dots; this was different. This was mysterious and obvious all at once. This was pure, unfiltered lust.

We stopped at a bar. Some of my relatives were there, recently having gotten off their bus shifts. Everyone was joking and rowdy, but not the way they would be in my grandmother's dining room. There was no censorship; just one dirty joke after another. It was then that my grandfather bought me my first beer. What was going on? I drank it. Cold and bitter, the foam hit my face like cotton candy.

It wasn't long before I was more than just a little bit tipsy ... and then the curvaceous black woman in the tight red dress walks in. My grandfather buys her a drink ... now he lights a Cuban cigarette, no filter, no chemicals, just the sweet smell of tobacco. And I notice. This room is what? Heavier somehow, than La Terasa. But heavy is not it either. Sweet? Like candy? Maybe, but only when you eat too much. Because tobacco, rum, and beer are not sweet themselves. But the smoke, the heat, the desire hanging in the air; they can all mix together and feel something like sweetness.

But maybe it's just memory. A mysterious room where everything seemed a little dangerous because at that time so little really was. Yes, tobacco, rum, and beer can be sweet when they fill your mind with 1958. Right before everything changed forever. Sweet. And sad. Because forever is like a wall: There is no way to climb over it or walk through it. *Forever* means that a period has come, full stop, on a sentence.

❧

The last real Christmas we ever had in Cuba was in 1958. Christmas in the tropics is a strange event, especially if you've ever actually had one in the cold. The weather is usually quite nice, mild and sunny, sometimes hot. Even so, the streets were lined with plastic Santa Clauses and fake snow proving that, even in Cuba, people like Bing Crosby.

By then, Fidel was nearing Havana. He had practically achieved rock star status at Oscar's

Oscar, Othin, me, and Manuela, Christmas Day, 1957

house, where his name was now said out loud by my aunt and cousins. "Fidel Castro!" As if Elvis was finally going to give a concert in Havana.

Everyone in my family was waiting for him to get there. My grandmother Cuca sat intently by the radio every night, her eyes full of hope and something else more vicious. She was like a cat, and the mouse she wanted to eat was Batista.

Although Batista had brought relative order and prosperity to Cuba, he was wearing out his political welcome after running in an unopposed election in 1954. He rapidly lost popularity among Cuba's middle and upper classes because of close ties to the United States and especially several American mafiosos. Many feared he was irresponsibly turning Cuba into a corrupt Carribean playground. Fidel had been trying to overthrow Batista since the mid-1950s. Batista made a point of aggressively tracking and eliminating his opposition, starting around the summer of 1958. By the fall news trickled down the pipeline that members of Batista's crew were tipping Fidel off about the General and his planned movement and attacks. When we started hearing about Fidel's minor victories, he showed the promise of becoming our country's great equalizer. If he had the persistence and moral strength to convert even the most corrupt Batistianos, maybe he could save the country from its slowly rotting core.

But on December 23 Christmas was too near to be worrying about morality. There were things to take care of. The pigs had to be slaughtered, the wine bought, the garlic diced, and the *yuca* dug out of the ground. There was *flan* to be made! And rum cake! Preparation was the name of the game at this time of year, and I was where I always was, directly at Oscar's hip, roaming the island in search of perfection.

We did all of our shopping in Guanabacoa, and every year I looked forward to my favorite stop: the little French-style bakery where they would make super-sweet marzipan animals to celebrate the holidays. Every year I picked out the same critter, a little baby pig nestled among candied leaves with a bright red apple in its mouth. I always ate the apple first because no Cuban I knew would put an apple in the mouth of their roast pig. It was probably a French thing, another way that Cuban *patissiers* aspired to continental European standards, but I just thought it looked out of place. It's not that I needed the pig to look perfect. It usually wasn't around long enough for me to admire it anyway. It was just a tiny detail that made this day with my grandfather feel more like my day. Our day.

We always bought extras for my brother Othin and all our cousins. By now my grandparents had taken in my cousins Dulce, Barbara, and Hugo after their mother died tragically. My cousin Alberto lived with us as well. He moved in after his mother left for New York and his father remarried. With all the cousins, the mothers, the sisters, and brothers and uncles and fathers, there were a lot of people to feed at Christmas. Fortunately it was just the young ones that needed marzipan pigs.

As we continued our shopping, the streets would be full of people, which was normal for that time of year. But there was a new anxiety filling the sidewalks, people whispering and throwing cautious glances over their shoulders to make sure nobody heard what they were saying.

"It's going to happen soon!" they would say, punctuated with nervous laughter.

"Fidel! He is already in Matanzas!"

"You think so?" A quick nod of knowing.

"Did you listen to the radio last night?" Raised eyebrows to signify yes.

"That S.O.B. Batista, time to get him and those crooks out of here!"

My grandfather found ways to respond in the codified signals learned in times of suspicion, but he never made a real commitment. It was not the time to trust strangers. Trust was something reserved for family and close friends.

It happened that Oscar's friends were usually his purveyors: the baker, the fisherman, the bartender. So when we stopped by the liquor store to pick up the traditional Christmas drink, the bubbly and boozy apple *cidra* imported from Spain, they came rushing up to him, asking with wide eyes, "When? How soon? What do you know?"

He placed an arm around their shoulders and whispered with complete authority, "It's going to happen very soon. A week. No more than two. Understand?"

They believed him because they knew he wanted Batista out as badly as they did. It was common knowledge among his inner circle that Oscar wanted an end to U.S. intervention on the island. He wanted Cubans to make money, not the Americans. He wanted the casinos to belong to him, not Meyer Lansky. Why the hell should foreigners get the bigger piece of his pie? And who was Batista to give it to them? No one was certain what Fidel would bring, but he was sure to change things. And as long as that happened before Batista ruined everything beyond repair, there was reason to hope.

Still, the spirit of Christmas persisted, and we had to buy a tree. We went to the docks knowing they were always fresher just off the boat. Expensive, too!

Now there are a lot of images in my head, but by far one of the strangest is that of people buying evergreens a few feet above the

Caribbean blue water at the dock in Cojimar. Still dreaming of a white Christmas in the tropics. I guess it's the power of the American movie mythology, a power we gave in to every year.

We'd pick out a tree from those lined up on the docks, cart it home on top of the Buick, and set it up for my grandmother Manuela to decorate. She put white cotton underneath, hung balls and tinsel, and finished it off with the tour de force: an oversized nativity scene complete with shepherds, sheep, glass rivers, paper mountains, and a grotto for Baby Jesus.

By December 24, everything was ready. The *cidra* was chilling, there were bowls overflowing with apples and nuts, and in both houses the pigs had been slaughtered. Every room was permeated by the smell of *mojo*, the citrus marinade used to flavor the pigs. Sour orange on top, oregano and garlic filling out the middle, and the hint of smoky cumin rounding out the bottom. That smell is very simply at the center of my being.

Cubans celebrate Christmas starting on Noche Buena, the evening of December 24, with a huge meal. It usually consists of traditional Roast Pork with *Yuca* and *Moros*. This is standard celebratory fare, but the extra care given makes the Christmas meal rise above all others.

Barbara, Raulito, me, Dulce, and Hugo, Manuela's house, 1956

I remember Manuela's *yuca*, fresh from the yard, peeled and boiled until it released its starch. The *yuca* is removed from its cooking water, then cracked open with a fork to remove its tough center core like a candle wick. The dense tuber retains immense heat, so when it's forked open it releases tremendous amounts of steam. The trick is to cover the *yuca* with a simple

Eduardo Machado & Michael Domitrovich

mojo of lime and garlic, then drizzle it with imported olive oil and maybe some drippings from the pork. If done correctly, the steam gently cooks the garlic, removing much of its pungent flavor. The lime, oil, and lard heat up, too, mixing with the starchy cooking water to form the simplest and most delectable of sauces.

Manuela's *yuca* was the best, but the roast pork at both houses was equally good. Fernando cooked his underground in banana leaves, while Oscar sent his to a bakery. This resulted in two vastly different animals. Fernando's was the juiciest, and the hardest to make. He began by digging a hole deep enough to fit the pig, although I doubt he ever actually touched a shovel. He'd put hard dry wood at the bottom and burn it until the embers smoldered like charcoal. The fire was then covered with banana leaves and topped with the marinated pig. More banana leaves were layered over the pig, and then the whole thing was buried. This is an age-old cooking technique, used everywhere from Polynesia to New England (where seaweed replaces the banana leaves and lobsters and clams replace the pig). The banana leaves act as a protective shield from the heat of the fire and the grit of the dirt. They also help to keep the cooking environment moist. The low steam heat, combined with the long cooking time of almost two days, resulted in a pig that was unbearably moist. Many stained shirt fronts and sticky fingers all around.

The only problem with the underground method was that it left the skin as moist as the meat. Never a problem for me, though, as all I had to do was amble down the block to Oscar's house. There I'd find the perfect roast pork, the skin lacquered deep reddish-amber, glistening with the caramelized sugars from the sour orange and garlic *mojo*.

It is still customary for Cubans to send their pigs out for roasting, although it's more likely to happen in a densely populated Cuban-American community than it is on the island itself. The burden of a whole pig is usually too much for a tiny home oven, as it was in Cuba in the 1950s. Today, a Cuban bakery is your best bet to get the job done. They have the manpower, the giant ovens, and, basically, they get it. The adventurous may like the challenge of roasting at home, but if you want a whole pig's worth of crackling, do yourself a favor and send it out. If you don't know why you'd want a whole pig's worth of crackling, I'm sorry. Truly.

Back and forth I'd go between Christmas havens, stuffing my face with roast pork two ways. I remember seeing our neighbors with their families lining the streets, their faces wrought with anxiety over Fidel's imminent arrival. No one admitted it, but everyone was waiting. We knew for sure that Fidel was in the mountains near Havana. We knew that Che Guevara and Camilo Cienfuegos had been putting up a strong fight against Batista, leading separate factions of civilians and guerilla fighters dispatched by Fidel. But it was only hearsay from there. Supposedly there was no way Batista would be able to keep his power, because by now his army was almost completely against him. Even those who claimed loyalty couldn't be trusted, and, naturally, the entire regime was getting more ruthless with each passing day. I worried that my father, grandfather, uncles, or cousins might be arrested before Fidel liberated us. I knew they had bought guns and rifles for Fidel because they sat in my toy closet before they were smuggled to the hills. My toy closet would be a good hiding place if Batista's police came to search the house. A little boy's toy closet would be the last place they'd look, and besides, there were plenty of toy guns mixed in with the real.

My head was full of nervous fears, too. I had reason to believe the men in my family could be arrested if the police came by again. They had already been by three times that year. Would they be back? I should have tossed and turned that night from all the tension in the air, but I slept soundly. Nothing like a couple pounds of pork to make you sleep like a rock.

When I woke up on Christmas Day, Santa Claus had left my brother and me two stockings full of chocolate. At the time, for some strange reason I thought chocolate came only from New York City. I'd say to my brother, "We are eating the finest New York City chocolate," just to make sure he appreciated it fully.

These would be the only presents we'd receive on Christmas, as it

Eduardo Machado & Michael Domitrovich

is a tradition to exchange gifts in Cuba and other parts of Latin America on January 6, Three Kings Day. The holiday is named for the Reyes Magos, or Magic Kings, also known as the Three Wise Men. The gifts exchanged represent the gifts they brought to Baby Jesus when they arrived on camels in Bethlehem. I know for sure they rode camels because I would put sand in front of the house and check for their footprints on the morning of the sixth.

New Year's Eve was the perfect dose of holiday frivolity, thrown into the middle of our sun drenched Christian festivities. I remember a small party in 1958. Nerves were higher than ever, as the week leading up to the New Year was full of rumors and truths. The Revolution was coming. Fidel was surrounding Havana. There were small bombs here and there. A beating. An arrest. Quickly mounting terror. Batista was on his way out, so people were excited. Ecstatic, even. And scared. Terror and ecstasy in every breath. The people, the city, the country, all breathing together. Waiting for the future.

And we had a little party. I helped my grandmother pluck grapes from their stems. We separated them into groups of twelve, then wrapped them in little pieces of tissue paper. Twelve grapes in a bundle were given to your loved ones to ensure good luck in the new year. There was music that got louder as the night went on. Voices that grew in volume, too, as the rum, *cidra*, and daiquiris were drunk. Manuela made *Camarones Enchilados* with rice and a salad of avocados and radishes. Dessert was little French pastries from Havana. Napoleons or éclairs eaten to celebrate the sweetness of the night. I fell asleep just after ringing in the new year.

And when I woke the next morning, everything had changed. My grandmother told me Fidel had won. Batista had left Cuba at midnight on a private plane. We were free. At last. Hallelujah.

"We have a future now!" my grandfather yelled. Days like this are never forgotten; they happen once if you are lucky, and they are printed forever in your mind.

What to do now but celebrate at La Terasa. My grandfather drove me in the Buick just before lunchtime. Every house we passed on the way had a Cuban flag in front. Some of them had pictures of Fidel in the mountains. Unbelievable. He had won. We had done it.

We ate basketfuls of fried shrimp. My grandfather and his buddies toasted to Camilo, Che, Fidel, and to the new world that they were all about to create; a world of financial and intellectual freedom for Cuba.

On Three Kings Day I got a huge erector set, a Rin Tin Tin costume, and a tent from the Reyes Magos. I put the tent in the middle of Manuela's *guayaba* trees. With my tent, my uniform, and my gun I was ready to be a soldier for the Revolution.

Fidel got to Havana a few days later. A couple days after that my cousin Rolando and his uncle Aquiles took me aboard a boat docked on the bay in Cojimar, in front of La Terasa. I met Fidel Castro that day, Camilo too. I don't remember if Che was there, but he could have been. It was after the sixth, but it felt like Three Kings Day. I was meeting the Reyes Magos, the Three Wise Men, bearing gifts of myrrh, frankincense, and hope.

That was when I began to stay up later and later at night. I thought it was just too exciting to sleep through a revolution. Fortunately there was plenty to do late into the evening. One night, Oscar took my aunt Chichi and me along with my cousins Hugo, Barbara, and Dulce, on an impromptu road trip to celebrate Fidel's victory. He drove us to an all-night roadside stand that sold burgers and sandwiches. The old guard ate *Media Noches*, a version of a Cuban sandwich with ham, pork, Swiss cheese, pickles, and a little mustard. The difference between the traditional Cuban Mix and a *Media Noche* is in the bread. The *Media Noche* is smaller and sweeter, shaped like a big hotdog bun with a flavor similar to challah or Portugese sweet bread. But as far as I was concerned, the only reason for a midnight snack run to the tin hut in the dark was a big juicy burger. They were really more like meatballs, a mixture of pork and beef with sautéed onions and garlic mixed in. Nothing else fancy, just a fresh bun and plenty of mustard and ketchup. The taste lingers: fresh meat and onions, enriched bread, and lots of ketchup. Something about those patties and their fixings, a little bit of Cuba and a little bit of Yankee . . . perhaps the burgers were clairvoyant?

Eduardo Machado & Michael Domitrovich

[Roast Pork]

The taste of roast pork is impossible to forget. The meat is marinated for a long time to soak up flavor, but after it's roasted it still tastes nice and porky. Usually the *mojo* used to marinate the pork is made with a paste of garlic and salt, but if the garlic burns during the slow roast, everything tastes pretty bitter. So this recipe uses cloves of garlic neatly tucked away in holes poked by a sharp knife. It's good to find a piece of pork with a thick rind of fat and some skin that will get nice and crispy. I like to use the butt portion of a fresh leg of pork, but you may use the shank portion if you like. Make sure that the bags you use to marinate the pork have not been treated with any chemicals.

1 fresh ham (butt portion), about 7 pounds with bone
12 garlic cloves, peeled
1 Spanish onion, peeled and sliced into ½-inch-thick rings
3 plastic grocery bags, rinsed and checked for holes
1 cup sour orange juice (or ½ cup orange juice and ½ cup lime juice)
1 tablespoon dried oregano
1 teaspoon ground cumin
2 tablespoons salt
1 teaspoon ground black pepper

1. Rinse the fresh ham with cold water. Using a sharp knife, score the skin with shallow diagonal incisions, then poke 12 deep holes all over the meat (but not the skin). Put a garlic clove in each hole, pressing it so it goes in deep. Place half the onions in the bottom of one of the grocery bags with a second bag around it. Place the pork in the bag and cover with the remaining onions.

2. In a small mixing bowl, combine the sour orange juice, oregano, cumin, salt, and black pepper. Pour the mixture into the bag with the pork. Tie the first bag tightly, then the second, squeezing out any air so the marinade is in direct contact with the pork. Place the double bag

inside a third bag that ties in the opposite direction to prevent leakage. Turn the bundle around in your hands a few times to bathe the pork in marinade. Set the bundle in a container that fits in your refrigerator, to catch any liquid that may leak out. Marinate at least 12 hours or up to 48 hours, turning a few times so the meat marinates evenly.

3. Remove the pork from the refrigerator about 1 hour before you're ready to cook it. Preheat the oven to 350°F. Cut open the plastic bags and discard the marinade inside. Pat the pork dry with paper towels. Transfer to a roasting pan and bake in the middle of the oven for about 3 hours and 30 minutes (30 minutes per pound), or until the internal temperature reaches 170°F on a meat thermometer. Rotate the pan once, halfway through, to ensure even cooking. When it's done, transfer the roast to a carving board. Cover with foil and let rest for 10 minutes so the juices can redistribute. Carve into thin slices with a serrated knife. Serve with *Moros y Cristianos* and *Yuca* with Lime *Mojo* (recipes follow).

Makes 8 servings

▌ *Moros y Cristianos* ▐

Moors and Christians. How controversial. How Cuban. The funny thing is that this is the most quotidian dish, even in Cuba today. It is often made with leftovers, because no Cuban household is complete without a huge pot of beans boiling on the stove. White rice is usually in abundance, too. All you have to do is add some bacon and *sofrito* and, voila, *Moros*. This recipe is made with canned beans for ease and speed, but if you tried Fernando's beans in the last chapter and managed to not eat them all, they'd surely jazz up this already flavorful recipe.

½ pound thick-cut bacon, sliced into 1-inch pieces
1 Spanish onion, peeled and cut into ¼-inch dice

½ green pepper, stems and seeds removed, cut into ¼-inch dice

4 garlic cloves, peeled and finely chopped

¼ cup Goya tomato sauce (from one 8-ounce can)

1½ teaspoons salt

½ teaspoon ground black pepper

1 teaspoon dried oregano

½ teaspoon ground cumin

2 cups medium-grain rice

Two 15.5-ounce cans black beans, drained and rinsed thoroughly

4 cups chicken broth or water

1. Fry the bacon in a large pot or Dutch oven over medium-high heat until crispy, 6 minutes. Transfer to a plate using a slotted spoon.

2. Add the onion and green pepper to the pot and cook, stirring, until softened slightly, 3 minutes. Add the garlic and cook, stirring, 1 minute more. Add the tomato sauce, salt, black pepper, oregano, and cumin. Stir and cook 1 minute more.

3. Add the rice, beans, and half the bacon to the pot, along with the chicken broth or water. Bring to a boil. Reduce the heat to low and simmer, covered, until the rice is cooked through, the beans are soft, and the flavors have blended, 25 minutes. Fluff the rice with a fork, then stir gently to make sure the beans are evenly distributed. Serve garnished with the remaining bacon sprinkled over the top.

Makes 8 to 10 servings

❙ *Yuca with Lime Mojo* ❙

Yuca is a mellow, hearty, stick-to-your-ribs kind of vegetable. It's served here with a bright and bracing lime *mojo* that wakes up the starchy root's flavors. This is a practical dish, simple yet luxurious, just like my grandmother Manuela. It uses the *yuca*'s salty, starchy cooking water to make a deliciously flavorful sauce. The leftovers are divine the next day. They heat up well, but I've been known to munch them cold, late at night.

For the yuca:
3 pounds fresh *yuca**
3 tablespoons salt

For the lime mojo:
½ cup lime juice
4 garlic cloves, peeled and finely chopped
½ cup olive oil
1 teaspoon salt
½ teaspoon ground black pepper

*Fresh *yuca* is a long, brown-skinned root that can be found in most Latin supermarkets' produce sections. If you can't find it fresh, frozen *yuca* is a wonderful alternative. It is already peeled, chunked, and partially cooked. If using frozen *yuca*, just start the recipe at step 2.

1. Peel the *yuca*, cut it in half lengthwise, then again into 3-inch chunks.

2. Put the *yuca* in a soup pot. Cover with cold water, then add 3 tablespoons salt. Bring to a boil. Reduce the heat to medium and cook, covered, about 30 minutes, or until the *yuca* is easily pierced with a knife.

3. Prepare the lime *mojo* while the *yuca* cooks: Combine the lime juice, garlic, olive oil, salt, and black pepper in a small bowl. Mix with a fork and set aside.

Eduardo Machado & Michael Domitrovich

4. When the *yuca* is done, reserve ¼ cup cooking liquid, then drain the rest. Transfer the *yuca* to a heatproof bowl. Be sure to remove any pieces of the *yuca*'s stringy core with a fork.

5. Add the reserved cooking liquid to the lime *mojo* and pour over the *yuca*. Cover the bowl with aluminum foil and let it sit for 5 minutes. Remove the foil, stir gently, and serve.

Makes 6 servings

Three

Rations

On a spring morning in mid-April, I awoke to see the sky outside my window clouded by parachutes. I bolted into the street to find my family staring upward. We thought it was the Americans landing, the final stages of a U.S. and Cuban exile invasion that would come to be known as the Bay of Pigs. Imagine our surprise to find that the parachutes didn't hold soldiers. Instead we were treated to parcels of anti-Castro propaganda, leaflets to fuel the fire. Even more bizarre than the appearance of the flyers was that my family agreed with their message. Get Fidel out of power.

How quickly things change. The savior had become the tyrant. Fidel was now the source of all suffering for my family, more than Batista ever was. I did my best to comprehend the contradictions in my family's feelings for the government. To this day it's still jarring to remember the rate at which everything changed. Still, I was only seven years old and I wanted to keep up, so I believed them. Fidel was a cockroach that needed to be squashed. A scourge. He was ruining everything.

First my grandfather Fernando was fired from his job at the docks. He had made it through the dictatorships of Machado and Batista, but Fidel was the guy who let him go. What a disgrace. My grandmother Cuca's properties in Guanabacoa were confiscated soon after, and then he did the unthinkable. He took over my grandfather Oscar's bus company in 1960 during a sweeping nationalization of major Cuban industries. Nobody was spared the reforms. Agriculture was collectivized, private property was expropriated, and when the banks were taken over by Che Guevara, the new head of finance, it was clear that Fidel's Revolution was not for us.

"A doctor as the head of finance. This is insanity!" my relatives exclaimed. The day before the banks were taken over it was a free for all in Havana. Everyone was trying to buy everything. The problem was, no one wanted to sell anything that could have possible value in the chaos that was about to ensue. Our neighbors buried bundles of gold bars in their yard. It seemed ridiculous at first, but as the day of financial seizure approached, we hid our own bundles. We buried dollars near Manuela's *guayaba* trees, feeling only slightly ridiculous amid the mass paranoia. Then the banks were nationalized. Our family's accounts were taken over and we were left bankrupt. The buried treasure was all we had to carry us through those impossible financial times.

Food was now rationed, and there were many shortages following numerous trade restrictions between Cuba and the United States. This led to the severing of all economic ties in January of 1961, and eventually snowballed into the U.S. embargo imposed on trade with Cuba that passed in February 1962.

But we were not yet in the realm of ideological dispute. We were hungry and dealing with the immediate effects of rationing. Everything seemed to be in short supply. The day before the pamphlets fell from the sky my uncle Pipo walked into the house carrying an enormous cloth bag, straining with the weight of something that seemed too large to be contained.

"What the hell is that?" Fernando asked.

"A swordfish," he said. "I went fishing."

"Oh, Jesus!" said Conchita, her eyes rolling at the thought of cleaning the monster.

"We need food, right?" asked Pipo. Nobody argued.

My father lit a cigarette and inhaled as he drank his café. I turned to him, seeking some stability, but he seemed lost. No smile, not an ounce of his usual manufactured charm, only angst. The mood was doubly bleak because our house was half empty. Almost everyone had left for the countryside to avoid being in the middle of a war. Most of my uncles, aunts, and cousins fled on the first day of the invasion, as soon as they heard the exiles had landed. We decided to stay, if only to see what would happen. That was just yesterday. It seemed like a month. It's hard to measure a change big enough to affect your whole life, but when a day seems like a month, you know something big is happening.

According to Oscar's marketplace rumor mill, the Bay of Pigs invasion was to be a two-part operation. First, a group of 1,400 exiled Cubans, trained and armed by the United States, would land in the city of Trinidad, about 250 miles southeast of Havana. There they would rally support among anti-Castro rebels in the area before approaching and overtaking Havana. If the ground invasion faltered or stalled, they would have the coverage of the nearby Escambray Mountains to set up camp and continue a guerilla campaign. The second phase of the invasion would involve multiple U.S. air strikes, mainly of Cuban military bases, followed by a deployment of U.S. Marines to aid the exile forces in their search and destroy mission against Fidel. The second phase never came.

At the last minute the exile forces were redeployed to the beaches of Giron and Larga, in the province of Matanzas, about 125 miles southeast of Havana. They were closer to Fidel, supposedly, but they were nowhere near the rebels who could strengthen their cause, and they would be dangerously exposed without the Escambray to cover them if anything went wrong.

We knew the exiles had landed. We knew that the plan had been set in motion. We even knew the exiles' chances were slim. We also knew there was plenty of U.S. aid on ships mere miles from the Cuban coast, and that if all else failed, the marines could march in to save the day.

So on that morning, standing in the street in front of my house, we thought, finally, they're here. It'll all be over soon. But as the parachutes drifted earthward, it was obvious that something was wrong. There were no soldiers touching down in Cojimar. Each parachute carried a crate that cracked open on impact, spilling piles of leaflets through the streets. I stooped down to pick one up. I don't remember if they were in English or Spanish, but we deciphered the message and were stunned by its simplicity: Go out into the streets and overthrow Fidel.

What? Obviously we would do that if we had to. But we were supposed to be bolstered by the military might of the U.S.A.! The air force and the marines! The exile army that had trained for two years in South Florida and Guatemala! We were waiting for the Yankees! Then we'd march proudly through the streets and defeat the tyrant!

But where were they? Why hadn't they followed as soon as our guys landed? Everyone was baffled. When? The word repeated. The question asked over and over as the propaganda landed on our heads from the sky. When would they save us?

We all got out of the yard and walked into the kitchen at Cuca's house for café and milk.

"Have they changed their minds?" Cuca wondered, stirring her cup.

"Never. They would never change their minds," my father argued emphatically.

"But when will they land?" she asked.

"Soon," Conchita assured her. "They'll be here soon."

All the questions swirled around me. I didn't understand how only two years ago we wanted the Americans out, and now we were waiting for their return, breathless with agitation. I guessed that marines were different from gangsters if we wanted them here so badly. The chatter rose in the room like smoke, then one of the cleaning ladies walked in and we all fell silent. We had to be careful. She was still a *Fidelista*. She believed in the Revolution. I took the silence as a cue to leave.

"Where's Mama?" I asked my dad.

"She's at her mother's with your brother."

"I want to go there."

"Fine," he said.

"In his pajamas?" Cuca asked, ever mannered, even in the middle of an invasion.

"Why not?" my father replied.

I ran out the door, listening to Conchita sighing. "We have to clean the swordfish now. Freeze some. Make *escabeche* out of the rest. If not the house will smell."

Escabeche. Yum. I faltered for a moment, wondering if I should wait around for a taste. Then again, *escabeche* is better when you let it sit for a while. That way the lightly browned swordfish can absorb the tangy vinegar marinade. Better to head over to see Mama and have some *escabeche* later. I looked up from the haze of my *escabeche* reverie to find myself walking through a war. It was not full-on combat, but it was war. Our lives were being directly affected by the military and their actions, and it was evident just by looking at the streets.

Nobody sat on their porches. Not a soul mingled in the street. A lone army jeep fitted with a machine gun and filled with cocky *milicianos* drove by. I looked to the mansion on my left and I noticed another group of soldiers throwing my neighbors' belongings into the middle of the street. My mother must have seen me coming while peering through a drawn curtain because she swept me up before I even reached the house, pulling me inside with Manuela and my aunt Chichi close by.

"What's going on?" I asked my mother. "Why are they doing this? Where are the neighbors?"

"They're gone," my mother said.

"Gone?" I asked.

"Yes," she replied.

"Why?" I begged.

"It wasn't safe for them here anymore."

"Not safe?" I dared to ask.

"Fidel was going to go after them. They had to leave," my grandmother said.

"It only took a night for them to take over their house," my aunt added.

"And now they're mocking them," said Manuela, "throwing their underwear out into the streets. No respect whatsoever. Motherfuckers!"

"Mama, please," my mother pleaded.

"Motherfucking bastards!" my grandmother repeated.

"They'll pay for it soon," my aunt said reassuringly.

The three women watched cautiously as our neighbors' personal belongings were thrown into the street. Undergarments, hats, papers, albums, and wedding pictures, spread through the street like garden trimmings scattered by a strong wind. The objects may have only been valuable to the owners, but to watch them discarded like garbage felt wrong. There was no room in Cuba for sentimentality anymore.

That night we ate swordfish *escabeche*, salty and pungent. The slabs of swordfish had nothing froufrou about them, no fancy spices or exotic fruit. We ate it simply, sliced into steaks then browned and brined. It was best to keep it simple, as this preparation was partially out of necessity. We had too much fish and couldn't possibly eat it all in one sitting. Still, there was something sophisticated about the dish, perhaps because the fish was allowed to keep its shape. Something about looking down at a golden slab, cutting into the thick flesh and marveling at the way it broke into juicy chunks, made the meal feel like a luxury. Maybe I just didn't want to admit it was a necessity. Either way, it got me through the night.

Soon after dinner we heard planes. "They're here," Cuca said.

I ran to my bedroom window to see the American planes. Then from across the street gunfire blared. My father ran into my room shouting, "DROP TO THE FLOOR!" I collapsed to the ground, waiting for the fire to stop. The smell of *escabeche* distracting my nose from what? Smoke?

An hour later my grandmother Manuela came over. I had never seen her out of control until that night. We gathered around her as she told us the news that my grandfather Oscar had been taken in for questioning by the *milicianos*. Silence. Creeping fear. My aunt Chichi appeared in the doorway.

"Any news?" asked Manuela.

"Nothing," said Chichi. "Our cousins will let us know if anyone calls."

Every breath felt dangerous. Manuela was fuming with the need for revenge. We wanted to get back at the bastard, but it was night, the Americans had not landed, there was no air force coming to the rescue, supposedly the fighting Cubans were being defeated. What happened to the plan? Would we be defeated next? How could the Americans betray us?

More paranoia all around, but we had reason to be paranoid. My entire family could have been implicated in the Bay of Pigs invasion. What was once a couple of guns in my toy closet had become an arsenal of fifteen or twenty machine guns. We were waiting for the Americans because we wanted to be a part of the uprising. We wanted to mobilize, to aid, to arm the resistance. Oscar was gone now and we didn't know if he was dead or alive. Any one of us could be taken in now. Who would be next?

Later that night, around two in the morning, we sat drinking *café con leche*. Some of the men sipped whiskey and everyone but the children had a cigar to fill each shallow breath with smoke. Oscar walked in. Manuela rushed to his side.

"Are you all right?" she asked.

"Of course I am," he said, dismissing her with a kiss on the cheek and a pat on the butt. "They questioned me."

"What did you tell them?" my grandmother Cuca demanded, her eyes flashing with fear.

"Be quiet!" Fernando ordered his wife, "let him speak."

"I told the truth," said Oscar. "I told them I was planning to overthrow Castro, that I was waiting for the Americans to land to start the uprising."

"You're crazy," Fernando whispered.

"They told me I was a mad man and let me go," Oscar winked. The room filled with laughter. My grandfather had done it again. He had told the truth and it had set him free. "But I think everyone should go into hiding. Manuela and I will stay here; the rest of you go to the countryside. They are watching us." We all nodded gravely as the laughter evaporated.

The next day we drove to a friend's house in the hills near Cojimar to get away from the action. Othin and I rode our bikes up and down the rambling roads of the countryside with our cousins Hugo, Barbara, and Dulce, watching the ocean from high points for signs of the American fleet that was supposed to be surrounding us. We could see the shadows of the boats in the deep distance. They never got any closer. Then Manuela called us with the news. The exiled forces had fought. Some had been killed. Many surrendered. Fidel had won. America had lost. We ate stale bread and butter with plantain omelettes until it was safe to return home.

José Antonio, Hugo, Dulce, Barbara, and me with Othin at Manuela's house, 1957

Even then, the nightmare continued. Every night we watched the trials of the captured exiles on T.V. The relentless sentencing infuriated my family. Execution for everyone? We had to think of a way to fight back.

When one of my great uncles was arrested and jailed, my grandfather had enough. Several of my cousins were already in hiding, so Oscar decided to try to save them. The best way to do this was to try to get them into the safety of a foreign embassy. This was more difficult than it sounds. Once you got into the embassy, Fidel's militia couldn't touch you, but nothing said they couldn't shoot you on the way in.

Oscar conducted several transports. Only one was unsuccessful, with the person ending up in jail, but this was not enough to deter my grandfather. He had a mission, and in this strange time of waiting that was all he needed to keep him going. He orchestrated too many transports for me to know about all of them, but there is one I remember well.

After hiding out for a couple of months, my cousin Eurgenio appeared one night at Oscar's door. He had taken part in the invasion, and Fidel's people were looking for him. His father was the great uncle already in jail, so he was doubly implicated. My grandfather told him to stay in my great grandmother's room with her. He was to leave the room only if he needed to go to the bathroom and only when my great grandmother told him it was safe. At that time there was always a family member guarding the house, sitting on the porch, looking for Fidel's militia. If any of us saw a *miliciano*, we'd tap on my great grandmother's window and Eurgenio would hide under the bed. The whole time he stayed with us he never sat down for dinner. We were discouraged from even entering the room, never mind talking to him. My great grandmother Maria was his only companion. She'd watch him from her rocking chair as he slept on her bed, if she wasn't dozing herself, that is. Waiting and more waiting. Eurgenio was tense.

News drifted in of Oscar's successful operations. He had helped my cousin Rolando, Eurgenio's brother-in-law, to drive a car through the gates of the Venezuelan embassy. His cousin Aquiles had a harder time. Aquiles had been a general for Batista. During Fidel's takeover he had strategically diverted his troops to allow Fidel's victory. A few years later, during a meeting with several high-ranking members of the Revolution, Aquiles got into an argument with Fidel. Fidel ended the conversation by shooting him in the shoulder, barely missing his heart. Aquiles's wife, Caridad, got a car to rush her husband to safety, but instead of taking him to the hospital she drove him straight to the Swiss embassy. She got a doctor to remove the bullet, kissed him good night, then went home to look after her children.

The plan for Eurgenio was to get him into the Swiss embassy. How this was to occur remained a mystery until just before it happened. Like we were riding to the countryside, my grandfather gathered me, my brother Jesus, my cousins Dulce, Barbara, and Hugo, and my grandmother Manuela. We piled into Oscar's Buick, surprised to see Eurgenio outside of Maria's room, waiting for us in the middle of the back seat.

My grandfather boasted, "They'll never suspect a car filled with children."

As we approached Havana, Oscar revealed his plan. When we got near the embassy, he would stop long enough for us to open the door to let Eurgenio out. A few of us would have to get out of the car for Eurgenio to make his escape, and my grandfather made sure to remind us that if we waited too long before getting back in the car, there would be trouble. Eurgenio's only orders were to run like mad and use all his strength to get through the gates of the Swiss embassy. We waited nervously until, mere moments away, Oscar changed his mind.

"Listen, when you kids run out of the car, I want you all to make a lot of noise. Try to appear normal and distract the guards as your cousin runs. Would you do that?" he asked.

"Of course!" we replied. Anything for family.

"I'm going to miss you guys," Eurgenio whispered.

"So are we," my grandmother said, a tear rolling from her eyes.

"I'm going to miss my country," Eurgenio said.

"You'll be back soon," said Oscar.

"We are going to beat the son of a bitch!" my cousin Hugo shouted with a very macho stance. My grandmother shushed him.

"I hope you don't die," I said as I squeezed Eurgenio's hand.

"Thank you," he said.

"Now! Now!" my grandfather shouted. We had reached the embassy.

All at once every young person in the car poured out the door chattering wildly, laughing and joking. The *milicianos* smiled at us as Eurgenio ran like a greyhound toward the gates of the Swiss embassy.

We rushed back to the car and drove away with the sounds of gunfire trailing behind us. I thought for sure he was dead. I said a couple Hail Marys to make sure he'd get into heaven.

When we arrived home, we got a special treat for our work. Our reward was ice cream, smooth and soft, and hard to come by, somehow procured so there was plenty to go around. We were given three different flavors—mango, coconut, and strawberry—and we all ate our fill. Then the decree.

"You must never speak about this," Oscar said.

It was not a moment to talk back, not like we could have anyway through mouthfuls of cool custard, but we knew. This was serious stuff.

Later that night we found out that our cousin Eurgenio was safe. I thanked the Virgin Mary for listening to my prayers.

❧

Food was rationed more and more and our money was quickly running out. We lived on red beans, white beans, and rice. We ate fish when it was available and meat or eggs only when Oscar would go inland to the farms to buy them from the farmers who had once been his friends. Things were different now. Friendship was measured by your loyalty to Fidel. Sure, they liked him enough to sell him food illegally, but he no longer trusted them. His life, his beliefs, his sense of good and evil were all being directly challenged by Fidel and his Revolution. Almost everything he worked his entire life for was gone, destroyed by the actions of the man who was supposed to secure it.

The priests at Los Escolapios had begun lecturing to us that Fidel was the devil on earth. They would tell us how the last headmaster (who had died a few years earlier) was appearing to them in the hallways. So now it was not only the lions and snakes that I was afraid of, but also the ghosts of past authority figures. If I had to go to the bathroom or walk from one classroom to another it was always in a total panic—rushing, running, praying that the ghost would not appear to me.

Panic is like salt and sugar, bitter when it starts, but in the middle of it, when it's making you run and dream, it's very sweet. It's better than sadness. Panic gives you a high. I spent the rest of my childhood panicked. I stayed at the school for lunch since there were no buses or chauffeurs to pick me up at lunchtime. The food at the cafeteria was now cold sandwiches with some kind of juice. The priests kept telling us that soon the school would be taken over by the Communists. Finally one afternoon the *milicianos* arrived. I first saw them outside the door as I sat at my desk working on a math problem. Our teacher saw them, too. He quickly closed the door. A few minutes later another priest came in looking like he'd seen the ghost of the headmaster and whispered something to the math teacher. The math teacher told us to walk in line toward the church.

As we walked down the corridors *milicianos* with guns were roaming the halls. When we got into the church, *milicianos* were standing on the altar. They passed out chocolate bars telling us that Fidel and the Revolution were giving us the chocolate bars, not Jesus, not the Virgin Mary, not the saints, but the Revolution. I think they danced on the altar afterward, but maybe I imagined that. At that point in my life imagination and reality were starting to mix with each other, like scrambled eggs when the yolk mixes with the white. I do know that I never went back to Catholic school after that afternoon.

At Manuela's house we now had more chickens running around in the yard for eggs and *Arroz con Pollo*. There was a whole family to feed us, and every egg could become another chicken. I remember marveling at this cycle most as my grandmother made breakfast. She'd crack the eggs into a bowl, showing me any with double yolks, a trace of blood, or a little unborn chicken inside that would have to be thrown out. The best was when she'd butcher a hen, splitting it open and removing its still-warm eggs. The plantain omelettes from those eggs were a special treat just for me, extra smooth and rich like custard. Manuela making a plantain omelette was proof that life goes on.

By now Manuela's family had felt the full effects of the Revolution. Her brother Pepe had been given a thirty-year jail sentence for helping in the Bay of Pigs. Most of her nephews were in embassies waiting to leave, but she still put on face cream and exercised. She, in the middle of all this madness, was completely calm. One day while she was making rice pudding with milk and lots of sugar and cinnamon, her mother Maria called her from her bed. My grandmother went in the room and walked back, stunned.

"Mama has a rash all over her body," she said to no one in particular. It was diagnosed as skin cancer. Death had come to our house.

We watched after my great grandmother for about a month. Someone was always holding her hand. We'd sit together in the dining room eating rice and beans and *yuca* and avocados. We gathered *guayabas* from the trees in the backyard and made *cascos de guayaba*. We busied ourselves with the day to day and waited for Maria to die. She was now eighty-eight.

One day my mother took me by the hand and told me to stay with my grandmother Cuca. My mother would keep my brother with her. I guess they didn't think he would know what was going on.

That afternoon I took a shower. I went into my room to get dressed and I heard my grandmother on the telephone. She told a relative that my great grandmother had died an hour before. The funeral was tonight, at the house. I could not button my shirt. I was frozen. My shoulders went up to my neck in fear. The fear that I had been holding back all year had finally won. Everything was over. Our lives were over. There was no escaping. The Revolution had destroyed us. I couldn't button my button. My grandmother walked into my room. She took a quick look at me and said, "So you heard me on the telephone?" It took all the strength I had to nod yes. My chest felt like it was falling into a deep hole. "I am sorry, but she had a good long life and died peacefully."

How could she die peacefully when she saw us lose everything we worked for? But I only nodded. Then the fear smothered me, conquered me, took over everything in me, and I fainted.

When I came to, my grandmother Cuca was rocking me in her arms. Conchita handed her some café. "Here, sip this," she said, and gave me a sip. "You are so sensitive."

"Am I?" I asked.

"Yes. What will the world do to you?" she asked, knowing the answer.

"I do not know," I whimpered.

"You're as cold as ..."

"A corpse?" I cut her off.

"Yes, as a matter of fact. Drink the café and it will bring you back to life." I did drink the café. I tasted its potent powers, and it brought me back.

After my great grandmother died, I began to have hallucinations of people haunting me. I would scream out in the middle of the night or faint suddenly during the day, always after seeing strange humanlike apparitions materializing before me. Whenever I had a spell, my grandmother Cuca would be there when I woke up, holding a sweet cup of coffee to bring me back. She believed my affliction to be spiritual. Manuela, however, decided that I was mentally unsound. Since one of my father's friends had become a psychiatrist, it was decided that I'd start seeing him.

I met with the psychiatrist for about six months. I remember one day when he gave me finger puppets and told me to act out everything that was wrong in my family, which I did happily. He was visibly shaken and told me that I had too big an imagination. Another time he asked me to draw pictures of everyone in my family. Armed with a box of pencils, I set about drawing the legs and genitals of every one of my relatives, but not their faces. My father was brought in and shown the pictures. Apparently there was something wrong with a six-year-old drawing genitals.

That day my father took me out and bought a bag of balloons with faces on them. He took me home, and upstairs to sit on the terrace of the house. As he blew up each balloon, he'd show me the face, naming one balloon after every member of the family. After I repeated their names, he would throw the balloons off the roof and into the street. The whole ordeal took more than three hours. This was the most time I ever spent alone with my father in my entire life.

While I was seeing the psychiatrist, time went by very fast. I was not going to school, and my brother had gotten old enough to keep me company, so we spent a lot of time together. It seemed more and more people were leaving every day, not on vacation, but on an extended excursion. I can't remember anyone ever talking about it. They would leave almost silently. There one day, gone the next. My uncle Oscar and his wife, Olga, had left for Miami with their children, Lupe and Oscar Jr. They had left behind the house that my grandmother built them on her property, in the area that had been a small park. After they left, no one went inside the house, as if they thought any day my uncle and aunt and my two cousins would return. The streets seemed empty like the night I walked to my mother's house during the Bay of Pigs, but they didn't fill up the next day. Or the next. We kept on.

It was in July of that summer that a rumor began spreading through Havana that the children of the bourgeoisie would be sent to Russia to be retrained and turned into Marxists. Our families would be torn apart in the name of the Revolution. I wondered why my mother and grandmother started to make my brother and me winter coats. I figured it was a project to occupy them, but what would we do with their warmth in the Cuban sunshine? Were we going to Russia?

In a flash the rumor was repeated by a Cuban bishop on the Voice of America radio station. Every night he intoned over the airwaves that the children would be sent to Russia. It didn't take long for the rumor to turn to fact, at least around my house. My parents were applying for visas to get out of Cuba, but not for all of us at once. They had heard about a special program that issued visas allowing unaccompanied minors to travel to the United States. The bishop on the Voice of America had called it Operation Peter Pan. That didn't sound so bad. Little did I know just how much that name would sting my ears years later.

In September the winter coats had been finished. Almost on cue, we got a call from someone at the airport that there were two Peter Pan Flights leaving that day for the U.S.A. My parents put my five-year-old brother and me into the car, took out an already packed suitcase, and drove toward the airport. When we got there, we were met with a major traffic jam and no way of reaching the terminal. Several hundred families were grappling to get their children on those two planes. Most of them didn't make it. We didn't either, but from that day on I knew I'd be leaving soon.

I loved my country even as a child. I was fiercely proud to be Cuban. As I waited for my day, for my plane, I made a practice of memorizing everything around me. The stools at La Terasa, count them. The flower beds in our family's rose garden, how big, how long? The sign on the side of the road in Guanabacoa, Capital Street, the right turn you made to get to Cojimar. The way my mother looked when she smiled, her front teeth slightly crooked. The way my father slumped his shoulders when he walked in his long sleeve pattern silk shirts. The sun. The heat. The way you smell the ocean even if you can't see it. I memorized it all.

Me reciting a poem by José Martí, with schoolmates and their parents, 1960

Then the day came. The day I had been waiting for. It was October 29, 1961. My grandfather Oscar took my brother and me for a haircut. Afterward we drove up and down the beach in Cojimar. He looked at me and I could see his eyes speaking. He was telling me, remember all this. Remember the sidewalks, the shells on the beach, the smell of jasmine. Remember me. I let him know silently that I would.

When we woke up the next morning, my mother and father told me we were going to the airport. We took two cars so we could bring both sets of grandparents and my aunt Chichi. When we got to the airport, my mother said nothing; she could only cry. My father said, "See you soon." My grandmother Manuela hugged me. My grandfather Oscar told me to take care of my brother, and then we walked into the waiting room. We sat by a neighbor, a young woman who was also leaving that day by chance. The day before we had visited her house as her mother dismantled her girdle and put dollars in between the rubber layers before sewing them back together. I spent the whole time in the waiting room thinking she was going to get caught and shot. That kept me occupied. Her doom.

It kept me occupied as I held my brother's hands, as he cried because he couldn't go and see his mother who was standing quietly on the other side of the glass partition nicknamed the fish tank. They stood and we sat for several hours. I would look at them every couple of minutes, noticing that my grandfather was leaving every once in a while, coming back, and not being able to look at me. None of them could. Look at me. And I wanted them to. I wanted them to look me straight in the eyes and show me the truth. They were letting me go because they were so afraid. Because the one thing they could not bear was that I might not end up exactly like them, or who they wished me to be. Ambitious. Aggressive. A capitalist. God please, not what Fidel wanted me to be. Not a Marxist, whatever that was. They were willing to give my brother and me up to a foreign country so that their wish could be fulfilled, so that their status quo could be guaranteed for the future. I knew all of this while I sat in the fishbowl, but I was not sad. I was furious. I hated myself for hating them, especially my mother. The angel. The kind-hearted, the innocent Gilda. I distracted myself by imagining Girdle Girl riddled with bullets, the seams of her girdle bursting into smoke, pieces of green paper flying everywhere.

Then a *miliciano* told me it was time for them to question me and check my bags. He walked my brother and me into a small room. My brother made friends with him, but I stayed quiet. He went through our suitcases and asked if there were dollars or jewelry hidden anywhere. I said no. Suddenly I was terrified about Girdle Girl. Should I tell him about her? About what she was trying to get away with? I decided not to.

He checked our suitcase. Two shirts, two pairs of pants, a coat, and so on. You weren't allowed to take a lot with you. He frisked me thoroughly, opened my pants, and felt inside. For what? For hidden diamonds, a hundred dollar bill? I imagined the treasures I wasn't concealing. I turned away as he searched me. I looked at my brother, who was sucking his thumb. They searched him, too. I was embarrassed by his weakness, but he was only five.

When the *miliciano* was finished, he walked us to the tarmac where we saw a Pan Am four-engine plane. Then without looking back, without a hug good-bye, without anything at all, I looked straight ahead and boarded the Pan Am plane. Girdle Girl was already on board. When I saw her sitting there on the aisle, I was relieved she hadn't died. She was crying quietly. She told us to sit with her, and we did. She told me I was lucky because my uncle was waiting for me. She didn't know where she was going. I didn't feel sorry for her because she was fifteen and had gotten to live in Cuba seven years more than I did.

I remembered my dad telling me that we were only going to Miami for a few days of vacation with my uncle Tatan. I remember not believing him, wishing that he had the courage to tell me the truth. My little brother was hysterical. He pleaded, "Where are we going! Where are we going?" I tried to reassure him.

"We are going on a great adventure. Don't be scared." I held his hand as tightly as I could as the plane took off.

I did my best to conceal my own uncertainty, but my head was popping with questions. What are they thinking? Why have they done this? Don't they love us at all? I am only eight. He is only five. Why do I have to take care of him?

Without our knowing it, we had crossed an invisible line. About fifteen minutes into the flight the pilot announced that we had reached American territory. We were free. Welcome to liberty.

Everyone applauded. The announcement cheered my brother up for a minute. I relaxed for a few seconds. I thought about the U.S.A. What's it going to be like? How cold will it be? My mind went back to the time my mother made Baked Alaska. What could be more American? Cake, ice cream, and meringue! That's what winter is like! That's what the U.S.A. will be like. White snow like meringue, but when you step in, you'll be stuck in cold frozen ice cream. The cake underneath is the soil. The earth. Terra firma. But we won't feel the earth; we'll only know the cold. I closed my eyes and felt my brother squeeze my hand as banks of sugared snow swept before me. We hit an air bump, and I squeezed his hand back. We were headed for the land of Baked Alaska. I was going to have to keep him warm.

[*Swordfish Escabeche*]

The longer this dish is marinated, the more briny goodness it picks up. But since most of us don't like anything sitting in our refrigerators for a week, I've kept the marinating time down to an overnight dunk in the pickling juice bath. Try to find thick swordfish steaks. If you can, get your fishmonger to portion them out for you, otherwise get three thick steaks and cut them into six halves. We ate this dish right before the Revolution, when food was scarce. At La Terasa, it was a special treat. Either way, it is best enjoyed in the afternoon sunshine with an ocean breeze blowing through your hair.

2 cups good-quality olive oil
Six 4- to 6-ounce swordfish steaks, 1 inch thick
1 tablespoon salt
1 teaspoon ground black pepper
1½ Spanish onions, peeled and sliced into ¼-inch half-circles
1 red pepper, stem and seeds removed, sliced into ¼-inch half-circles
4 garlic cloves, peeled and coarsely chopped
3 bay leaves
10 whole black peppercorns
2 cups wine vinegar (white or red)
One 3.25 ounce jar capers, with brine*

*I prefer smaller capers in a brine that has no preservatives (just salt, vinegar, and water).

1. Heat ¼ cup of the olive oil in a large skillet over high heat. Season the swordfish on both sides using 1½ teaspoons salt and the black pepper. Sauté the swordfish until golden, 3 minutes per side. Transfer to a 9 × 13-inch baking dish.

2. Add the remaining 1¾ cups olive oil to the pan along with the onions, red peppers, garlic, bay leaves, peppercorns, and remaining 1½ teaspoons salt. Cook until the vegetables are softened, 5 minutes. Turn off the heat, then add the vinegar and capers with brine. Stir carefully to combine.

3. Pour the mixture over the swordfish, distributing the vegetables evenly. Cool to room temperature. Cover with plastic wrap and refrigerate overnight, turning the steaks once in the morning to absorb the marinade evenly. Remove the *escabeche* from the refrigerator about 30 minutes before serving. Serve the *escabeche* with Cuban bread and a small green salad, topping each fillet with some of the vegetables and a few spoonfuls of marinade.

Makes 6 servings

[*Plantain Omelette*]

The combination of eggs and bananas may seem odd at first, but it is just that combination of sweet and savory flavors that keeps me coming back for more. The texture of this omelette is like a Spanish *tortilla*, with a uniform doneness on the outside and a tender, though not runny, center. Do not fret if the tortilla doesn't make it through the flip—the eggs will be just as good and the plantains just as sweet. Of course, I recommend using the freshest eggs possible, just like Manuela did.

8 eggs
½ teaspoon salt

¼ teaspoon ground black pepper
¼ cup vegetable oil
2 ripe plantains, peeled and sliced ¼-inch thick
1 tablespoon salted butter

1. Using a fork, beat the eggs with the salt and pepper until well blended.

2. Heat the vegetable oil in a 10-inch nonstick skillet with rounded edges over medium-high heat until hot but not smoking. Fry half the plantains in a single layer until golden brown, turning once with a spatula, 1 to 2 minutes per side, depending on how ripe the plantains are. Transfer to a separate plate when done. Repeat with the remaining plantains.

3. Reduce the heat to medium. Add the butter to the pan, along with all the plantains. Using your spatula, stir the plantains to coat them with butter and prevent them from sticking.

4. Pour the eggs evenly over the plantains. Cook, pulling the eggs away from the edges of the pan with your spatula, swirling the pan to fill the spaces with uncooked egg, 2 minutes. At this point, the egg should cover the entire bottom of the pan. Spread the plantains out into an even layer using the back of your spatula and cook the omelet without disturbing it for 1 minute more, until the bottom is set and the top is still a little runny.

5. Carefully run your spatula around the edge of the omelet to make sure the sides are not sticking. Shake the pan gently, then slide the omelet onto a big plate. Place the pan on top of the plate and carefully invert. Remove the plate and cook the other side of the omelette until just set, 1 minute more. Return the omelette to the plate and slice into 6 pieces. Serve with rice and beans or buttered toast.

Makes 6 servings

Four

Exile

Hialeah was a lot of things; cold was not one of them. From a bird's-eye view it looked like a burned-out field; just little square boxes surrounded by little square yards, all dingy green and ashy gray.

After we landed, my brother and I were separated from Girdle Girl and made to sit waiting for about as many hours as we had waited in Cuba. At this point everyone was terrified. Two U.S. officials took Othin and me into a small, sterile room and questioned us for a while. Then they gave us a set of vaccinations. I think it was the same set we had been given in Cuba right before we left. We were told that my uncle had "requested us," whatever that meant, so there was nothing to worry about. We were going to live with him and we wouldn't be sent to an orphanage. We only had to enjoy our freedom and good luck for getting out of Cuba. I tried to contain my excitement.

My passport photo, 1961

The officials led us outside, and the moment they left us, I feared what was next. My brother looked to me for reassurance, then, upon seeing my obviously anxious state, he launched into a series of his own questions.

"Where's Mama?" he whined. I could tell he was tired.

"In Cuba," I told him.

Othin's passport photo, 1961

"Where are we?" he snipped. He was getting angry.

"Miami," I replied.

Before he could get anymore answers, I spotted my uncle Tatan running toward us. With his fair skin and muscular six-foot-six frame, he towered over the crowd and was instantly recognizable. Tatan was followed by his wife Olga's cousin who had driven him to the airport since he did not have a car of his own.

We drove a short distance through the barren streets and arrived at a shack. "Welcome," my uncle said. I looked at him like he was crazy. "Everyone's inside. Come."

It was late in the afternoon and the heat of Hialeah was predatory. The bodies in the house made it almost impossible to breathe. Four people were living in a two-room shack. Olga and Tatan had left with their children Oscarito and Lupe before U.S.-Cuba relations soured. And although they had settled and made the home as livable as possible in those circumstances, the effect of the little shack was jarring, to say the least.

Devastation overcame me upon seeing the room we were supposed to share with Oscarito and Lupe. It was furnished with a bunk bed and a double bed. Nothing else. Grim. I was to share the bottom part of the bunk bed with my brother. Lupe and Oscarito had dibs on the big bed and top bunk because they were there first. It's not like we could have drawn straws, or raced, or played some other appropriately childish game to see who won the better space. These cousins didn't like to play. They were cold and reserved when they confronted our presence, and they made it clear that the sleeping situation was non-negotiable. Even though we lived a house away from them in Cuba, we had never been close. There was a wall that surrounded everyone in my father's family, a wall that would take decades to tear down, even a tiny little bit. They weren't entirely rude. They were polite, just not warm. I mistook their reserve for apathy. I thought they didn't care about what had just happened to my brother and me. As I saw it, they came with their parents. We were alone. Therefore, they were the enemy.

What had just happened to us? From a mansion to a shack. From

Eduardo Machado & Michael Domitrovich

the sea breezes of Cojimar to the suffocating heat of Hialeah. When were my mother and father getting here? A day? A week? Months? A year? Never? Would we ever go home again? What was home? How could they do this to us? Did they know how much it hurt? Were they sitting at La Terasa having a drink and eating *paella*? I was furious. Shocked. Disbelieving. Then anger. More anger. Rage.

Before we went to bed, Olga's cousin had brought all the kids masks. I could tell by the price tags that they were cheap. Five cents? It was insulting. Why was he bringing presents, and why were they cheap masks?

He told us it was for something called Halloween.

"What's Halloween?" I asked.

"It's a Yankee holiday where everyone dresses up."

"It's happening tomorrow," Oscarito said.

Okay, I thought, like a costume ball. Could I be Rin Tin Tin again? No. I was given a clown mask, my brother a ghost mask. It was all too confusing.

I imagined a variety show I had seen with my mother the year before in downtown Havana. Whenever it was time for a song, the set would roll away and a single spotlight would illuminate the singer. I willed the set of Hialeah to go away so a spot would come on me. Alone. Without any of them. I felt the humiliation of being sent away. How the Revolution had led to abandonment. Exile. I wanted to die. No. I had to take care of my brother. If I were gone, what would happen to him? So I let him walk into the spotlight of my isolation, and he became part of my imaginary world. We were not in Miami; we had gone all the way to New York City. Our two-room shack was a suite at the Plaza Hotel, and we were eating Baked Alaska every night for dinner with real New York City chocolate for dessert.

In reality, that night, my first night in the U.S.A., we feasted on white rice and SPAM. Not the kind of SPAM that comes in a cute little box with a blue label and sunny yellow lettering. This was a giant cylinder from a huge can courtesy of the army. I don't know which color induced nausea faster, the dirty gold of the tin or the sickly pink of the processed meat. Army-rationed SPAM, like ham that has been sitting out in the sun for a day, is a flavor that will forever haunt my nose and mouth. Little did I know, I would have to get very used to SPAM and all its permutations.

My brother was shaking when he went to bed that night. He cried in his sleep and sometime in the early hours of the morning he wet the bed. Poor little thing was only five. If I was devastated, I can only imagine how he felt.

We both woke up terrified. It was the next day, and mother was not there. My brother must have known this in his sleep. He must have dreamed of a world without her, a world without her lullabies and soft kisses and virginal smiles; without short walks down the beach and her *flan* made with a dozen eggs and syrup that tasted like angel nectar. To sleep and in dreams to search for her crooked smile, only to see soldiers and planes and clowns and ghosts, it's no wonder he wet the bed.

The next morning my cousins went to school. My uncle told me he would enroll me in a couple of days, but that for the time being he wanted me to rest. Othin and I were left alone with our aunt Olga, who was now a very nervous young woman. After moving to the United States, she discovered a new religious fervor within herself, which she channeled into the small gatherings and intense Bible study of a local religious community. She grew closer to her cousin's wife, the one who picked us up at the airport, and before long it was official. She had become a Jehovah's Witness.

This new brand of Christianity, however, had not taught her to be kind. When she found my brother's soiled sheets, she made us wash them by hand and hang them out to dry. She instructed my brother to stand near the sheets and wait. Whenever anyone passed by on the streets he was to call out, "Those are my sheets; they are hanging there because I peed on the bed."

She spent the day inside studying scripture while we remained in the yard until she decided we had had enough. I was thinking in all-too-American terms. "She is a bitch. Or worse than a bitch, she's a whore. Cruel. Satan with a Bible."

She could have had some sympathy, given that we were just children. Then again, this was a woman who had devoted her life to marrying up the economic ladder, only to lose everything. When your prized husband is stripped of his social and economic status, it's impossible to not ripple the shock wave of loss through those around you. Still, I couldn't get over the hypocrisy: She was a devil to us while she was learning about Jesus.

October 31, 1961 was our first full day in Hialeah. It was a day filled with heat, overheard Bible studies, humiliation, and rice with eggs for lunch. The day was bad; the night got much worse.

At around five we had a dinner of cold Velveeta cheese sandwiches on white bread with a salad of lettuce and canned garbanzo beans in vegetable oil and distilled vinegar. It was an exercise in gustatory sterility. The food tasted more like the chemical processes used to preserve it than any kind of actual flavor. The salad was a disappointing Easter basket, all plastic frills of soggy iceberg covered in wet beans that tasted like metal. I grew accustomed to the texture of the sandwich after a while, but I was irked by the way the enriched white bread conformed to the roof of my mouth as the cheese oozed from the inside. The tang of the Velveeta, contrasted with its creamy texture, dulled by the cottony feel of the white bread, made the whole thing seem like a science experiment. And just as my tummy ache started to dissipate, there came the next humiliation. Olga's costume-giving Jehovah's Witness cousin came back with his Bible-studying wife and their fat four-eyed daughter.

"Put on your masks!" my aunt yelled, and we did. Lupe told me we were going to have a lot of fun, and I believed her. She was reserved, but I was inclined to trust her, if only because I thought she resembled Audrey Hepburn. Still, I wasn't entirely sure what was going on.

"What are we doing?" I asked Olga's cousin.

"It's an American holiday," he replied.

"But what are we doing!" I demanded without restraining the superiority I felt to his class position and his second-rate religion. Even though he believed in America as the great equalizer, he was still forced to explain.

"All we are going to do is knock on doors and ask for candy."

My brother heard the word *candy*, and he was ready for anything. After two days of SPAM, garbanzo beans, and Velveeta cheese, candy for Othin was worth getting at any price. I was not so easily mollified.

"I'll go," I said, further enforcing distinction, "but I won't beg."

Olga's cousin handed us grocery bags and out we went. I hesitated for a moment in the doorway, feeling like an outsider. Hialeah was not filled with Cubans back then. It was house after house of Yankees, and here I was getting ready to ask them all for candy. Was this part of being an exile?

As we left the house, the block was dotted with children in all sorts of costumes. It was like Mardi Gras without the bands. We neared the first house, approached the front door, and Lupe leaned over to whisper, "We are supposed to say, 'Trick or treat'."

"What?" I had no idea.

Olga's cousin tried to help: "If they don't give us candy, we throw rotten eggs at their house!"

"You have rotten eggs?" I asked, horrified.

My cousin Oscarito also looked appalled, but I didn't have the energy to say, yes, Oscarito, I understand we have sunk very low. I empathized, but what was his problem? He had his parents with him. No mercy for the enemy. Instead, I put on a brave face of holiday cheer.

I instructed my brother, rolling my *r*'s with gusto, "We say trrrrrip or trrrrrick."

"Tick a trrrrrick!" he repeated.

"Good enough," I said. Othin jumped up and down. He opened his grocery bag and hid under his mask. He was ready for candy!

We knocked on the door. A plump blond woman wearing a pink

T-shirt and striped Bermuda shorts answered. Like little grasshoppers, we yelled, "Trrrrrick of trrrrreat!" and she rewarded us with delicious M&M's. Chocolate and sugar? For that? Maybe it won't be so bad.

The candy came in floods for the rest of the night. Milky Ways, Hershey bars, hard butterscotch candies. Whenever we got an apple, the Jehovah's Witness would take it from us, as his fat four-eyed daughter explained with righteousness, "They can have razor blades inside."

Yankees are cruel, I thought to myself. Today we beg for candy, tomorrow we will be begging for pennies, because that's what we've become. We are beggars now.

Before the night was over, we found a house that had no candy to offer. We were given pennies instead, five each, then sent along. I had my proof, case closed.

That night was restless like the first. I got up every hour and took my brother to the bathroom, but he didn't need to go until dawn, when he peed all over me and the bed. I wanted to kill him, but I didn't let myself get angry. He was the innocent and I was the adult.

When morning came, we awoke to the same hysterical aunt Olga, all nervous tension and frenetic religiosity. She made my brother endure the same humiliation in front of the clothesline.

"The sheets are on the clothesline because I wet the bed!" Othin's little voice sounded from the yard, piercing through the muted tones of Olga commiserating with her Bible study group.

Thankfully I started school soon after, and while it wasn't any more familiar, the chatter of young people speaking English in a classroom was comforting. I was in a school that was not run by priests but by attractive young people who seemed to enjoy life.

As the weeks passed, I began to see a glimpse of a whole new world. I was moving about in a place that was supposedly freer. And while I still missed Cuba with my entire being, I was beginning to get a sense of the repression that we lived under that everyone talked about. I was far from happy in America. I still wanted my mother, but maybe there was hope.

When we read stories about Peter Pan in school, I loved to

imagine him flying high over his island paradise, and I took to calling Cuba Neverland. I felt like Peter—after all, I came to America on one of his planes. But I wasn't free like him. Neverland was a dream from the past, a place I had been sent away from. I was stuck in the real world, and all I wanted to do was fly back.

After two months of fried eggs, white rice, Velveeta cheese, and garbanzo beans, we were dreaming of something different. By now there was one more person living with us, my cousin Elena, who had come from Cuba on her own without her parents or her little brother. She was like my brother and me. Alone. Allied. She was now sleeping on the top bunk bed while Oscarito and Lupe shared the double bed. My brother and I still huddled on the smelly bottom bunk.

One day when I was walking back from school, I saw my brother, as usual, waiting for me on the front lawn. There was a smile of pure joy on his face, which I understood as the door to the house opened. Out came my cousin Rosita's husband, Rolando. He had been involved with the Bay of Pigs invasion and had been one of the people my grandfather Oscar smuggled into the Swiss embassy. A relative of my mother's, thank God!

Even in Cuba my mother's relatives were warmer, kinder, and a lot more fun than my father's. I ran toward Rolando and embraced him. I didn't want to let go.

"Easy now!" he said warmly, "I've got a surprise for you. Let's go for a walk."

He took my brother and me by the hand and led us down the block. The building he took us to was white and structured, and the sign was painted in blue letters.

"What is this place?" asked Othin. I shrugged, not so sure myself.

"Welcome to White Castle," Rolando intoned.

White Castle? Are there kings?

"What are we doing here?" Othin wondered.

"Here," said Rolando, "we eat."

He took us inside and we were wrapped up in the smell of fried onions. Rolando sat us at a table and returned moments later bearing miniature hamburgers on delicate buns.

"Are they real?" my brother asked.

"Delicious," said Rolando.

I eyed the burger suspiciously and then took a bite.

Onions. Grease. The bun was soft and soaked up the juices on the bottom. The top was dotted with mustard and oh!—a crunchy pickle slice! It was like the top of a *Media Noche*, but the meat was totally different. It melted. Dissolved. Sweet little flecks of onion indistinguishable in texture from the beef. Top it all off with a sip of fizzy Coca-Cola, satisfying and sweet, and the effect was comprehensive, a mass of flavor drifting down my gullet in one congealed lump. This was a science experiment I could get used to.

At last we had been rescued from the wrath of Velveeta cheese.

By the end of the meal, Othin and I were drunk with the satisfaction that accompanies a new treat. Rolando led us home. As we approached the house, he delivered the bad news. He said he was living in an apartment with a bunch of other guys and that he would not be able to take us to live with him. I begged and pleaded and I told him that Olga was becoming a Jehovah's Witness and that she was crazy and that my uncle had stopped speaking and taken a job cleaning cars, and what's going on, anyway? Where were my parents? It had been three months!

He tried to reassure me that they would be here soon. He promised to visit as much as he could. Then, before he sent us inside, he held me fast by the arm.

"Eduardito. This is very important."

He handed me a little blue plastic bag about ten inches long and four inches wide that zipped with a long zipper.

"Open it," he said.

I pulled the zipper slowly and had to look away when the setting sun reflected the contents inside.

"These belong to your family."

I reached into the bag and sorted through. I held my history, every piece of jewelry my family owned. My mother's engagement ring, my grandfather Oscar's diamond tie clip, rings, earrings, and bracelets in countless colors, and on the bottom of the bag, little red and green stones with their own brilliance.

"Beautiful, no?" said Rolando. "Emeralds. Rubies. I smuggled them all through the Swiss embassy. Eduardito," his tone grew more serious, "I need you to take these jewels and keep them safe."

I was speechless.

"Where I am living I am afraid someone will steal them," he confided.

"You want me to keep them?" I managed.

"Yes. Keep them with you all the time. Keep them safe."

"Me?" I whimpered.

"I know you can do it," he said, and something about the seriousness of the moment made me believe him.

"Fine," I said, straightening with responsibility. "I can do it."

"I know you can," said Rolando, "and don't worry. This exile will be over soon. We will be home soon and everything will be back to normal." That was harder to believe, no matter how serious he was, but I hoped he was right. "I have to go now—remember what I told you—keep them with you all the time. Keep them safe."

That night I slept with the bag under my pillow. The next day I took it to school. I did this every day. They were always with me. The Family Jewels, I called them. I didn't tell anyone in the family that I had them, except Othin, who swore to secrecy. I don't know what would have happened if he hadn't kept his word, but they stayed safe.

As one month came to an end and another began, I got into the habit of taking the Family Jewels out every night after everyone was asleep. I'd huddle under the covers and turn on a flashlight, marveling at the way the stones reflected everything back. "This," I'd tell myself, "this is who you really are. Don't forget that. We will beat Fidel Castro, and in a couple of weeks we will be home."

A couple weeks came and went. No word from Cuba or my parents.

No phone calls, not even a letter. *Nada*. Nothing. Maybe they tried to send letters and they were confiscated. Maybe that's just easier to believe. I could ask my mother what happened, but even now I am afraid of the answer. All I remember is waiting. More waiting. Week after week.

One morning when I woke up, Yolanda, Elena's mother, was there sleeping on the couch with her son Bebito. She had gotten in very late the night before. I never got along with Yolanda, so I did the civil thing. I tried to sneak off to school before she woke up. If I had not liked Yolanda when we were in Cuba, what would she be like now in this place that brings out the worst in people? In this tiny house at the beginning of her exile, how could I expect anything but bitterness?

Then again, my mother might have sent a letter with her. My father might have let her know when they were planning to come. I stopped at the door.

"Good morning, Yolanda!" I shouted sweetly, waking her up. She nodded drowsily. "How are you?"

"Dead. So tired," Yolanda replied.

I waited. I heard a clock ticking somewhere.

"Do you have anything for me?" I dared not ask above a whisper.

"Nothing," she snarled.

"I see." I wanted to leave, but she emptied the load of her travels onto my little back.

"I got my visa two days ago. I was on a plane yesterday. Your mother had no time to write you a letter. Besides, she has morning sickness."

"Morning what?" I was irritated, so I spoke a little more loudly.

"Your mother is pregnant. She's replacing you."

"I'm irreplaceable!" I said, lifting my chin.

"I was kidding," she spat. "Maybe they'll come for you. Maybe they won't. They haven't even gotten their visas yet. They might never get out."

"Please don't tell my brother," I blurted out.

"I won't; he is a baby. I would not want to hurt him." She smiled like a reptile.

"Good." I smiled back.

"Yes," she smirked, "everything is good."

I turned on my heels and left as quickly as I could manage.

I had to stop on the way to school. One foot in front of the other was too much to manage if I was expected to hold back the tears.

She is replacing me, I thought. We will have to live with these morons for the rest of our lives. They have always hated mother and me because mother's parents had money. They're jealous because we never had to kiss Fernando's and Cuca's asses for our pocket change. They are so hateful. I cannot be related to them. I must save my brother from all of this. I must.

That day they had macaroni and cheese for lunch at school. I was beginning to depend on the school's lunchtime staples, if only for a brief moment of escape from all the SPAM and Velveeta. The macaroni and cheese at school was a different kind of science experiment. The noodles were like test tubes bathed in a gloppy cheese sauce that would have looked perfect bubbling over a Bunsen burner. The top was crunchy, from breadcrumbs saturated in oil that dripped through the nooks and crannies of the noodles, surrounding the whole dish in a shiny puddle. The noodles were overcooked, the whole thing leaden and greasy, but, as I said, it was a departure from the dreaded SPAM, so I savored every bite.

For a couple of months my uncle Tatan's house was very crowded, with Yolanda and Bebito on the couch, the Jehovah's Witnesses over every afternoon, and all the children. Yolanda found a job at a factory (a fate I thought she deserved) and soon after moved Elena, Bebito, and herself into a small apartment as she waited for her husband, my uncle Fernando, to get out of Cuba.

I was glad she was gone, if only so I wouldn't have to hear that casual biting tone of hers day in and day out. "Your parents are never coming. Hah! I'm only kidding! I just got here sooner because I could not bear to live without my daughter."

Good riddance.

My uncle Tatan barely spoke anymore, and my aunt Olga was trying to save us with Jehovah. Sometimes she'd push me to the breaking point and I would yell at her, "We are Catholics! CATHOLICS! That's the church we were baptized in!"

"I am only trying to bring you the truth!" she'd scream back. This argument occurred now every hour on the hour as her religious fervor grew. I am still amazed at the number of my relatives who were willing to go head to head with an eight-year-old.

Then one afternoon when the whole world seemed as bleak as Hialeah, an angel drove up in a dark green Cadillac. Maria Juana, my mother's best friend. Maria Juana had married the ex-husband of one of Batista's daughters, and they had left Cuba in January of 1959, before relations between the United States and Cuba went sour. They had gotten everything out of Cuba, including the rose bushes from their front yard. In this transient land, Maria Juana was the first person I saw who did not have the look of an immigrant. Better still, she came bearing gifts.

"Children!" she said. "You're coming with me!"

She loaded Othin and me in her car. We drove to a fancy restaurant. I had my first American fried chicken and my brother ate a steak. I'll admit I was bowled over by the flavor of the chicken and the juiciness of the meat, but I was a little distracted by the clumpy coating on the outside—this was not *Pollo Frito* as I knew it. My brother devoured every morsel on his plate.

Maria Juana let us open our presents at the table in the restaurant. She had bought us erector sets like the ones we had in Cuba.

"I'm sorry it's taken so long to visit. I've been in Europe, but I came as soon as I could."

I told her how awful everything was, and she assured me that my mother and father would be getting here soon.

"What if they don't?" I challenged her.

"Then I will take over."

"We can come live with you?" I asked. My brother's eyes darted in her direction.

"Boys, be patient. If it takes longer than a couple more months, I will come for you myself, but until then you wait."

Maria Juana visited us often, and every time we begged her to rescue us. But it wasn't until one day a few months after that meal that she delivered the news that we had so longed for.

The Cadillac pulled up to the house, and Othin and I ran to greet it. "They're coming," she said, "today. Your mother and father are coming to Miami today."

The rest was like a dream. All I remember is that soon after the news came we were standing on a rooftop at Miami International Airport with a crowd of Cubans. The families around us were out of balance, a mother and son here, a cousin and an uncle there, like a family tree drawn at random. As I looked around and saw the various relief funds, Catholics, Protestants, and Jehovah's Witnesses, I realized that everyone was waiting for the same thing. Family? No. Salvation.

It was 1962 by now, and there were so many Cubans flocking to Miami every day that their arrivals had become quite organized. I'm sure the scene I remember was played out over and over at Miami International, and while most of it was unfamiliar, there was one element that I was pretty used to. The wait. We waited. And waited. Tears welled up in the crowd here and there, sometimes a scream, a moan. It was like a funeral, but what were they mourning? Was it the loss of hope? No. It was deeper. With the joy of arrival came the reality of departure. Nobody could have known just how final that departure was, but it felt like they did.

Then the Pan Am plane landed and the shroud seemed to lift. Relief! Cheers! Applause! Flags waving, Cuban and American. More tears, joyful now, and shouts as many people came down the stairs from the plane. Families cheered and called out names as they were reunited. About thirty people came down the stairs, but no Mama and no Papa. Not for Othin and Eduardo. My brother sounded hopeless. "They're not on that plane," he said.

"Don't say that," I shushed him. "They have to be."

Then I saw my father. He was very thin and was wearing an impeccably tailored gray flannel suit. His hair was greased back so that he looked like a 1940s movie star. I was struck by how handsome he was, and how scared he looked. My brother started to cry.

Then my mother walked out of the plane. Her hair was set in tight curls atop her flushed face, and she wore an embroidered linen maternity outfit. She looked frightened, as if she was being led into the gas chambers instead of the company of her sons. Her face and arms where thin. Her stomach was huge. She was nine months pregnant and obviously ready to pop.

My brother started yelling, "Mami! Mami!" She saw him and began to cry. A joyful reunion, undoubtedly, but my heart was filled with nothing but hate. Cold, steel hate. I did not even smile. I didn't understand this feeling. I was ashamed of it. But I could not bring myself to love her. The person I had been praying for all these months was here, but there was no rejoicing. Even later, when she came into our room to kiss us good night, all I could feel was contempt. Then guilt.

My father joined her, hovering over our bed as they told us how much they had missed us. My brother was overjoyed, but I did not believe a word they were saying. They were so obviously lost and frightened. But I didn't care. I resented them both, especially my father. He was the spoiled child now, and I was the protector. Was I supposed to protect all of us?

As they were about to walk out of the room, I remembered something and asked them to wait. I got out of bed, pulled back a corner of the mattress, and removed the Family Jewels. I handed the bag to them nonchalantly.

"Maybe this will buy us some real food," I pronounced. My father laughed nervously, and my mother left the room without a word.

At the very least it was a relief to hand the jewelry and my brother over to my parents. They never thanked me for a job well done or asked me what it had been like. Months later when I mustered up the courage to tell them how cruel their relatives were to us, they refused to believe me. My father accused me of having a wild imagination. Fine. The best response they could manage was that they had sent us here to save us from communism and that we should be grateful for their sacrifice.

I was not grateful. Ten months in America had made me hate capitalism, before I even fully understood what it was. But that was a subject even I was not prepared to raise.

Othin, Mom holding Jeanette, and me, Hialeah, 1962

Somehow my father got the money together to rent us a tenement apartment in downtown Miami. It was practically falling apart. It had one bedroom for my mother and father and the new baby, my sister Jeanette, who had been born three weeks after they arrived. Jeanette was the first Machado Yankee. Her birth made things worse for Othin and me. Any special attention we might have received as they tried to assuage their own guilt ended abruptly. Now we had to share the love with a new baby. Poor Jeanette.

There we were. Finally, actually a family living in our own little run-down one-bedroom apartment with a tiny living room and a kind of walled-in terrace where Othin and I slept. The best feature of our new apartment was the kitchen. Better still was the head chef. No matter how angry I was with my mother, I was oh-so-glad she was back behind the stove. We still ate SPAM, but with mother cooking it was like an adventure. She started making her own American science experiments: breaded SPAM, SPAM Chili, SPAM with Pineapple, and SPAM *Croquetas*. She even chopped the SPAM and fried it until it was crispy, adding it to garbanzo beans with a little tomato sauce. It wasn't chorizo, I knew that much, but it was close.

Then there was the ever-present Velveeta. When mother made Velveeta sandwiches, she heated them in a pan with a little butter. It was like a grilled cheese sandwich, but the Velveeta, with its otherworldly consistency, will never qualify as cheese in my book. Still, it was so much better heated up. With the buttered bread, grilled golden in the skillet, I didn't mind the Velveeta at all because it had something crunchy to contrast its weird smoothness. I didn't have to pry the bread from the roof of my mouth or wait for it to dissolve. Wonder of wonders, I could actually chew it! No matter how I felt, it was mother's cooking that felt most like home in this strange, strange land.

A few months later my cousins Hugo and Barbara arrived from Cuba and moved in with us. Now there were four of us sleeping on the terrace. The family was slowly coming back together. Hugo and Barbara were teenagers, and so they were always listening to rock and roll and making up games. Life seemed full and fun again.

One night after the Catholic Relief had been particularly generous, my mother made *Arroz con Pollo*, without saffron. Instead she used *bijol*, a sinister mixture of annato seed extract and various dyes and flavorings that would give the appearance of saffron without the expense. There was only one piece of chicken per person, but there were plenty of *petit pois* and *pimientos* on top. It was the rice that did me in. I felt my whole life in every bite, resistant to the tooth, eventually yielding into creaminess. We were neither here nor there, and our dinner tasted exactly the same. In between. So-so.

As we ate, my father explained to us that when he had gone by to pick up the rations of SPAM, lima beans, eggs, rice, and Velveeta, the Catholic Relief had made him an offer he could not refuse.

"They offered you more chicken?" my cousin Hugo asked. We all laughed.

"No," said my father, "they said we could relocate somewhere else. That they would help us leave Miami."

"What do you mean?" Barbara asked. "We just got here!"

My father explained, "Look, the Catholic Relief will pay for all of our airplane tickets, including Barbara's and Hugo's. The church in the town we relocate to will adopt us. They'll find me a job, have a house waiting for us. They will even furnish it and give us a refrigerator filled with steaks!"

"I love steak!" Othin shrieked.

"So do I, son," my father said evenly. "They'll even pick us up at the airport." I thought about holding my tongue but decided against it.

"I thought we were waiting in Miami just to go back to Cuba," I said innocently.

"So did I," my mother joined in.

"Look," my father was angry now, his voice shaking as he cast a derisive glare my way, "the Bay of Pigs failed. It's going to be at least a year before we go back. I can't get a job here, and we deserve better."

"Where are we going now?" I asked.

"We had a choice of Boston, New York, or Los Angeles. I picked Los Angeles."

"Why?" I asked.

"I've always wanted to meet Elizabeth Taylor," he replied, only half joking. Everyone laughed.

"Hollywood," Barbara cooed.

"When are we going?" Hugo asked.

"In four days," said father. My mother took a small bite of her chicken and rice.

"Are you upset?" I asked her. She looked at me as tears filled her eyes.

"California is three thousand miles away from home," she said. I knew what she meant. Jeanette started crying and Mother left the room to breastfeed her.

My father saw me scowling, and so he decided to name all the movie stars we would meet in Los Angeles: "Rock Hudson, Doris Day, Jerry Lewis, Frank Sinatra, Ava Gardner, Tony Curtis, Jack Lemmon, and Marilyn Monroe." I was not impressed, but I wasn't entirely disappointed either.

Garbanzos with SPAM "Chorizo"

I cannot pretend that I love SPAM. There are just too many bad memories associated with it. But I will say that if you cook it crispy enough, pinch your nose, and close your eyes, it at least *feels* like fried chorizo in your mouth. And while this dish has roots in Spanish *tapas*, the SPAM puts it in a category all its own. I know there are even some people who love this strange smelling "meat food." I hope this dish makes them happy.

½ cup olive oil
One 12-ounce can SPAM, cut into ½-inch cubes
1 Spanish onion, peeled and cut in half, then sliced thin
2 garlic cloves, peeled and finely chopped
Two 15.5-ounce cans cooked garbanzos (chickpeas), drained and
    rinsed thoroughly
Two 8-ounce cans Goya tomato sauce
½ teaspoon salt
½ teaspoon ground black pepper
1 cup water

1. Heat the olive oil in a large skillet over medium-high heat. Add the SPAM and fry until crispy, stirring occasionally, 8 minutes.

2. Add the onion and cook, stirring, until softened slightly, 3 minutes. Add the garlic and cook, stirring, 1 minute more.

3. Add the garbanzos, tomato sauce, salt, pepper, and water. Cook, stirring occasionally, until warmed through and thickened slightly, 7 minutes. Serve with white rice.

Makes 4 servings

❚ *Velveeta Grilled Cheese* ❚

"Cheese food" is a whole different story. The tastes of white bread, ecru butter, and golden Velveeta are so mild, I am hard pressed to find anything offensive about the flavors in this dish. I believe the dish is actually all about the texture, something I wish my aunt Olga had understood. It took my mother's saintly hands to bless the cold slabs of Velveeta and squishy white bread with her own culinary imprint. She made the horrible bearable, and even enjoyable.

8 ounces Velveeta cheese (half of a 16-ounce block), chilled
8 slices white sandwich bread
4 tablespoons salted butter, softened to room temperature

1. Cut the Velveeta into eight 1-ounce slices. Place 2 slices of cheese on a slice of bread. Place another slice of bread on top. Butter both sides of the sandwich using 1 tablespoon butter. Repeat with remaining bread, cheese, and butter.

2. Warm a nonstick pan over medium-low heat. Fry each sandwich in the pan until the cheese is melted and the bread is golden, 2 minutes per side. Be sure to press the sandwiches flat with the back of your spatula after flipping them. This will help the cheese to melt and will result in a crisp and chewy crust.

3. Transfer to a warm plate and slice on the diagonal. Serve immediately.

Makes 4 sandwiches

Five

The New Frontier

Our trip west began on an early morning in August. We weren't sure what the opposite coast would hold, but anything seemed a better option than the late summer heat of Miami.

As my mother prepared Jeanette's bottles for the trip, she clucked to herself, "Three thousand miles from home!" She said it to no one in particular, but loud enough that my father could hear her.

"Only for a year," my father insisted. "Let's have an adventure for God's sake!"

"One way?" she asked, even though she knew the answer. My father had acquired six one-way tickets to Los Angeles from the Catholic Relief. Mother refused to accept that there was not a ticket back to Miami. She wanted a guarantee that we'd be ready to return to Cuba when the opportunity presented itself. My father's unwillingness to answer confirmed her fears.

"One way." Mother repeated her new slogan, shaking her head. I think she feared getting lost in America, and in some ways we did get lost. We didn't know how final all those decisions were. We were so caught up in fighting with the present that we didn't have time to accept the past. The momentum of our lives kept building, hurtling us away from a reality we would not, or could not, accept, until suddenly everything was irreversible. But I didn't know any of that yet. For the time being I chose to believe my dad's story: one year in Los Angeles and then back to Cuba when Castro was overthrown. Sounded good to me.

I felt no small relief that we packed our bags together, as a family. Even if we didn't know what would happen, we knew we were leaving, where we were going, and that it was not "just for a couple of days." We knew the trip would be nothing like a vacation, but the whole process was bearable because we were together.

Rolando, who now owned a car, and Tatan, who borrowed one, came to pick us up and drove us back to Miami International, where our descent into the hell called exile had begun. We said quick good-byes at the airport, no tears this time, just resignation and smiles and excitement. Hollywood. We were going to Hollywood, a magic land. If it was good enough for Audrey Hepburn and Grace Kelly and Desi Arnaz, it had to be good enough for us.

The day we left Miami, August 6, 1962, my father had eleven dollars and fifty-two cents in his pocket. We had an eight-hour plane ride to L.A. with two stopovers on the way. I couldn't look at him on the plane. His face was twisted with emotion I had never seen from him before. Was it fear? No. Nervousness? Couldn't be. What was it then?

"Are you okay, Papi?" I asked.

"Of course," he said, "I'm just thanking God for the help of the Catholic Church."

Of course! That's what was all over his face. Piety! He looked like an icon of one of the martyrs. Terrified, for sure, but filled with such faith in the Catholic Church that the contortion of his features signaled a happy ending, even if it was only after certain death.

He was probably just terrified. In fact, as he has confirmed over and over in the years since, his worst fear was that we'd arrive in Los Angeles and no one would be waiting for us.

But that day all he could hold on to was a belief in the Catholic Church, that they would come through for us. They would not abandon us, not the clergy, not the priests, not the bishops or cardinals, certainly not the Pope. If he was scared, terrified, shaking in his boots, he gave his fear up to God.

Then, out of nowhere he said, "You gotta believe. You have to believe there is goodness in the world."

By now airplanes were old hat for Othin. He liked the excitement of travel, especially with his nerves soothed by the presence of his mother. He seemed to marvel at being close to so many other people in the airtight confines of the cabin, and he giggled whenever the stewardesses walked by. His optimism was contagious, and as we began our descent into the Dallas Airport for our first stopover, we were all joking and in a party mood.

It might have been the plane's descent giving me butterflies, but as we landed I felt a giddy kind of relief at the thought of being away from all the Cuban exiles and especially my extended family in Miami. I looked at my mother feeding Jeannette from a bottle the stewardess had warmed for her. I heard Hugo and Barbara humming their favorite songs. Othin was playing with the set of wings we had both been given. This was all the family I needed.

I turned to my father. "Will there be snow?" I asked.

"I think so," he said, softening around my curiosity, "but also palm trees and orange trees and movie stars."

The plane took off for the second time from Dallas, Texas. We talked about the movie stars we each dreamed of meeting. Mickey Mouse for my brother, for me Doris Day. Hugo thought Sandra Dee was the prettiest of all, and Barbara was gaga over Tab Hunter. Mom liked Rock Hudson for his wholesome appeal, and Dad? It had to be Marilyn Monroe. He had seen *Some Like It Hot* three times when it showed in Cuba, and he didn't go for the comedy.

The flight from Dallas took forever compared to the quick jump from Miami. As we crossed the United States, what began as jovial excitement slowly turned into the harsh reality that we were going to the other side of this very big country to begin a new life.

More than a year, I thought. You are going to live there longer than a year—it will be a long time before Bay of Pigs Two ever happens. Maybe ten years. Maybe twenty, thirty, maybe a lifetime? We all had that sinking suspicion whispering in our heads, but we dared not admit it. More than getting lost, I think we all feared that when we landed we would become different people altogether. As I looked out the window of the plane at the Rockies descending into the Mojave Desert, the foreign landscape of craggy mountains and sandblasted earth made my jaw hang in wonder.

Somewhere toward the end of the flight Jeanette started to cry. The cry turned into a sob that would not stop. It embarrassed my mother and father; their children were supposed to be perfectly behaved. Jeanette was letting out the first scream of many to come. A scream that said, "The old ways are dead, I can be myself!" I screamed silently with her that day. A scream of defiance resounding with freedom, and not just political freedom, personal, too. Freedom from a culture, a language, a set way of life. But even freedom is scary when it happens all at once.

The plane began to land, and we all looked out our windows. Los Angeles was surrounded by mountain ranges, but where the land around the peaks in Cuba had been green, Los Angeles was tan. There was a thick haze in the air that shrouded the place in mystery. It was like no landscape I had ever seen, but as the plane turned for its final descent, I saw the Pacific Ocean for the first time. Thank you, God! Ocean! Something familiar at last! My father explained, "It's called the Pacific. It was discovered by the Spanish conquistadores, Balboa I think."

So other Spanish people have been here before? What a relief.

When the plane landed, my father got very nervous. He wanted to be the first person off the plane for fear that the Catholics would disappear if he didn't show up immediately. My mother needed his help with Jeanette, who was still whimpering, so Barbara and I went out first. We walked down the stairs onto the tarmac and toward the gate. When we entered the gate area, there were three very blond couples with signs that read WELCOME HOME MACHADOS. Home, huh?

Barbara whispered to me, "I guess I am a Machado now," and we hurried toward the sign and waved hello. They spoke in English with warm and soothing tones.

"We are so happy that you are here!" The men looked very serious.

"You are away from the Communists now, young man," said one of them.

"You're safe," said another. They shook our hands and gave us tentative hugs. The greeting was drawn out as the rest of the passengers debarked the plane. I turned around to catch the look of relief on my father's face when he saw the signs. I think there was even a tear in his eyes. A single tear, just like the icons. My brother ran toward us with Hugo while my father strode confidently behind them.

As he opened his arms to embrace the couples, the mood changed suddenly. The intimate gesture was too much too fast. The women turned coy and the men stood up straighter. It was all very territorial. I could tell the women thought my dad was a real Latin Lover with his slicked-back hair and pinky ring. He was tan from days of working in the sun cleaning cars in Miami, and he wore his gray flannel suit and polished Italian shoes.

When my mother finally joined us, her thick brown hair done in curls that framed her large oval eyes and clean white skin, the tension eased as the men felt less threatened. One of the women asked, "Mrs. Machado?" My mother shook her head, no. The Catholic ladies were confused. Had they let an unwed mother into their fold?

"In Cuba the women do not take on their husband's name," my father explained to them in the standard English he had learned at university.

"Well, here you are Mrs. Machado," said one of the ladies, looking at Mother askance.

"Really?" my mother replied cautiously.

"Beautiful rings!" said another lady, grabbing Mother's hand. "I guess you were rich in Cuba?"

The third housewife butted in, "You certainly are a very beautiful and exotic family." My father thanked her with a tight smile.

Exotic? We looked like we always did. Father had his suit on, mother wore one of her Paris couture dresses. She had her emerald earrings on, and the ring with the rubies, in addition to the wedding band and diamonds. She didn't always wear the rubies, but she was glad to have them back after I had kept them safe for so long. Hugo, Othin, and I were in our linen shirts and pants. Barbara was seductive in her tight skirt and revealing shirt, but at fifteen it was nothing indecent.

And then I looked at the Californians. Beige skin, blond hair, white teeth. They were suited up in their best Sears casual outfits, not a natural fiber in sight, staring at us in our tailored linen and cotton. I saw one of the wives look nervously at the bracelet of black balls on mother's wrist. No big deal—it's just the keep-away-the-evil-eye bracelet. She must have thought we practiced voodoo.

It's a strange feeling to suddenly become foreign, but there we were, so obviously the "others." We were inches away from them, but the distance was enormous. We must have looked like aliens, or mobsters at least. It took all of a moment to go from feeling perfectly natural in our own skin to suddenly being the circus freaks. To understand the feeling, imagine blinking once, and when you open your eyes you're suddenly in a Fellini film, and you're the star.

My father saved the day by saying, "We are so thankful and grateful." Suddenly everyone had a smile on their face.

We were led to the parking lot and put in two separate cars. Othin and Jeanette went with Mom and Dad in one car; Hugo, Barbara, and I rode together in the other. As we began the drive to the San Fernando Valley, I thought to myself, Fernando—my grandfather's name. Seemed like a good omen. But how to make sense of the town we were about to move to? No matter how you said it, Canoga Park still sounded strange.

Canoga Park. I made a mental note to rib my father about it later, but my mother beat me to it.

"Not Los Angeles," she said, "not Beverly Hills, and certainly not Hollywood. You brought us to Canoga Park."

We reached the Valley by way of Sepulveda Boulevard. *Sepulveda*, I thought, another Spanish name. But there were also names like Inglewood and Burbank and Sherman Oaks. The emphasis was definitely on Spanish, though, so I felt good. We passed La Cienega, Los Robles,

Santa Monica, and then we turned onto a highway called Ventura. Proof! Maybe there had been Spanish people here before us!

As we drove for many miles down Ventura Boulevard, I took in the sights of the San Fernando Valley, at that time not much more than orange groves and corn fields surrounded by mountains. There were green lawns in front of rows of identical tract houses. The air was dry, the sunset orange like the fruit on the trees. It was rural and domestic all at once.

We turned onto a street called Sherman Way, and after passing a small hamburger stand turned again down a dirt driveway flanked by two furniture stores, one on either side. At the end of the road was a whitewashed ranch house with a shingled roof that had probably been built in the 1930s. It sat, quietly, waiting just for us.

There were more Americans waiting at the house. They opened the door and proudly showed us around as they cooed, "Welcome to your new home!" Hugo and Barbara each had their own room, but Othin and I shared ours. Mom and Dad had the master bedroom, with room enough for Jeanette. There was a living room, a kitchen, and a separate dining room for six.

Looking out the back windows, I noticed a dilapidated stable at the rear of the yard with a little path leading to an alleyway. Next

Hugo with Jeanette, Othin, and me outside the house in Canoga Park, 1962

to the two-car garage stood a wooden hut that looked as if it had been plopped into the yard from above. The lawn was patchy at best.

Inside the house every room was furnished with donations from the church, bits and pieces of what people did not need or were willing to give away. The couch came from one person, the television from another. The six chairs in the dining room were from six different sets.

Half the curtains were blue, the other half white. There was a washer and dryer and shelves of dishes in every size, shape, and color.

The refrigerator was full of food, the pantry shelves stocked to overflowing, but we couldn't have cooked right then if we had wanted to. The Catholics had taken care, setting the dining room table with a grand spread to welcome us. There was glazed ham from a can, not quite salty, with strange gelatin clinging to the rubbery meat. They had boiled hot dogs on spongy buns with neon yellow mustard. There was sticky white bread and butter, steamed zucchini, and a string bean salad. The tuna salad wasn't made with cream cheese, and the macaroni salad tasted both saccharine and bland all at once. Both dishes probably had Hellmann's or Miracle Whip in them, as neither tasted like the mayonnaise Manuela made with fresh eggs and oil.

With so many new flavors to digest all at once, I was relieved to see a familiar fruit present for dessert. The thick slices of homemade pineapple upside-down cake had a familiar tropical tang, but the texture of the fruit was new. Pineapples were only readily available in cans at the time, and though I would come to love their soggy sweetness, this was an entirely different fruit from what I was used to. There was no sour bite, no refreshing snap as the fibers gave way to the tooth, and the sweetness was synthetic, more corn syrup than sugar cane. But hey, in this land of science experiments, I was happy to at least be able to recognize it as pineapple. The oddly chewy maraschino cherries were another matter. I still can't make sense of those.

I didn't quite know what to think when one of the California wives presented Hugo and me with large scoops of an unidentifiable green substance, dotted with white blobs and smothered in what seemed to be whipped cream. JELL-O with marshmallows, an early version of Ambrosia Salad, was "like eating air," as Hugo put it. Whatever it was, it certainly tasted man-made, as if dessert had been passed through the engine of the plane we had debarked a few hours earlier.

That night my dad became the life of the party—he spoke English fluently and even told a few jokes. My mother was polite and charming but uncharacteristically quiet because of the language barrier. Jeannette behaved, only letting out a tiny wail when her first spoonful of green JELL-O wasn't followed immediately by a second.

As the adults drank copious amounts of whiskey and beer, the tight-lipped politesse of the evening gave way to a more rowdy atmosphere. At one point a photographer from the local newspaper dropped by to take the family's picture. They were used to Mexicans in the area, but Cubans were definitely newsworthy. With all the excitement, the booze and publicity, the whole family stayed up past midnight. It felt more like Hollywood than I expected.

All in all it was a big wonderful welcome, made even more wonderful when one of the Americans offered my father a job. Mr. James R. Anderson, part of the welcoming committee that greeted us at the airport, was short and all-American, muscular and tanned. He looked as though he had played every sport in his heyday, reduced now to remembering those glorious times from behind his desk. He owned and ran his own accounting firm, and after what seemed to me like too short a time he invited my father to work for him. Dad impressed him so much, fit in so well, that Mr. Anderson asked him to start work the next day.

After everyone left, we ate again. My father found a package of thin-cut breakfast steaks in our cavernous refrigerator, and he insisted that my mother cook them. She fried the steak in a skillet with a drop of vegetable oil, then sautéed chopped garlic and thin slices of onion in the caramelized drippings. She topped the steaks with the browned aromatics, then finished them off with a squeeze of lemon. We each had a piece of meat between two slices of toasted white bread smeared with bright yellow mustard.

"This is not a Cuban Sandwich," I said flatly, but it was late enough that I could close my eyes and pretend we were on a street corner surrounded by Cubans feasting on *Media Noches*.

"I think it's better," Barbara said.

"Maybe," said Hugo.

"Impossible," I said. "Nothing is better than a Cuban Sandwich." But I didn't open my eyes.

What kind of sandwich was it then? Mama had made it. It had meat and bread, garlic and citrus, the flavors were familiar enough to call them Cuban, but this was too new to feel like home. Or was it? We all agreed it was the best food we'd had since we got to the United States.

After our second dinner, my father opened a newspaper, only to read that Marilyn Monroe was dead. The horror. One Cuban's wet dream brought to a crashing halt. As he told us the news, his face clouded over. Was that it? Was that all the joy we'd have on our first night in California?

Just as quickly as they darkened, his eyes lit up. "Well, at least Elizabeth Taylor is still alive." He looked around the table, and his smile spread through all of us. "Come on, let's go for a ride."

Dad pushed his chair back and led the family to the driveway, where he started the beat-up Ford that someone had donated for whenever my father found a job he had to drive to. "Better make sure it runs," he said, oozing with pride that his first day of work was only a few hours away.

Mother hung back in the doorway, but Hugo and I wouldn't let her poop out on the party. "You're all crazy," she said, but we didn't care.

We didn't go very far. We just drove up and down the driveway a few times. If we were to split up and go to bed, it seemed like the dream going on around us would end. We were so together going up and down that driveway that even Mother couldn't suppress a smile.

I crawled into bed close to one o'clock in the morning, only to confirm that I still couldn't sleep. The simple joy of being in a bed that was mine, that would stay mine for at least a year, was enough to keep me up until dawn. I was under a spell. Being in a new place, surrounded by new people, on the other side of the earth, the idea that this could be our new home, the impossibility of it all felt like magic. Even though the house was not in the best shape, even though the furniture was second-hand, even though the horse stalls in the backyard and the garage on the side were falling down more than a little, even though the hamburger stand and furniture stores out front were like American-made walls trapping us at the end of our dirt driveway, even though everything was so different from what we knew in Cuba, it was ours, and that propriety was magical in itself. That kind of spell—the kind that allowed a family of refugees to finally relax, if only for a moment—possessed a new kind of magic I could definitely get used to.

The next morning we woke up to the worst coffee any of us had ever had. When we first got to California, there was no such thing as good, strong coffee. Starbucks was obviously decades away. There was no such thing as grind 'n brew; in fact, it was nearly impossible to find whole beans. We had to settle for a can of Maxwell House and a stove-top percolator that my father found.

He read the directions on the can and by instinct put in twice as much coffee as instructed. "Yankees have no sense of café," he said.

We waited as the coffee percolated up. It sounded like the noises my stomach made after too much roast pork. My mother boiled some milk with a pinch of salt in it after noticing how, just like in Miami, the milk had no cream.

"Pasteurized," my dad told her. "Safer."

"No taste!" my mother announced. Nobody argued.

My dad told me to make toast, and Othin buttered each slice. Hugo and Dad sat at the table talking now, as we served them first, making more toast for ourselves. The two men of the house—they had the right to be waited on.

Finally the coffee was ready. When we poured it into our cups, it looked pale brown like river water, sick compared to the rich, dark, almost red espresso we drank in Cuba. Even in Miami they had espresso, but I figured they knew better because they had been so close to Cuba for hundreds of years.

My mother and Barbara poured the milk into the coffee and added two teaspoons of sugar to each cup. We all sat around the table, hesitant. We opted for bites of toast first. It was papery, a little boring, but at least it soaked up the butter so there was some richness to it. Then we took our first sips of American coffee.

"Sugar water," my mother pronounced, making a sour face. Jeanette began to cry, so she left the table to soothe her.

"Next time we will add more coffee," said Dad.

"It won't make it any better," called Mother over her shoulder. Hugo tried to intercede.

"Italians drink espresso—there's gotta be some Italians around here."

"That's right," Barbara urged.

"I am going to find an Italian food market," Hugo said proudly. Then silence. Jeanette stopped crying, my mother sat back down, and we drank the dirty sugar water with the paperlike toast and tasteless milk.

That morning my father started work. He was all set to start his day; he even warmed up the Ford in the driveway. Then Mr. Anderson arrived and reminded him that he wouldn't be able to drive to work until he got his license. In all the excitement, not to mention the fact that he was a perfectly good driver, Dad forgot this minor piece of red tape. Not to worry—Mr. Anderson offered to pick him up every morning until he was ready for his driving test.

Even in the morning Mr. Anderson was cheerful. Hugo asked him if there were any Italians around, my father acting as the reluctant translator.

Mr. Anderson seemed confused—why did Cubans want anything to do with Italians? He must have pictured some newfangled Cosa Nostra, or rather, a Cosa Nosotros. But he said he thought there was a small Italian community in North Hollywood. Off he and my dad went before Hugo had a chance to ask him if there was a bus that went to North Hollywood.

Our first full day in Canoga Park was hot, but it was a wonderful dry heat that motivated us kids to explore our immediate surroundings. We went by the burger place and saw the prices and knew we could not afford any for lunch. We looked at the furniture in the two furniture stores for kicks. Then we went into the wooden hut in the backyard to discover that it was packed with boxes full of different drapes, more donations. There were drapes of all colors and materials. Hugo flicked the light switch and, amazingly enough, the electricity worked. Then Barbara found the hidden treasures—a radio and a record player and a stack of old records! Everything was in working order.

As we played a Doris Day album, Barbara declared, "The music room! This can be our clubhouse!" She and Hugo and I began to decorate as Othin watched. Barbara decided there should be drapes everywhere, even on the walls. They found a hammer and nails and we set about transforming the room. Othin and I walked to the old horse stalls and found rope and a tire. We got Hugo to tie it to a tree next to the house, and voilà! We had a swing. My mother went into the garage and found boxes and boxes full of clothes, most of them styles from the fifties. They didn't appeal to her high fashion sensibilities, but nevertheless they were clothes that we could wear. She made piles of things that would be suitable for each of us, then she returned to the kitchen.

For lunch mother made Campbell's Tomato Soup along with ham and cheese sandwiches. She came up with the idea of using a serrated knife to cut the crusts off a whole loaf of white bread in four big slices. She spread mustard on the inside, layered them with ham and cheese, then buttered the crusty exteriors. She fried them in a skillet, pressing them flat with the back of a spatula. When she called us in to eat, we marveled at how the sandwiches looked just like the ones we used to buy at Tarara, the local beach. Of course we agreed the sandwiches were better in Cuba—how could you try to reproduce the perfect sandwich that quelled the hunger of a long day swimming in the turquoise Caribbean? As we reminisced and talked about that perfect, precious beach, nobody pretended this moment came even close, but I saw my mother beaming with satisfaction at having created as faithful a replica as she knew how.

I cannot stress the importance of that moment enough. My mother, lost in the old, defiantly swallowing the new. All at once she understood her future. If she could make some part of every meal she cooked look and taste like Cuba, maybe then her children would not forget where they came from. Maybe then they wouldn't get lost.

Barbara, Othin, and Hugo with Jeanette on Othin's birthday inside the house in Canoga Park, 1962

After a couple days our family picture was printed on the front page of the local paper. The Americans made a huge deal out of telling us what a special honor this was. We felt important until we finally saw a copy of the paper. They had spelled our name "Namachados," I'm not sure why. The story was about a family escaping communism and the Catholics who saved them. They had quotes from my dad, Mr. Anderson, and a priest who spoke as though he knew us intimately. We wondered why we had no idea who he was. Dad said we would see him at church on Sunday.

"You mean we have to go to church?" I asked.

"Yes. If they are helping us, we have to go." We were lapsed Catholics at that point. I didn't see any reason to resume practicing . . . unless I thought about where the food was coming from.

During that first week my mother poured herself into her cooking. She made a roast chicken that she marinated in lemons and garlic, no oregano, as the pantry wasn't stocked with any. When she made powdered mashed potatoes, she added lots of black pepper. We must have had five jars of black pepper in the pantry—I guess the Californians couldn't take the heat. She made ham steaks that she fried with slices of pineapples, reducing the syrup and drippings to a golden brown sauce, with overcooked broccoli and a squeeze of lemon on the side.

She seemed to put lemon on everything, to wake the food up with a little bit of freshness. I think she really did it just so she could make a point, always saying, "This should really be made with sour oranges; they have the right combination of sweet and sour."

It was all worlds better than the SPAM experiments, though no-where near as good as Cuba. Oregano, lard, and cumin were desper-ately needed. Hugo was sure they would be waiting for us with the Italians in North Hollywood. Alas, we had no way of getting there, as Dad still hadn't gotten a license. He studied every day, though, from a book Mr. Anderson had given him.

As Saturday approached, we were running out of food. Mr. Ander-son had advanced my dad two hundred dollars, so it was time to go shopping at the Food King supermarket just a few blocks away from the house.

On Friday night, as we watched a rerun of *I Love Lucy* on the televi-sion set, we only understood what Desi was saying, while my dad got all the jokes. During the commercial, we planned Saturday's expedi-tion to the Food King. My mother started making a list of the bare essentials.

It was decided that for the first trip, my mom and dad and I would go shopping while Hugo and Barbara babysat Othin and Jeanette in the music room. So after our morning cup of river water and by now stale toast, we dressed and began the journey that would change our status, internally at least, from political refugees to immigrants.

As we walked the five blocks toward the Food King, my mother repeated her list out loud: "*Yuca*, plantains, *malanga*, lemons, limes, avocados, radishes, real bread, butter, olive oil, and, for God's sake, lard! Mangoes, bananas, papayas. Shrimp. Lobster, fish, short-grain rice, oregano, cumin, saffron.... Oh, yes, and *naranjas ágrias*. If they even exist here."

"Of course they do," said my father. "This place is surrounded by orange groves. We'll find it all." He hesitated but went on. "It is a SUPER market."

It was hot and dry, not at all humid. The air smelled liked a smol-dering campfire. I had not been outside our immediate block. It was flat. Completely. The buildings were uninteresting, not like in Havana with its Colonial and Art Deco splendor. It wasn't even like Cojimar with its colorful fishing houses, mansions, and scattered modern structures.

Sherman Way was all square and functional. Every building had a parking lot beside or in front of it. There were drug stores and bicycle shops, office buildings, a church or two, although not the Catholic one. We were the only people walking—everyone else was in a car.

"How can they call this a town?" my mother said without it really being a question.

"It's a suburb," my father said, pronouncing the word in his standard university English.

My mother mocked him, "Sub-BOORB!"

"Los Angeles is the town," he explained. "These are all the communities around the town. Suburbs."

"Havana is a city," my mother snapped. I could see the supermarket a block away. I prayed we'd get there before a huge fight broke out.

"What do you mean?" my father asked.

"This place," mother scoffed, "my God. It has no beauty. Don't they care about beauty?" She looked at him straight in the face. A challenge. He looked away, ashamed of himself.

"But you lived in Cojimar, not Havana." He couldn't help himself. Silence. Mother stopped walking, completely exasperated.

"Othon, Cojimar is a beautiful fishing village with sea and hills and homes. Even Guanabacoa is a town. It's an industrial town, true, but still a town. A colonial town. This Sherman Oaks Boulevard. This Canoga Park. This. Is nothing."

My father was shattered, but he tried to appeal to her.

"Look up. The mountains are beautiful." We looked up and around us. "Aren't they?" I nodded my head yes. My mother glanced at the mountains as if she was inspecting a cockroach she had killed. The disdain that she had been hiding for a week could no longer be masked by the look of a grateful immigrant.

"In Cuba we had plenty of mountains," she snapped as she took off toward the market.

When he got to the glass doors of the Food King, Dad offered a sort of truce as a last resort.

"Food," he said. "You can buy whatever you want."

But mother had already gone inside.

We walked in and the delicious air-conditioning hit our faces. The first thing we noticed was that the vegetables and fruits looked like nothing we had in Cuba. There were green, red, and yellow apples of all sizes. Piles of pears, grapes, and oranges were stacked under brightly colored price signs shaped like sunbursts. There were no *guayabas*, mangoes, or papayas in sight, not even a lime as far as we could see. And there were certainly no sour oranges, just sweet ones.

My mother looked at my father with obvious contempt. "I told you, no *naranjas ágrias*," she said.

"I can see that." My father could no longer fight her.

"Only one kind of bananas, with labels on them," she said, as if they were plastered with horse shit.

"At least they are bananas," I finally said.

"They're called Chiquita," she scoffed, "even though they're huge. Everyone knows huge bananas have very little flavor. And where are the plantains? They don't have plantains." She was losing her grasp on reality. "No *yuca*. No *malanga*. What's wrong with these people?"

My father pointed out the potatoes and yams, but even they were not up to mother's standards. "They're not white. They're orange. Do they think they're pumpkins?"

She approached the Hass avocados and seemed to stare them down. It was as if their size and their black nubby skin was a direct affront to her integrity. "These!" she scoffed, "these are pathetic. Dirty. They're smaller than my hand." She was obviously hoping for the Caribbean variety, bright green and watery, perfect for avocado salad. How could she have known that their dense flesh was creamier, richer than the kind we had in Cuba? I dared not express my curiosity on that day because when my mother proclaimed, "This is not an avocado!" the conversation was over before it had begun.

From the dejected look on my father's face, I could tell this trip to the Food King, this trip that was supposed to change everything, was quickly turning into a disaster.

As we went down the other aisles, it didn't get any better. When we got to the grains and beans, we found no black beans anywhere on the shelves. There were only split peas, lima beans, and a dusty package of dried chickpeas. There was no Serrano ham in the deli section, and the steaks at the butcher were all cut too thick.

"London broil?" Mother asked aloud, "how do I cook this? It's cut like a tire!"

"We'll find a way," my father said halfheartedly. If steak couldn't make her happy, nothing could.

"I wanted *Bistec Empanizado*!" I whined, seeing the chance of having a thin breaded steak go right out the window.

"Impossible," said Mother.

"We'll get a pot roast," said Dad. "It will taste just like *boliche* if you make the sauce the same."

Mother gave him a dirty look and I thought she'd get into it with him again, but even she was getting tired of it all.

We managed to find onions and garlic, dried oregano and ground cumin. We even got some cheap-looking olive oil, barely green, nothing like what Fernando used to bring back from the docks. Of course there was no espresso, no whole beans, just cans of the same stuff we had been drinking, and other brands that seemed even less hopeful. We did not even try to find French baguettes. Without pineapples, pears and apples would have to do. At least there was fresh corn. It wasn't bad—maybe mother would make *tamales* with it—but the store was so bland that very little could offer reassurance.

That night my mother baked a pot roast with garlic, oranges, lemons, onions, and oregano. She made boiled potatoes with olives from a can scattered over the top. It was worlds better than unseasoned garbanzo beans or Velveeta grilled cheese, but it was certainly not *boliche*, not black beans with *yuca* on the side, not sweet fried plantains. That would have been something. That would have been home. This was just okay.

We woke up early Sunday morning to get dressed for church. We toned it down quite a bit compared to the day we arrived at the airport. Mother didn't wear nearly as much jewelry, Father wore linen instead of his suit. Still, we were quite a sight.

After we walked nearly a mile to get to church, Barbara and my mother paused for a moment on the front steps to adjust the lace veils they had smuggled past the *milicianos* when they left Cuba. Barbara opened her fan and mother took out her amethyst rosary, part of the stash I guarded in Miami.

I don't think anything could have toned us down sufficiently. As Mom and Dad walked down the aisle toward an empty pew, the heads of the faithful turned like a wave breaking. The room looked like a sportswear convention, with clothing barely a step above what the Catholics were wearing when they greeted us at the airport.

Barbara fanned herself. "Don't they dress for church?"

"No," My mother answered, closing her fan with a quick snap of her hand.

Somewhere in the middle of the mass the priest introduced us and we stood up. He congratulated his flock for helping us and my father thanked him again. After the mass no one approached us, no one spoke to us, no one offered us a ride home. Even Mr. Anderson only managed a quick wave across the lawn in front of the church. Dad refused to wait more than a moment, so we walked home without fanfare.

"I guess they don't want to be friends," my mother whispered to my dad.

"I guess not," he said, grabbing her hand. My mother was thirty, my father just thirty-three. They must have hoped for some kind of social connection. They were perfectly justified in wanting to have a little fun, especially if it was initiated by a meeting under the roof of the holy Catholic Church.

Mother made a quick lunch when we got home, but it had all the power of some potent witchcraft from the past. She made tuna fish sandwiches with the crusts cut off, with cream cheese, not mayonnaise. It must have inspired her deeply, because in the weeks that followed, there was a new sense of adventure in her cooking.

She started frying the Chiquita bananas in oil and adding eggs to make banana omelettes. She made hamburger meat into a new kind of *picadillo*. It was impossible to be authentic, because we could not find capers or green olives. The dish was missing that pickled bitterness the condiments bring, but the saltiness of black olives from the can along with the sweetness of juicy California raisins was delicious.

Eventually she even tried to make *Bistec Empanizado* with London broil.

First she set out to tame the unruly piece of meat. She sliced the oblong steak into smaller chunks, then made Hugo bring her a hammer from the garage. She covered the meat with a piece of wax paper, then used the side of the hammer to pound it as thin as she could.

There was nothing like the *galletas* we had in Cuba for breading. Maybe we could have used water crackers to simulate the discs, but only if we ate them whole. Something about the richness of the *galletas*, their flaky texture and fluffy snap, makes the breading more appealing than what you'd get from water crackers. As with most things, it probably has to do with lard.

But *galletas* were not a luxury we had available, so Mother improvised. She used stale bread toasted in the oven until it was really dried out. She then crushed it in a paper bag until the texture was fine enough for her liking. She beat a couple eggs in a shallow dish, seasoned the breadcrumbs with salt and pepper, and readied a frying pan with enough vegetable oil for a shallow fry. Then she set about making the sides.

She took a thick-cut ham steak and sautéed it with onions and garlic. She added a bag of split peas and a diced green pepper that had been charred in the broiler to remove its bitterness. A little tomato sauce from a can and enough water to cover, and we had beans of a sort. She served these with rice made with a splash of olive oil and a dash of salt.

Frying the steaks was disastrous. The breadcrumbs couldn't match the powdery texture of *galleta* meal. This would have been okay if Mother had tried dipping the steaks in flour, then egg, then breadcrumbs, but she was preparing the dish as if the bread was a natural substitute for the *galleta* meal. Since it's so powdery, you can actually double dip in the *galletas* and get a nice even coating for the egg to stick to. The breadcrumbs just clumped. So after the lackluster double dipping, she fried the steaks until they were cooked through and the breadcrumbs were browned.

There were more problems with the meal. The rice was not high quality. The split peas were not black beans. But worst of all, the steaks were tough and the chunky breading was greasy. She had tried her best, but it was not close enough, and for her that was the same thing as a failure.

Every Sunday we went through the ordeal of going to church to pay respects to the people who had been so kind to us. Every Sunday they would stare at us politely, but still no one wanted to be friends.

"Americans are very private," my father would say.

About two weeks after arriving in Los Angeles, my father took his driving test and passed. He started driving the old Ford in the driveway. It was heavenly to not have to walk to church anymore, but it was a shame to not see Mr. Anderson's ever-smiling face when he would pick Dad up in the morning. Still, he'd give us his polite little wave whenever our eyes met in church. Usually he'd be sitting with his three blond children, but for some reason, Mrs. Anderson was never with them.

Then in the first week of September, right before we were about to go to school, my father came home on Friday night after a week of hard work and told us we had been invited to a barbecue. "What's a barbecue?" I asked. He wasn't quite sure, but Barbara knew.

"It's a party where they cook all the food outside on charcoals, and if they have a pool, you get to swim."

Hugo was worried because he didn't have a bathing suit. None of us did. My dad reassured us that on the Sunday of the barbecue, the day before Labor Day, another unknown holiday, he would take us shopping.

"Whose house are we invited to?" my mother asked.

"Mr. Anderson's," my father replied proudly. It was no small feat that we had been invited to take this first step up the social ladder. Even if the whole idea of social climbing was beneath us in Cuba, we were all a little bit relieved. Finally someone wanted to be friends with us.

We went to a Sears store in Reseda, another suburb in the San Fernando Valley. It was filled with kids and their parents buying stuff for school. The only thing I could compare it to was El Encanto, the fancy department store in Havana that carried all the latest fashions from Europe. Sears was a whole different story. There were no marble floors or eager salespeople dressed better than the mannequins. I doubt if anyone in the place had ever heard of Coco Chanel, much less worn one of her dresses. It was a meat and potatoes kind of place.

At first Hugo didn't want anything. He was too embarrassed that my dad would have to pay for it. "I got plenty of clothes from the boxes in the garage," he said.

"But not a swimsuit," my mother teased him.

My father insisted, and Hugo reluctantly gave in. Barbara was not as shy and bought herself makeup, a bathing suit, and a dress. Othin and I got bathing suits and new shirts. We all got packages of pens and pencils as well as notebooks for school.

Around noon we made our way to Woodland Hills, the richer suburb next to Canoga Park. As we went up the hill toward the Andersons' house, we noticed the nicer houses that looked more like the newer towns in Havana, with 1950s-style architecture. With the green lawns and Arabic palms that were brought in because they grew better in the desert than tropical trees, the neighborhood felt expensive, more like the Hollywood movie we imagined from Miami. Halfway up the fantasy ended, as the Ford came to a clunking halt. My dad panicked as we started rolling down the hill. He put the emergency break on and shouted at us to get out of the car. My mother stayed put as the rest of us piled onto the street. What a disappointment. Maybe we'd never reach the barbecue, stranded forever halfway up the hill.

After a few moments my mother gave Jeanette to Barbara and

shook her head. She directed my dad, "Let's turn the car around so it's going down the hill. You boys push it, and I'll pop the clutch."

"You know how to do that?" Hugo asked.

"Of course I do. I grew up around buses. I know all about cars."

With the boys pushing and mother steering, we managed to turn the car around in the middle of the hill. With a final shove the car started rolling and picked up some momentum. Mother worked her magic and got the motor running. Dad took the driver's seat and maneuvered his way up the hill to the Andersons'. He made sure to not use the driveway, parking on the street just in case.

We were greeted by Mrs. Anderson, the kind of lady who never seems to give her first name. She was tall, thin, and wiry, with little veins that popped out on her neck when she got excited. She had been a ballerina in her youth and still practiced regularly. We walked into her house and it became immediately clear that she had taste. Her walls were filled with paintings and her furniture was a classy combination of modern and antique. She was gracious. She didn't look at us like foreigners; she welcomed us as friends. My dad could not keep his eyes off her. She told us to change into our suits, which we did, and then led us out into the

Dad and Mom at Mr. Anderson's house in Woodland Hills, 1963

backyard. Mr. Anderson was holding court in a bathing suit and open shirt, mixing drinks and, as usual, full of jokes and goodwill.

We were the first to arrive, my parents being the only Cubans I have ever known who are always on time. Mr. Anderson hugged my mother, told her she looked good in a swimsuit, and poured her a drink. She was beaming. We were finally at a party. The three blond

Anderson children called out to us, and Othin, Barbara, Hugo, and I all jumped into the pool at once.

I swam down to the bottom of the pool and closed my eyes. I imagined I was in the water at Varadero swimming above the beach's clear white sands. Perfect. I was alone and clean. A fish. Maybe a mermaid. The water made everything feel so safe.

By the time I resurfaced we had been joined by two other couples, newlyweds, too young to have children. The husbands both worked with my dad, and as they made professionally polite conversation, their wives looked on with wide eyes.

Mrs. Anderson made a grand entrance carrying a platter stacked high with thick-cut steaks that had been marinated in bourbon and barbecue sauce. Mr. Anderson took them from her and started grilling them immediately. The smell was intoxicating.

Mrs. Anderson came over to the side of the pool, handed me a Coca-Cola, and asked, "Hot dogs or hamburgers for you?"

"Bistec!" I said, my mouth watering. She didn't understand. She called my father over and asked him to translate. I told him, *"Quiero bistec, Papi."* He shyly explained that I wanted steak. She patted my head.

"Smart boy," she said with a knowing wink.

I swam all day, only leaving the pool to eat my steak. I polished off every bite of the mammoth piece of meat, along with hearty helpings of potato salad, fresh tomatoes, and corn on the cob. We had banana splits for dessert, which made the tasteless Chiquita bananas a lot more enjoyable.

We left around eight p.m. and thanked God when the car started. My father told my mother as we drove away, "We are going to have a house just like that."

"When and where?" she asked. What a pistol. Dad didn't say a word for the rest of the ride home.

We started school the next day. Othin was now old enough to go to kindergarten, so my mother went to his classroom to drop him off. His eyes were misty on the way there, and when we got close enough he burst out into sobs. I was nervous, for sure, but I was firm in my conviction to not show any emotion. What could be worse than four months in Hialeah?

Othin didn't practice such restraint. He was a river of emotions. Wailing and flailing, he refused to let go of my mother's skirt. She kept telling him she'd be back in the afternoon. He did not believe her. I could not blame him.

I went on my own to my classroom. I was early and the teacher asked my name and pointed to where I should sit. I watched as the students came into the classroom. Some were very American, but some were dark and definitely Spanish. The dark ones had names like Ramon and Linda. Good, I thought to myself, as soon as lunch comes I will be able to talk to someone! But lunch was hours away.

When you don't understand what people are saying, everything about a new experience becomes very visual. How someone looks at you, if they're scratching their head, if their fingernails are dirty, or how they hold their hands when they approach you, they're all clues. If you don't have a common language to communicate with, you have to use these visual signs to assess the situation. The world ends up feeling like a silent movie where the English language is just the tinkly piano score playing in the background. I sat, I watched, and I waited for lunch, eager to articulate with my soon-to-be friends.

When lunch began, I sat near Ramon and Linda and ate my ham and cheese sandwich. I worked up the courage to say something to them but stopped short when they took out their lunches. Out of their paper bags came strange little packages rolled in thin sheets that looked like crepes. One of them had what looked like *picadillo* on the inside, topped with shredded lettuce and cheese. That was it. I had to know what they were eating.

I approached Ramon because he looked the nicest, and I started rambling about a thousand words a minute. Finally I asked him what he was eating that looked like a crepe roll-up.

"No entiendo," he said to me, in very broken Spanish. "I don't understand." None of them did.

Wow! Mexicans that don't speak Spanish! What next? *"Son mexica-nos?"* I asked them.

They replied, laughing at me, *"Mexicanos?* No! Chicanos!"

Chicano? A new nationality. I guess I learned more on my first day in school than I had bargained for.

That night we all shared our adventures. Barbara had made lots of Chicano friends during the day. The ones she met called themselves low riders, and one of them had driven her home in his souped-up convertible. Hugo did not approve. He liked the California girls, saying they all reminded him of Sandra Dee. Othin made it through kindergarten in one piece, and after my mother arrived to pick him up on time, he was seriously considering returning the next day.

I couldn't stop talking about the food the Chicanos were eating. Had they ever heard of anything so strange?

"They're called tacos," my dad said.

Barbara chimed in. "The ones with beans inside are called burritos."

"Black beans?" my mother wondered, searching for her holy grail.

"No, red," Barbara said. "One of my new low rider friends let me taste some."

"What the hell is a low rider?" my father asked.

"A girl friend or a boy friend?" Hugo demanded.

"Boy," said Barbara.

"I don't like this," he said, shaking his head.

"Look, Hugo," Barbara said, "if you choose to hang out with white girls at school, then that's your choice. I like being near the darker people."

"Why?" he asked. "You jealous?"

Barbara spat, "Look at me, Hugo, I'm dark. Not like you." Jeanette started to cry, and my mother went to pick her up. Barbara glared at Hugo, her cheeks deeply flushed. Hugo didn't know how to respond. Barbara had acknowledged the difference between her skin and her brother's in a way that never would have occurred to her in Cuba. There they both had been considered white, and even though neither of their skin tones had changed, America had made Barbara's slightly darker complexion noticeable. She wanted to be a Chicana, and Hugo was horrified.

When Mother came back to the table, she repeated my father's question: "So Barbara, what's a low rider?" Barbara's fury turned to pride as she spoke about her new friends.

"They're like a club. Their cars ride low to the ground and they cruise them up and down Van Nuys Boulevard. That's where your office is, right, Othon?" Dad nodded yes.

"No sister of mine is going to go cruising!" Hugo snapped. Barbara ignored him.

"They dress really cool, the boys slick their hair back, and the girls do it up real high. You look tomorrow, Hugo. You'll see them." Hugo was seething with anger, but Barbara pretended not to notice. In a cool tone, she said, "I have to do my homework now, and so do you. White girls don't like boys with bad grades." She left the room before Hugo could respond, but he followed her to continue the fight. Mom and Dad had a good laugh at Hugo's protectiveness.

The next morning Barbara spent an hour in the bathroom getting ready. When she appeared, there was a new girl in front of our eyes. Her hair was teased into a big bouffant. She had gobs of eye makeup on and her lips were hot and red. Hugo was beside himself. "Gilda, tell her to wash her face!"

"Tell her yourself!" my mother said, knowing full well that there's no way to get between a young girl and her rebellion.

"I will never wash my face!" said Barbara, "I want to fit in!"

Mother looked at her and kissed her on the cheek. "I think you look pretty," she said sweetly, and off to school we went.

Hugo led us through the alleyway near the horse stalls, deciding it was the best way to get to school. "Shortcut," he said, ever the alpha male.

Once Othin was sure that Mom would be there to pick him up, he was fine with Hugo and Barbara dropping us off before they went on to the high school. For the first couple weeks he still cried his eyes out as he said good-bye to Mother, who waved to him from the doorstep while holding Jeanette. Eventually he got used to it, though I don't think he would have if I hadn't been there to take him all the way to his classroom.

In the evenings after school, I began to watch more television. My favorite show was still *I Love Lucy*. I was always thrilled when Lucy announced she was making Ricky Chicken with Rice. I loved the way she called it *Arroz con Pollo* in her correct but funny-sounding Spanish.

Through television I slowly began to teach myself English. There were no special classes at school to help me learn, no favoritism for children with English as a second language. I was on my own.

One day a group of kids, a daunting mixture of Chicanos and Americans, started heckling me as I waited for Hugo. "Communist!" they shouted, repeating the word as though somehow it would exorcise the red demon inside me. I ran home without Othin, but they followed. I took Hugo's shortcut and tried to hide in the abandoned horse stalls. The angry mob chased me down and kept taunting me.

"Communist!" they yelled.

They were about to hit me when Hugo appeared suddenly and chased them away. Barbara and Othin were standing next to him. Hugo took my hand and said, "Always tell me when anyone tries to hurt you."

Barbara butted in, "I'll get my Cholo friends to kick their ass."

"Were you in a fight?" Othin asked. I was too shaken up to answer. Hugo looked at him severely.

"This is our secret," he said.

"Don't worry, I won't tell Mom or Dad. I won't tell anybody." So sweet. Little Othin was defending his older brother's honor. He never told a soul.

One Friday night Dad announced we were going out to eat, so all seven of us piled into his jalopy and went to our first Mexican-Chicano dinner. We had tacos, enchiladas, and burritos. My mother wanted to know how they made their guacamole. She couldn't believe it was those ugly little Hass avocados that had this kind of flavor. My dad refused to ask the owners.

I loved the Mexican food. The flavors were familiar but exotic at the same time. We were all laughing on our way back to the house. Something about that food, so new but so satisfying, it made the whole night come alive. The restaurant, the drive down Sherman Way, even the cool, dry air of the desert at night—after a meal like that, somehow it all felt normal.

The seasons went by, at least they did as much as they could in Los Angeles. Either it was a very cold year or we just felt like it was compared to what we were used to. Whatever it was, I remember that right before Christmas it rained on Sherman Way, and as the night grew colder a few snowflakes even fell. I won't wax poetic about the beauty of a Cuban seeing his first snow. I was more interested in the puddles that lay frozen in the backyard when we woke up the next morning.

People always talk about how weird it is to have Christmas in Los Angeles. They think the heat makes it feel strange for one to buy and put up a Christmas tree. Heat, for me, at that time of year was nothing new. I felt the holiday cheer as Christmas approached, but nothing could prepare me for the joy I felt when I looked up to see the San Gabriel Mountains, covered in snow. They were such a clean white, and in my little mind, reeling with joy, I couldn't help thinking they looked just like a Baked Alaska.

We searched for a week before finding the ingredients that would serve as our Christmas dinner. Nobody anywhere would sell us a whole pig. We finally settled on a pork butt. Mom marinated it for a day and then cooked it slowly in the oven. Since *yuca* and black beans were out of the question, she made it with mashed potatoes and a carrot puree. We could not find *turrón* to save our lives. The nougat and almond candy was something the Italians probably would have had if we'd made it up to North Hollywood, but we settled for a big bag of walnuts. For dessert, mother made a perfect *flan*. Eggs, milk, and sugar you can find anywhere, but no one turned them into *flan* quite like Gilda could.

Santa Claus brought presents for us on Christmas day. "The Reyes Magos only work in South America," Dad told us. Othin got a blue tricycle, Hugo and Barbara got new records. Mom gave Dad a pair of flannel pajamas, and Dad gave her a new sweater. Jeanette was happy with a little doll and I got a brand-new bicycle. It was shiny and red and had a light so I could ride through the streets even if it was dark.

That night we went to a fair in front of the Food King. Hugo and Barbara rode the Ferris wheel, but Othin and I were too chicken to go on it, so we watched with Mom and Dad, who was holding Jeannette. Then from somewhere near us we heard something very familiar. Could it be? Yes, it was. Spanish! But not just Spanish—one word, nearly impossible to translate for its infinite possible uses, ringing through the festive crowd like a bell. The word *"coño"* resounded in our ears.

My mother clutched her throat as if she'd seen a ghost. "I could swear I just heard someone say *coño*."

"So did I!" I screamed. We turned around and saw a couple in their late twenties with one daughter looking at us. All of us were bewildered, and though we didn't know exactly what was going on, we were pretty sure we were face to face with another family of Cubans! Without a word we ran into each others arms and hugged before we even introduced ourselves.

We were not alone anymore. There were other Cubans in town, and if they were here, in the suburb of Canoga Park, in the city of Los Angeles, in the San Fernando Valley, in the state of California, maybe, just maybe, there was hope for us in the United States of America.

❙ *Suburban Pineapple Upside-Down Cake* ❙

This cake is so easily prepared, and delicious, too, if for no other reason than most of its ingredients were engineered to be both things. This was one of my first experiences of truly American food. Because it was offered to my family by the suburban welcome wagon of Canoga Park, I would further suggest preparing this cake as a quick and easy hostess gift. Everything old is indeed new again, and it doesn't get much more retro than this.

One 20-ounce can pineapple slices in heavy syrup
¼ cup (½ stick) salted butter, melted
¾ cup dark brown sugar
One 6-ounce jar maraschino cherries
One 18.25-ounce box yellow cake mix
One 2.75-ounce box instant vanilla pudding mix
3 large eggs
⅓ cup vegetable oil

1. Preheat the oven to 350°F. Drain the pineapples, reserving the syrup in a measuring cup. Add enough water to equal 1⅓ cups. Set aside.

2. Pour the melted butter into a 9-inch round cake pan. Sprinkle with the brown sugar. Place one slice of pineapple in the center of the pan. Arrange the remaining slices around the first. You won't use all the pineapple in the can. Place a maraschino cherry inside the hole at the center of each pineapple slice. You won't use all the cherries, either.

3. In a large mixing bowl, combine the cake mix, pudding mix, eggs, vegetable oil, and syrup mixture. Mix with a whisk or electric mixer at medium speed, 2 minutes. Gently pour the batter into the cake pan so the pineapple slices are not disturbed. Place the pan on a baking sheet to catch any batter that bubbles over.

4. Bake in the middle of the oven until a toothpick inserted in the center of the cake comes out clean, 1 hour. Set aside to cool for 10 minutes. Invert onto a plate or cake stand. Slice and serve.

Makes 8 servings

Six

Adaptation

I wish I could remember the other Cuban family's names, but I can't. I wish I could say we became lifelong friends, but we never did. For about a year they were like family, but it was a relation borne out of necessity, a result of our shared isolation.

They came by the house at least once a week, usually on the weekends. We'd share stories and news about Cuba, whatever we had heard during the week. When they were over, my mother seemed happier and more at home. She'd put on a dress from Cuba whenever she knew they were coming, making sure to select just the right earrings and bracelet to go with it. She seemed easier, more laid back when they were around, and while she always entertained hospitably, she never seemed to be working too hard. Maybe she was just enjoying herself more.

Like any good (or not so good) Catholic girl, Mother was pregnant again. Jeanette was one year old, walking and running around like crazy but not quite speaking. She made sounds, but they couldn't be traced to any one language in particular. She called my father Tata, and if she wanted something, she said, "Geevee." It might have seemed like your average baby talk, but I knew better. Jeanette, like the rest of us, was stuck between two languages. She, however, had taken a more radical approach to navigating this uncertain terrain, inventing her own way of communicating. I, on the other hand, understood English, but my accent was still thick enough to keep me from speaking easily. Where Jeanette just went and used her tongue no matter what came out, my inability to pronounce *v* or *th* had made me painfully shy. My *r*'s rolled off my tongue with uncontrollable gusto, and all it took was a few Yankee chuckles for me to decide that I'd rather remain silent around Anglos. I made up for this silence the moment the other Cubans came over.

At one of our weekend get-togethers, we discussed the lack of any real Cuban food in Los Angeles. The father of the other Cuban family told us they had made a great discovery. There was a market in downtown Los Angeles, huge and full of exotic foods, called the Grand Central Market. There, he said, we would find all the things we were missing.

"There has to be some Italian espresso!" Hugo announced. It was decided we would go to the Grand Central Market the following weekend.

This time everyone was going food shopping. All that week, Barbara and my dad looked at maps in the music room to find the fastest route to downtown Los Angeles. Barbara even asked some of her low rider friends for advice. They had offered to drive us there, an idea that Barbara was trying to sell for the whole week, but my mother repeatedly told her the answer was no.

"There is no way I'm driving anywhere for an hour in a car with low riders!" Mother said, making the sign of the cross.

Barbara accused my mother of being a racist, but Mother's answer was still no.

So after much careful planning, the other Cubans arrived at the house, and we were ready to go. We piled into two cars and went on our first trip to downtown Los Angeles. My father took the lead, even though it was the other Cuban father who had first heard of the market. Dad had done some serious mapping and he wanted to see his planning through.

Los Angeles was more of a city than any of us were used to. With its tall buildings and paved sidewalks, the modernity might have caught our attention first if it weren't for the huge numbers of Chicanos (or were they Mexicans?) walking the streets. All the white Americans seemed to be driving cars or taking buses. The sight of the buses set us off on a ream of chatter about Oscar and Manuela, their brothers and sisters, and the bus company that seemed like such a distant memory. This, of course, led to talk about how much we missed Cuba. No matter how many times we spoke about them, longing, heartbreak, and loss of our island paradise were inexhaustible topics between our family and the other Cubans.

But as we drove downtown I had to admit to myself that maybe, for the last few months, I had not missed Cuba. I missed the food, for sure. I felt my tongue getting lonely with every day that passed. But the place itself? I was starting to feel at home in Los Angeles, but I'd never let my mother know. It would kill her if she did.

I looked out the window and saw a street corner bustling with people carrying bags and eating food as they drove.

"We must be near it!" I screamed.

My father threw me a derisive glance that asked why I had to be so shrill. I was hungry.

"This is it," he said with conviction. "We are here."

He honked the horn and gestured to the other Cubans in the car behind us. This was the place.

Suddenly we were in the thick of it, with people and automobiles crowding our vision as far as we could see. We had to find a parking lot and pay to leave the car, as it would have been impossible to find a spot on the street. It was nearly impossible to *see* the street.

Hugo kept chanting, "There will be espresso here! They'll have it, I know it."

As Barbara got out of the car in her black halter top, the sound of snapping necks rippled through the crowd. Every Chicano in a twenty-foot radius checked her out as we approached the entrance to the market.

My mother tried to give Jeanette a bottle, but she didn't want it. Even the baby knew something monumental was unfolding, and that it would result in more satisfaction than any formula. Othin and I grabbed my dad's hands, and in we went.

The Grand Central Market was better than any of us could have dreamt. It was sheltered by a roof overhead, but the doors on all sides opened up, letting the air in. This gave the whole place the feel of a country farmers' market even though we were in downtown L.A. And while we weren't quite sure what kind of market it was yet, it was clearly a hell of a lot better than the Food King.

The first thing I noticed was the smell. Clouds of smoky perfume wafted through the warm air. I saw their source—little stalls with rows of spices lined up in giant cylindrical tins. Piles of earth tones, yellows and all shades of red sat alongside mounds of crinkly browns and blacks. There were peppers of every variety, but I had no idea what they even were. I was able to spot and identify the containers of dried oregano, cumin, and saffron. After yearning for those spices for so long, I was surprised that they now seemed ordinary next to vats of things I had never even conceived of.

I started putting two and two together and realized that the market should be called Central Mexico. There was Spanish writing telling us what most of the things were. Tortillas? Mother decided she was ready to try them, so she bought a bagful. *Tamales?* They didn't look like *tamales*, but Dad was not going to miss the opportunity, so he bought a dozen.

Then my salivary glands sent a flood rushing into my mouth. My nose pointed up into the air like some kind of bassett hound, and I knew there was roast pork nearby. I dragged my father toward the scent.

The sign said CARNITAS, so I was suspicious. Mother was even more so.

"It looks like beef," she said. I think I saw my father roll his eyes, but he bought three orders anyway.

The vendor layered a piece of aluminum foil with a piece of wax paper. He took two tortillas and piled them high with the *carnitas*, then topped them with chopped onions and shredded radish. He handed them over the counter, and my father gave one each to me and my mother.

I quickly brushed the onions and radishes onto the floor of the stall so I could get a better look at the meat. It was a deep caramel color, the pile of thick-grained chunks dotted with gelatinous nubs of fat. I took a bite.

Oh, my God. Pork. Roast pork. Dissolving in my mouth. Filled with the scent of lemons and garlic, a hint of oregano, no cumin, that's for sure, but I almost didn't miss it. It was melting. Positively melting. Just like the pork I knew.

"*Carnita* is not beef," my mother said, "it's just roast pork." How could she talk at a time like this? "I think there's cilantro in it." Who cares? I was busy stuffing my face.

Dad bought two pounds of *carnitas* to bring home for dinner that night, no tortillas or radishes, thank you very much.

Further inspection of the central market revealed several different kinds of bananas, but still no plantains. There were mangoes and papayas, but not a single *yuca*.

"*Boniato*," my mother said proudly, when she spotted the starchy white sweet potatoes we loved in Cuba. "I can make *boniatillo*," the sweet potato pudding that only sticks to your ribs when it's made with the real thing. Not "those orange things."

We turned a corner onto a row of butchers selling every possible cut of meat. Mother shut up and set out to find *palomilla* steaks. She didn't say a word; she just scanned the rows of beef looking for the right cut. She was deep in thought, and it looked like she'd stand there all day till she found it, but Dad beat her to the punch.

"They have *boliche* here, too!" Brisket was a familiar cut now, and Dad ordered it as Mother's eyes clouded over. She shook her head. How could it be so hard to find a *palomilla*? She had given up, but she made sure to take the parchment package the butcher handed to my father. But there was still more to discover, and Mother trudged onward. Part of me knew she'd return to the butcher soon.

"Mami!" I shouted as I stumbled on a dry goods stall with red, white, yellow, green, and, "Look! Black beans!" She bought a few pounds, and then, revitalized, scanned the next stall until she found a pile of brightly colored peppers.

"*Habanero*," she said, "maybe they're from Havana." I looked at her askance. Havana? Not La Habana? Was it that far away that she had dropped the article? Switched the pronunciation, made it sound so American? Had her failed search for *palomilla* steaks beat her into submission?

No. Not quite. Because she moved on to another stall. She had spotted a wealth of short-grain white rice, pounds and pounds of it, so she bought a huge bag. She was about to send Dad back to the car to lighten our load because who knew what else the Grand Central Market would present us, but she stopped short as Hugo and Barbara came running toward us.

Hugo had found the Italians at last. They led us to the coffee counter, where we found French roast, Italian roast, and, look! Espresso!

"Are you sure this is the right stuff?" my father asked. "I can't take any more Maxwell House."

"This is it," said Hugo. "Buy it all."

Dad ordered several pounds and we all said a silent prayer as it was being ground. The silence became a jubilant rejoicing when Dad decided we had enough money to buy a stove-top espresso maker. Mother took off to hunt for "real" milk but returned a few minutes later empty-handed.

"I'll just have to use pasteurized. It tastes better when I heat it with a pinch of salt."

My family had come alive in the course of one trip to the Grand Central Market. Everybody's face radiated possibility, because of what, food? It was more than that.

The food made us feel rich again, with its bounty and endless offering of opportunities. Sure, the end result was just a list of menus, but we had to find the place, we had to get the ingredients, we had to put the dishes together. It was a lesson in self-sufficiency. Having nothing and finding everything. The obvious analogy is that of the American dream, but we weren't quite there yet. And anyway, this didn't feel like America. This place, this market, it obviously belonged to the Mexicans, but we had staked our claim in such a short time, and we had done it all on our own.

As we were leaving the market, my mother spotted French baguettes, not quite Cuban but good enough. At the deli counter my dad had found something that the butcher guaranteed was close to Serrano ham and he picked up a pound, making sure it was sliced extra-thin.

On the drive home we snacked on ham and bread. The crust of the baguette scraped the roof of my mouth, but I didn't mind. The texture was chewy, not like the soft Cuban bread, but the saltiness of the ham on the inside transported me into visions of Spain, just like when Fernando would return from the docks bearing gifts of delicacies from across the ocean. I opened my eyes to be reminded that this was just California. Today that was good enough for me.

As we got closer to Canoga Park, Mother couldn't help herself, so she went through the list of all the things we hadn't found. "*Yuca*, *malanga*, plantains, sour oranges," etcetera, etcetera, etcetera. I shared a glance with my dad in the rearview mirror and took another bite of my ham sandwich.

As soon as we got home, we made espresso for our Cuban friends. Mom spooned heaping tablespoons into the filter portion of the stovetop espresso maker. She filled the bottom container with water, screwed the whole thing tight, and set it on the stove to brew. Since there was no "real" milk, we would drink the coffee black with lots of sugar. Mother did her best to match our American coffee cups to saucers, but I don't think anything in our cupboard went with anything else. She lined up the cups in a row and readied a large mason jar into which she spooned several tablespoons of sugar. When the coffee finished brewing, she added it to the jar and stirred, then filled each cup a little less than halfway. She shrugged, as if to say that the absence of demitasse cups just couldn't be helped.

She passed the cups around. The other Cubans thanked her politely, but I just went ahead and took a sip.

It was not called Cuban roast per se, but how could I argue as the thick black taste of beans so dark they were almost burnt rolled over my tongue for the first time in ages. Mother had brewed it extra-strong, too, so each sip sent a caffeinated shiver down my spine. The room was silent except for murmurs and quiet moans. Some part of all of us was complete again.

Our friends drove home quickly after that. They said they were eager to eat all the stuff they had bought. I think it was probably just the first dose of real caffeine they had received in a while.

My mother set about cooking up some of our own treats, putting a pot of water on the stove to heat up the Mexican *tamales*. She also preheated the oven to a low temperature to heat up the roast pork, or, as we now called it (with an extra rolled *r*), *carnitas*.

That night over dinner, the great *tamal* war began. Cuban *tamales* are made by grating fresh corn, and only fresh corn. They're filled with sautéed *sofrito* (onions, pepper, garlic, and tomatoes) and chunks of shredded pork and fatback, and it is rare to find one that isn't bright yellow and supremely moist. They don't need a sauce to make them yummy. Mexican *tamales* do, as they are usually dry. This is not a judgment; it's just a matter of ingredients. They rarely have fresh corn in them; instead they're made with dried ground corn flour, or *masa harina*. Instead of pork and aromatics distributed evenly though, they have a thin sauce of chiles and spices with chunks of chicken or pork in the center. The *masa* is then wrapped around the filling and the whole thing is cooked.

As we tried our first bites of this strange cousin to the *tamal* we all knew and loved, Hugo announced, "This is not a *tamal*."

"Just because they're different doesn't mean they're not good," Barbara chimed in.

"Of course you would like them, you love anything Mexican," Hugo said.

"At least I'm not a racist," Barbara spat.

"If you love Mexicans so much, why don't you marry one?" Hugo challenged.

"Maybe I will," she snarled back.

My dad interrupted. "I agree with Barbara. They are different. But they are tasty. What do you think, Gilda?"

"The pork is delicious," my mother answered without missing a beat. My father frowned.

"The pork is good!" Othin yelled. I remained silent. I was deeply disappointed.

My favorite thing in the whole world is a real Cuban *tamal*. I associate *tamales* with a full belly and an afternoon nap under a tree. Cuban *tamales* taste like sweet flowers and buttery breakfast meat. The Mexican version tasted like chalk in comparison. I will never eat a real *tamal* again, I thought.

That night I dreamt of Cojimar. I was standing behind the wall in the front yard of Fernando and Cuca's house and I heard the words coming down the street: "*Tamales!* Twenty-five cents. *Tamales!*" A savory siren song. I got my quarter and waited by the gate, but the vendor never came. All of a sudden I was standing in front of the hamburger stand in Canoga Park and someone handed me a hot dog. I woke up crying and I heard myself say, "I want to go home."

This was the first time I had admitted it out loud. I cried alone, remembering. This feeling, longing, missing, it was not just food. It was fullness, satisfaction, dozing in the afternoon with a belly so full even the idea of moving was an impossibility. I missed the food. But even more, I missed feeling so safe that I could eat until I was completely immobile. I missed my home.

At that moment I knew I was more like mother than I had realized. Every moment that felt real to me in this new place was imagined. I was just pretending to fit in. I was homesick and I would be homesick for the rest of my life.

The next morning I practiced my English with a bitter streak of resolution. I vowed that I would fit in. I would learn perfect English, if only to tell the Yankees how their home was nothing, and would never be anything like mine.

That November, two years after I arrived in Miami, my sister Gilda Elizabeth was born. We called her Didi. She was different from Jeanette, quieter, calmer. She was in no way a refugee. She was conceived and born in Canoga Park. She was a Californian, a thought that provided endless amusement for me, and a little pity.

In the months that followed, we started meeting other Cubans. There seemed to be a lot more of them coming to live in Los Angeles—after all, it was warm and it did have an ocean. There were more opportunities for better-paying jobs than in Miami. Plus, there were the streets and towns with Spanish names. All these things seemed so foreign when we first arrived, but we now wore them with a badge of pride and familiarity. The strange land had been conquered, or at least infiltrated, by the Machado clan.

Most of the newly arrived families were moving to Panorama City. Maybe it was the name that attracted them. They expected something beautiful, with expansive vistas, but it was really just another little town in the Valley next to Van Nuys. It was closer to Mr. Anderson's office, though, so when a house became available on the street where all the Cubans were congregating, we moved away from Canoga Park.

Our new house was a tiny bungalow with a smaller guest house behind it. There was a family of Spaniards that lived in the guest house, though they had spent most of their lives in Cuba before moving to the United States. Barbara made friends with their daughter, but the cultivated young girl was no replacement for the gang of low riders she left behind in Canoga Park.

There were two other Cuban families across the street. They became fast friends with my parents, and our weekend get-togethers with the other Cubans grew to include them. My mother would cook, and my father started a regular dominos game every Sunday. With his keen mind for numbers he was the king of the table. He always seemed to win.

My mother used the gatherings as an opportunity to expand her culinary repertoire. She started to cook Italian. She loved the Southern Italian specialties she ate in her youth in Cuba, and she did her best to piece the flavors together from memory. After discovering the Grand

Central Market, she had a whole range of ingredients at her fingertips. She was having a ball putting fresh basil into everything she could. She especially liked making tomato sauce with lots of oregano, serving it with boiled spaghetti and grated cheese from the cheese stall.

Her favorite dish to prepare for the Sunday socials was her version of a lasagna. She'd boil the wide noodles and layer them with ricotta cheese and a light tomato sauce made with chunks of browned bulk Italian sausage. Instead of adding ground beef to the layers, she'd make miniature meatballs full of onions and garlic that she'd slice in half to fill out the middle. The time-consuming absurdity of this step feels very French to me now, but the proof really was in the pudding. The meatballs would pop out from the layers of slippery noodles as my fork made a beeline through the crust of lightly browned mozzarella on top. Every time they'd slide directly from the fork into my gullet, I recognized every time that those little half-moons of goodness were what set Mother's lasagna apart from all the rest.

Around that time she also started cooking Mexican. She was picky, though, so she gave the dishes a Cuban twist. She refused to eat red beans, so she used black beans to make her version of refried beans. And although she eventually bought Hass avocados, for a long time she'd use the Caribbean variety and end up with a watery guacamole.

She loved the idea of tacos. They were easy and fast with the home-made tortillas from the Grand Central Market, but it was her version of enchiladas that were her greatest success in the world of Mexican cuisine.

Mother made her enchiladas by stuffing tortillas with homemade *picadillo*, browned ground beef flavored with tomatoes, olives, raisins, and spices. She'd roll the enchiladas tight and tuck them side by side into a casserole. It was her version of *mole* sauce that really set them apart from Mexican tradition. All she did was use her Cuban tomato sauce but with more olives, raisins, and a few capers. She'd cover the bundles in sauce, then finish the dish off with a liberal sprinkling of cheddar cheese. The whole thing would go into the oven until the cheese was bubbling hot. The balance of complex flavors has ties to the basic ideas of Mexican *mole*, sweet, salty, and pungent. The sauce would tenderize the tortillas in just the right way. The enchiladas sometimes fell apart while she served them, but that didn't matter. There were no rules in this strange land of fusion cuisine. Cumex. Or Mexiban. Mother was way ahead of her time.

Over the next couple years a mass of relatives made it out of Cuba. In late 1964, my cousins Rolando and Rosita moved in with us for a few months with their baby son, Rolandito. Eventually Rolando found a job with the Budweiser Beer company, and they moved into an apartment as soon as they'd saved enough money.

Soon after, the Miami contingent started arriving on the West Coast. I didn't even try to contain my hatred when Yolanda moved into our house with my uncle Fernando and their children Elena and Bebito. Every moment Yolanda was in my presence I stared her down with an icy gaze, a mixture of avoidance and defiance. My eyes said, "See. They're here. And you told me I'd never see my parents again." Fortunately they moved out after only a few weeks, but they became part of the Sunday socials as well.

In early 1966 we moved again. This time we stayed in Panorama City but relocated to a spacious three-bedroom apartment in a complex filled with Cubans. It was like our own little version of Melrose Place. Upstairs were the other Cubans we met in Canoga Park at the Food King. Next door to them was a family of eight, a mother, a father, three daughters, and one cousin with two children of her own. Across a courtyard in the complex was another building that Rolando, Rosita, and Rolandito eventually moved to. Soon after came Rolando's sister and her family, who moved in next door. Just two blocks away was another similar complex, with three other huge Cuban families and a large assortment of relatives. We were practicing a subtle form of cultural imperialism in our own little corner of Los Angeles.

With the proximity of so many other Cuban households there began an exchange of recipes throughout the neighborhood, especially among the women at the Sunday socials. I remember the first time Mother made American pot roast. The meat, as far as I was concerned,

Eduardo, Othin, and Jeanette,
outside the apartments in Panorama City, 1968

was second rate *boliche*, all the texture with none of the flavor, but I loved the softness of the carrots and onions and celery cooked with it. My favorite part was the potatoes that soaked up beef juice and burst open like overstuffed pillows when cracked with a fork.

When the women gathered, they loved to prepare typically tedious recipes in large batches with food enough for everyone to take home. Someone had a new way of making *tamales* in tin foil. They made the filling with whole frozen corn kernels, adding dry cornmeal and *sofrito* to fill it out and using the Mexican *carnitas* from the Grand Central Market. The mixture would be stuffed into foil rectangles, then folded over once and tucked in at the edges. The foil packets could then be dropped into boiling water and cooked for several hours. The *tamales* were good, don't get me wrong, but between the dry corn *masa* and the lack of corn husks it was all a little too inauthentic for the purist in my belly.

I preferred the communal *croquetas* that never seemed to last the whole weekend. Mother had purchased a meat grinder that she used to pulverize chicken or ham steaks. Someone else would make the base that would be used for both flavors. It's really just a béchamel sauce, made with flour, butter, milk, and seasonings, but the mixture has to be reduced to a stick-to-your-ribs consistency, and that requires lots of stirring. It's perfect for a large group.

So while two people would work the base, one stirring, one adding milk, someone else would make the breadcrumbs from stale bread and seasonings.

The real communal aspect came when the bases were done. The meat would be added to two separate batches, then left to sit and cool in the refrigerator. This was the perfect time to cut and stuff the foil packets of *tamales*, or, more accurately, the ideal moment to sit around and gossip. When the base had cooled sufficiently, the women would set it in the middle of the table. Armed with spoons and plates of breadcrumbs, they'd mold the dough into little cylindrical nuggets with their hands, rolling the baby footballs and stacking them in pyramids until they were ready to fry.

Something about busying the hands always seems to free the tongue. Stories, recipes, and jokes would fly through the air. I remember watching the repetitive motion of fingers cupping the *croquetas*, gently rolling just the right amount of crumbs onto each, dropping them onto piles. It was like a meditation. Eventually someone would take a break from their cooking to click on the record player. The women always listened to Olga Guillot. Their favorite song, "*Añorada Cuba*," went something like, "Unrequited Cuba, I think of you so I have the strength to live. When I remember your beaches, Tarara, Santa Maria del Mar and all of the others where we swam, I love you more and more." There was never a dry eye in the kitchen when that played.

We were definitely not alone anymore. Our family was getting bigger and stronger as more of us moved west. One night when Rolando and Rosita were over for my mother's now-famous Italian *café con leche*, Rolando had news that the family was growing larger still. Another baby? I thought. But no, it was a bigger deal than that. Rolando told us that his uncle Aquiles had decided to move from Miami to Panorama City to be closer to all of us. Aquiles was that mythic figure, the general in Batista's army who helped turn the men around to guarantee Fidel his victory. We knew Fidel had shot him and that his wife, Caridad, had dragged his bleeding body to the Swiss embassy in hopes of escaping, but now Rolando told us the rest of the story.

It turned out that Fidel had actually come to visit Aquiles while he recovered from his wound. According to Aquiles, every time Fidel visited, he would make a trip to the bathroom. When Aquiles was strong enough to get up, he followed Fidel when he went to relieve himself.

Fidel would leave a gun on the edge of the sink to see if Aquiles would follow him and then, upon discovering the weapon, use it to shoot Fidel through the stall. Aquiles saw through this bizarre mindgame and never picked up the weapon, assuming that Fidel would shoot him back through the stall with another gun he had hidden on his person. I listened wide-eyed and drop-jawed. I don't know how true it was, but it was a great story. But then my family has always had great stories to tell. Tragic stories, myths, even. I always marveled that these people were related to me.

Another one of my favorite family tragedies was that of Isolina Chinea, Hugo and Barbara's mother. Barbara had told me the story in the music room back in Canoga Park. Her voice had an eerie air of detachment and fascination. Her mother had burned herself to death.

Isolina was a twin. When she and her sister were infants they lived in a farmhouse that mysteriously caught fire while the family was sleeping. The only person roused from slumber was her father, Barbara's grandfather. He came rushing to the rescue but unfortunately was only able to save Isolina. Her sister and mother perished in the flames. Years later, when Barbara was only three or four, Isolina had just finished refilling a small kerosene stove. As she went to light the burner to start cooking something, she slipped and knocked over the fuel canister. The kerosene caught and she was suddenly covered in flames. She looked at her children, who had come to see what was wrong, and said, "This is my fate. Do not try to save me." The children ignored her and ran for help, but it was too late. Their mother was covered in third-degree burns, and she died two months later.

This is the history I pondered in my alone time. I tried to make sense of a middle-aged woman's death at the hands of fate. Tragedy was her destiny. Was it mine, too? These were my relatives. This was my history. Maybe my fate would be different. Maybe, in a way, my tragedy was already equal.

Aquiles and Caridad moved in to our apartment building when they arrived from Miami about a month after Rolando told us they were coming. Life became very exciting. They had four children, a son and a daughter that were Hugo's and Barbara's ages, another daughter closer to my age, and a younger son. I made friends with all their children, but it was Caridad who became my closest consort. She was my first adult friend. She was humorous, honest, and worldly. She was, after all, a general's wife and part of the Revolution. Best of all, she treated me with respect, as though she understood that I had been through the same part of history that she had survived, that somehow we were equal.

Caridad and Aquiles's arrival also brought a new sense of paranoia and intrigue to the neighborhood. According to Aquiles, the CIA believed he was still working for Fidel. Caridad would tell me that the spooks made weekly, sometimes daily, visits to our apartment building. One day she mentioned offhand that she had walked in on two men searching her apartment. Her relaxed tone and casual manner kept me from believing her completely. I guess that's how you sound when harassment by government institutions is an everyday affair. Like most things Caridad told me, I kept the information to myself, until one day when I went over to her house to say hello. Caridad wasn't home, but the door to her apartment was ajar. I walked in to find three men in suits hunched over drawers and cabinets, looking for something. I was petrified. The spooks stood up, waved hello to me, and left. I waited outside in the courtyard until Caridad came home, at which point I told her everything.

"You see?" she said. "How are we ever going to be able to have a life if they're always looking for a way to destroy it?" I didn't quite know what she meant, but it was from that point on that I realized the American government played a role in the lives of all Cubans, that somehow, just because of where we came from and who we might be, we had to be closely watched.

It was also around that time that I started noticing just how grown-up Barbara and Hugo had become. They were only in their late teens, but they had matured past the point where I could really associate with them the way we had in Canoga Park. Hugo had been working part time in a factory until he was able to buy a secondhand car. He and

Barbara had started traveling to visit friends of theirs from Cojimar in Downey, a little town about an hour and a half away from Panorama City. They made the trips on most weekends, and it seemed innocent enough until one day there was a knock at our door.

It was a young man named Bruce. He was twenty-one, a few years older than Barbara, and he had come to ask my father and Hugo for her hand in marriage.

I don't think Dad quite knew what to say. I should mention our shock that this boy was white. Pale white. All-American white. Not a drop of Latin blood in him. I was SURE Barbara would marry a Mexican. Hugo was relieved, I think my dad would have preferred a Cuban, but everyone agreed it was a good thing when they found out he was Catholic.

All the families in the neighborhood got together to give the happy couple a small wedding in Downey. My father gave Barbara away and the Cuban ladies from Downey and Panorama City made her a long white wedding dress with a veil and everything. She looked classy and rich, especially since she had stopped ratting her hair like a low rider several months before. She had matured into a beautiful young woman with dark black hair, olive skin, big eyes, and full lips all perched atop a perfect little figure with curves in all the right places. We had California champagne and roast pork with black beans, which Bruce's divorced parents and their friends seemed to love. My dad also made sangria from scratch. There were no pears or apples in his version of the Spanish concoction. He made it with red wine, brandy, lemons, limes, and lots of oranges. It was like a citrus punch fortified by the brandy. A perfect salve to ease the transition. Even though my mother had a houseful of children, she was sad to see Barbara go. She left that night with her husband, and the era of our family of circumstance had come to an end.

Things changed after Barbara's departure in more ways than one. The pressure cooker of Cuban life in our neighborhood was a good litmus test for our cultural sentiments. It was clearer every day that all our situations were not as temporary as we may have liked.

My dad's parents, Cuca and Fernando, had made it out of Cuba but were now living in Mexico with my uncle Pipo, waiting for visas to enter the United States. My mother's parents, Manuela and Oscar, had filed their own papers to leave, and so had Hugo's father, Miguel, his other sister Dulce, and his stepmother, Rosa. The message was clear—they had all given up on anything changing.

My mother's dream of going home was no longer realistic, though she never admitted it. Neither did I. The only evidence of our crushed hopes was the look in our eyes whenever we heard news of the family.

One of those looks was shared when we received a letter from my aunt Chichi that Fidel's men had done an inventory of Manuela and Oscar's house in Cojimar. The inventory was the last step before they gave you the visa to leave the country. The *milicianos* would show up, make a list of everything in the house, from candlesticks to underpants, so that if you didn't hand everything over when you left, they would know. They wanted to make sure nothing was given to the people who stayed behind. Everything belonged to the Revolution. Nobody else could tell that my mother's hopes were dashed—when she was nervous she just cooked more—but when she looked in my eyes I knew. She was a wreck.

Ours was not the only family to be affected by this mass realization of paradise lost. We were all horrified to discover that a single mother of two who lived in the apartment complex had hanged herself. In the note she left she stated that she had tried to inject air bubbles into her children's veins the night before in hopes of taking them with her, but she had failed. Whether it was a lack of will or anatomical know-how I'll never know, but her letter said that she simply could not bear the knowledge that she wouldn't be able to return home.

It was bleak. Even Caridad was disturbed, especially as she recounted the whole story to me. She confessed that even she had thought of suicide to escape the constant presence of the CIA agents. Even if they weren't searching her house every day, she feared they were always close by. That much paranoia is a kind of torture in itself.

But even more than government intervention, Caridad feared the harsh realities that a permanent life in the United States might require of her.

"A factory," she'd repeat, "me in a factory making dresses."

All the women around us except my mother worked in factories. My father was making more money at Mr. Anderson's firm, even as he prepared for his CPA exam. Caridad saw that Aquiles's career opportunities were limited at best, the harshest reality of all.

In the spring Dad passed his exam on the first try. He was promoted to a junior partner position in Mr. Anderson's firm. Soon after we received news that his parents had arrived in Miami from their extended layover in Mexico. He bought a new blue Pontiac that he planned to drive to Miami for a visit over his summer vacation. I was dying to go with him—I wanted to see the Mojave Desert—but he went with Rolando and Fernando instead.

The closest I got to the desert that summer was a postcard Dad sent from a roadside gas station in New Mexico. The card had a picture of a shiny Chevy convertible on it with a note on the back saying, "See if you can catch up to me with this car." I know he meant it as a joke, but that little dig made me hate him. It was as if that single postcard crystallized all the resentment I felt toward him for never including me in his life. There was an added fear that came with his cross-country trip. If he abandoned me once, he could do it again. The car just added salt to the already festering wound. But I did not tear up the card. I saved it as evidence of his cruelty. I told Caridad all about it, and she agreed with me completely.

That fall most of the rest of my family made the trip to Los Angeles. The family dog, Terri, miraculously arrived first, I have no idea how. He was quarantined for a couple of months, having arrived in Los Angeles in late July. The call to pick him up didn't come until early September. He remembered us all when he saw us, even though he really belonged to my grandfather Oscar. The bizarre part was that Terri got to the United States before his master. I had a special affection for Terri because his favorite food was leftover *Moros*. As cute as it was to watch him eating mounds of rice and beans, the unpleasant odors that followed were not exactly adorable.

My grandparents Oscar and Manuela arrived next, along with my aunt Chichi. Hugo and Barbara's father, Miguel, his wife, Rosa, and daughter, Dulce, were right behind them. We went to the airport to greet them, and there was profound joy and pain all at once. We all cried, with happiness to see each other, and regret that it had not been in Cuba like we had dreamed.

We took my grandmother Manuela to the Food King the very next day—better not to shock her with the Grand Central Market right away. She was overwhelmed anyway, after living for some time in Cuba under rations similar to the food we had in Hialeah.

I remember thinking how funny it was that she bought bags full of cheese and apples. It wasn't like the Food King had triple-cream brie or aged gorgonzola—she was elated at the prospects of Swiss, cheddar, and Jack. As she bit a big chunk out of a juicy Red Delicious apple, she told me she had always wanted to have an apple tree.

"Maybe here I'll be able to grow one," she said. She seemed strangely ready to start a new life at sixty-one.

Everyone moved into the three apartments our family had in the complex—Rolando's, Aquiles's, and ours. Manuela, Chichi, and Rosa found jobs in a wig factory, Rolando got Miguel a job with Budweiser, and Oscar found work as a mechanic. Everyone settled in surprisingly fast.

Things changed just as quickly. Miguel, his wife, Rosa, and Dulce soon got an apartment down the street. Hugo was so used to our family that he stayed with us. My aunt Chichi went to New York to visit her fiancé, whom she had not seen for five years. She never came back—she married him and moved there. Then, just as I was about to finish elementary school, my father announced we were moving again. We could now afford a five-bedroom house in a suburb called Granada Hills. It didn't have a pool, but at least there was a barbecue.

We celebrated in grand style the first weekend we moved in. Family and friends came down from Panorama City, Downey, and Van

*Othin, Mom with Michelle, Dad, and me in the back,
Didi and Jeanette in the front, outside the house
in Granada Hills, 1969*

Nuys. We cooked steaks for dinner. They were not *palomilla* cut, and there was no breading involved. We marinated and grilled thick-cut London broil that filled the back-yard with the aroma of oranges, limes, and oregano. Mother made a huge pot of *Moros y Cristianos* to accompany the meat, as well as a salad of tomatoes, onions, and big green Spanish olives from the Grand Central Market with a light oil and vinegar dressing. Dad held court next to a keg of beer, and he was obviously proud to be able to feed so many people. For dessert we had a giant rum cake cooked in a sheet pan. The spongy cake was thick with syrup so sweet you needed a little booze in it to cut the sugar. The whole thing made my head spin.

It was a good thing we had so much family to keep us company, since most of the neighbors in Granada Hills stayed away from us. We had moved to a truly suburban suburb. There were no Chicanos or Mexicans, definitely no blacks, and most certainly no Cubans.

Othin and I thought we'd be able to make friends with somebody's children, but nobody really wanted to play with us. We stuck together during that time. We found a small creek at the bottom of the hill at the end of our block. There he and I would pretend to be soldiers, like we did in Cuba during the Bay of Pigs. The difference was that this time we weren't waiting for the real soldiers to arrive. We set up camps on either side of the creek and waited, our only battle to fend off boredom.

Every weekend the house would fill with our Cuban friends and relatives. You could tell we were having one of our get-togethers be-cause the driveway would spill over until the entire street was lined with cars. No one else on that block ever had a party as big as ours. It's funny how normal the gatherings seemed to me. Eventually I decided that the neighbors must hate us because of all the noise we made. I started hating us a little, too, thinking that we Cubans were too loud compared to the rest of America. Some part of me still wanted to fit in.

One weekend my grandfather Oscar decided we should make *tamales* from scratch for our Sunday social. So that Friday night on his way home from work he bought ten dozen fresh pieces of corn from a corn stand on the side of the road. We made makeshift graters out of metal cans, using the lip to snag the corn kernels until the container was full. The whole family shucked and grated the corn, being sure to save the best husks for wrapping the *tamales*. No way would Oscar ever use tin foil. That's why I loved him.

My mother slow-roasted a pork shoulder, then mixed chunks of the meat with *sofrito* and tomato sauce. We set up an assembly line and stuffed the husks with ground corn and roast pork. We used string to secure the husks, twisting and tying them to make sure none of the corn seeped out during cooking. I suppose we should have used strips of corn husk instead of kitchen twine, but I was happy there was no foil or dry cornmeal in sight, so I kept my mouth shut.

The stuffing went on late into the night. I fell asleep before it was over, so when I woke the next morning, I was blown away by the piles of perfect corn bundles stacked higher than my head on the dining room table. Oscar started playing records early on, then started a huge pot of water boiling. He refused to let my mother cook the *tamales*, so she came outside and helped me clean the driveway.

Our neighbor Mr. Gunter approached us from the house across the street. He was an older white man, probably in his fifties. I couldn't tell if he looked scared or suspicious, but he spoke anyway.

"Another party?" Maybe he was just amused. Yankees.

"Yes," I said. "Would you like to come?" Now he was scared but obviously curious.

"I would, actually. Can I bring my wife?"

My mother looked like a deer in headlights, but she was always ready to welcome a woman to the house. She nodded and tapped me on the shoulder.

"Sure," I said. "The party starts at three." He retreated to his house and gave a nervous wave over his shoulder.

At exactly three o'clock the doorbell rang.

"Who could that be?" my mother wondered. Three o'clock meant three-thirty at the earliest. Any Cuban would know that.

"We told them three," I said, and I went with Mother to answer the door.

Mom and Dad were nervous. It was the first time in two years that we had an American neighbor over. But Mother's face went from nervous, to surprised, to relieved when she opened the door to find Mr. Gunter standing there with his wife. Surprised because the wife was Korean, relieved because she didn't speak English much better than my mother herself.

The lunch was a little awkward, but we all got friendly very fast. It turned out Mr. Gunter was a retired soldier who had served in Korea, where he had met his wife. They were very much in love. He was the strong silent type, she a little more lively and sweet. By the time the carloads of Cubans arrived, the ice was more than broken. It's hard to get a word in edgewise when my family shows up. Thankfully that spared us any more awkward small talk. I just hoped they wouldn't scare our new friends off.

They weren't scared. In fact, they enjoyed themselves, so much so that we received an invitation the following week to dinner at their house. Mr. Gunter specified that the invitation was for Mom, Dad, Othin, and me. I figured it was some faux pas the rest of the family had committed that didn't get them invited. Maybe they didn't like Oscar's *tamales*? My dad assured me that to invite the whole house would have been too many people. Manuela agreed that must be the case. She was a little miffed, though. I could tell by the way she said, "No matter. I'm making oxtail for dinner tonight." As if that would be far better than anything we would get from the white man and his little Asian wife. Boy, was she wrong.

When we arrived for dinner, I was fascinated by the mixture of East and West that made up the decor of the house. Simple delicate floral arrangements sat alongside big squishy easy chairs. Delicately colored silk screens were hung next to shelves of shiny football trophies. I never found out why they didn't have children. I didn't have time to ask because for most of the night my mouth was full.

That was the first night I ever ate shrimp tempura, and I couldn't get enough. I was used to fried shrimp breaded in *galleta* crumbs, but my mouth was not prepared for the fluffy crispness of tempura batter. We polished off the whole platter Mrs. Gunter set before us. I think I took care of most of them.

The main course was barbecued steak. I'll admit I was a little bored by the idea. Everybody made steaks in this country—I was hoping we'd get something a little exotic. After all, we had fed them our very best homemade *tamales*. But as the platter of meat was set on the table, my mouth watered uncontrollably. There was a smell filling the room that I could not identify. My mother looked perplexed—I could tell she smelled the same thing. What was that smell? It was both bitter and fragrant, sour but earthy, like vinegar or red wine, but not quite.

The flavor intensified as we all tucked into our steaks. It was my father who asked the question that was on all our minds.

"What is this marinated in? It's delicious!"

"Soy sauce," said Mrs. Gunter with a mischievous smirk, "and secret spices." Mother made a mental note.

From then on Mother had a new secret ingredient at our Sunday socials. She started putting soy sauce in all her steak marinades. Sometimes she added garlic, sometimes hot peppers, and she especially liked it with orange juice and dry mustard. Everybody knew something was different, but Mother was such a magician that they knew better than to ask. I'm sure she would have given a little wink and said, "Secret spices," even if they had.

We were getting used to living in Los Angeles. Showbiz was an ever-present part of life. We had bought the maps to the stars' homes a few years earlier, stopping to see if anybody came out of Desi and

Lucy's place. My dad had even spotted Elizabeth Taylor walking to her car after a business lunch downtown. He declared her the most beautiful woman on earth and talked about the sighting for months after. "She did give me a look," he would say, as if it would be inconceivable any other way.

Some of my classmates at Porter Junior High had closer connections to the industry. One boy's mother had been the cute girl with curly hair who sang in *The Little Rascals*. According to her son, she was just on the verge of making a comeback, and when she did it would be huge.

Another friend of mine named Tim had played a role in a movie called *Camelot* that was due to come out the next year. I pounded him with questions about what it was like to make a movie. He seemed to think it was pretty easy, but only because he had such a good voice. He convinced me I should try out for the school choir so that I, too, would be ready if Hollywood came calling.

I auditioned for the music teacher, Mrs. Ruth Davidson, and was shocked when I got in. I thought my accent would prevent me from singing with the rest of the group, but it didn't make a difference. I loved Mrs. Davidson. I spent every lunch hour and time after school in the music room, singing with Tim and a few other kids and talking to Mrs. Davidson. She told me she had a daughter going to a school called Juilliard in New York City. A school where you got to sing all day? I wanted in. I immediately went to the library and started memorizing subway maps.

It was around the same time that I first read Shakespeare in English class. The first play I read was *The Tempest*. Reading the words was like doing linguistics exercises in my head. I didn't yet have the courage to read them aloud, but I was hooked.

I was glad for the friends I made in school, but I was still sure that if they met my crazy family they wouldn't want anything to do with me. I thought my parents and grandparents were loud and out of control and that nobody would accept me if they knew where I came from. I didn't bring any of my new friends home, so I spent most of my time with them in Mrs. Davidson's music room.

Fortunately the time was well spent. The music department was putting on its annual show where kids from the music class would perform songs in front of the whole school. Mrs. Davidson announced we would be singing selections from *Mame* and *West Side Story*. I was terrified at the thought of auditioning, but I figured if I could get into the choir, I might as well try out for a solo.

I got parts in two big songs: I was one of the Jets in "Cool" from *West Side Story* and I played the part of Older Patrick, the nephew in *Mame*. Tim was cast as the younger version of myself, he being smaller and blonder than I. Mame was played by a brassy young redhead.

On the day of the show I was full of jitters, but I felt safe knowing that Tim was out there onstage by my side. Our number, "The Letter," started with Tim singing and typing on a typewriter to the beat of the song. As he began to sing, all I could do was shake. What made me think I could do this? They were all going to laugh at me. The entire school thought I was weird enough as it was; why show off my embarrassing accent? Patrick did not have an accent.

As Tim's final phrase resounded, I crossed the stage and without thinking the notes just started pouring out of me.

I stood stock still for a moment, waiting for laughter to erupt, but there was none. Applause. Applause for me! I have heard people's stories about their first moment onstage. Good or bad, it is always unforgettable. Mine was almost therapeutic. I felt that my debut on the stage healed some part of the trauma from my past. It wasn't complete; I was still far away from home. I still had the ache of a child whose exile was starting to feel like the only thing he'd ever know. But in that instant, for the first time since arriving in the United States, I felt accepted. I felt I belonged. I would go on to need that feeling in greater and greater quantities, so that showbiz developed an ache of its own.

The number from *West Side Story* brought more applause, and for a few days kids at school would go out of their way to wave hello or pat my back. Even my math teacher made an announcement. "I know you all saw Mr. Machado in the show. Let's give him a round of applause. I want you all to know that Mr. Machado has something very rare. It's called charisma." More applause. I was thrilled, and a little ashamed to have so much attention. Was I betraying my home by feeling so happy here? Nevermind, I told myself, just enjoy it.

It was a good thing I did, because one day not long after, when Tim and I were walking home, an older boy followed us with his trashy-looking girlfriend. He started shouting after us, calling us sissies, and before I knew it his girl ran up to me and hit me over the head with her purse, which had a rock in it.

I pushed her away, dizzy and confused, which gave the boyfriend reason to get in my face.

"Want to fight it out with me sissy?" he growled. Bullies are so predictable.

I didn't answer, though. I just pushed him back, which was answer enough. A real life, honest-to-goodness fist fight ensued and a small crowd gathered around us. I was miserably defeated.

As the crowd dispersed, Tim helped me up. "Let's get you home," he said.

"I don't want to go home," I replied. Even though I was dizzy I knew I didn't want to bring him home.

"Let's go to my house then," he said. I hobbled along with him, hoping his mother would have a bag of frozen vegetables to help dull the throbbing in my head. We stopped in the driveway of Tim's house. "My house is a mess," he said, casting his eyes toward his feet.

"That's okay," I said.

But he was right. I had never seen a messier house. There were piles of newspapers and old magazines on every visible surface. In between were tucked empty beer bottles and crusty glasses. Tim's mother was sprawled out on the couch smoking a cigarette and clutching a half-empty bottle of Bud. Tim introduced me and she muttered something. He pulled me by the arm to his bedroom.

Eduardo Machado & Michael Domitrovich

In the safety of his room he opened a box of records and played a Dean Martin album. The walls were sparsely decorated with magazine cutouts and posters, but as the crooning sounds wrapped around us we were transported to a safer place.

"When *Camelot* comes out, I'm going to get away from all of this. I'm going to be a big star," he said wistfully.

"I know you will," I said, even though I had no idea.

How strange it was to know somebody who wanted to escape from the very place I wanted to feel like home. Did I really want to fit in here? Was L.A. where I wanted to belong or was it just the only option when Cuba was an impossibility?

As I walked home from Tim's I thought, maybe my parents aren't so bad after all. But I still never took an American friend home.

Things were changing all around us. My family was rising up in the world. We had more money, between Oscar's work as a mechanic and an even better job Manuela had found at a hat factory. My father's junior partner salary was stuffing the coffers with more money than he could have dreamed of when he was on the plane to Los Angeles with eleven dollars and fifty-two cents. We had new furniture and two cars, and though my mother still refused to speak English or get a license, she was happy to be living in a nice big house.

People in the community were starting to turn to my dad for financial advice. He did taxes for every Cuban we knew and all the respect was great for his ego. I think he felt almost as important as his own father. Maybe he didn't own his own company, but he was a prominent member of the community, and he had started with nothing.

Hugo had fallen in love with an American girl named Diane whose parents were Seventh-day Adventists and vegetarians. I'm not sure which shocked my parents more.

"You mean she doesn't eat pork?" my mother wondered. Definitely a bigger sin than straying from the one true faith. "What the hell do you cook for them?"

She found out soon enough, as Hugo started inviting Diane over regularly. The first time she came, my mom made her tomato and on-ion salad, as well as rice and beans with only a little bit of bacon, which she picked out of Diane's plate before serving it to her. The gesture was sweet, and Diane adored Mom for it.

After a few meals at our house, watching us eat plates full of steaming pork, grilled fish, or barbecued steaks, Diane had had enough. She announced that she was no longer a vegetarian, and that she was coming over for dinner as often as possible, to sneak as much meat as she could.

"But if my parents come over . . ."

"We'll have them over," said Mother.

"You mustn't tell them," said Diane.

"We'll keep your secret," said Mom. "Have some more pork."

With prosperity in the air to justify the expense, Manuela decided that it was time for Diane to try *Langostas Enchilados*, Lobster in Spicy Tomato Sauce. She would prepare the dish when Diane came over on Friday. She didn't want to break the bank by trying to feed lobster to the crowd at the Sunday social.

Now, where to get the lobster? They were frozen at the supermarkets, and the piers in Malibu and Santa Monica only seemed to have freshly caught fish. If we were to find lobster, in the quantity and quality Manuela desired, we'd have to go to the Grand Central Market.

So it was decided that my grandfather would leave work early on Friday so he and I could buy lobsters. Manuela also wanted hot peppers like we had in Cuba. This prompted an hour-long conversation among all the grownups about how the flavor of the peppers in Cuba is better, really, because the sun was stronger and the air cleaner in Havana. I did a double take when I noticed that it was not just Mother who neglected to say La Habana by slurring the two words together. They were all saying "Havana" like Yankees with accents. Though it was just a small change in name, it signaled a much larger shift in identity.

But, toe-may-toe or toe-mah-toe, we needed lobster. Oscar was waiting for me in front of Porter Junior High on Friday and I ran ahead of my classmates so no one would see him or his rundown Ford. This was the first time since our drives through the countryside that my grandfather and I had gone on a trip alone. I was old enough now, I suppose, for him to let out a truer version of himself. The whole way to the market he talked to me about beautiful women and sex. He kept saying, "You're getting to be the right age where you probably want a woman. No. You need a woman." I was terrified, and I hoped our trip wouldn't have any detours.

We got to the market without any stops along the way. First we found the hot peppers that my grandmother had requested, the fiery orange *habaneros*, but then we came face to face with the tank of live lobsters and got very confused. They were huge! Not small and delicate like the ones from the Caribbean Sea. These were murky shades of green and brown and their shells were ridiculously thick.

"How the hell do you clean that?" my grandfather asked.

"How'm I supposed to know?"

"Are you sure these are lobsters?" he asked. I read the sign.

"It says lobster," I said. "Look at their claws!"

"Ask him if they have real ones!" Oscar demanded. I got the fishmonger's attention.

"Do you have any smaller lobsters?" I asked.

"This is how big lobsters are here in the U.S.A." He was definitely patronizing.

"This is all they have," I told Oscar, defeated.

So we bought ten of them.

Even in those prosperous times it cost a lot of money, far more than any lobsters we had ever bought. In Cuba the Caribbean lobsters were an everyday food. All the meat comes from the tails, which are proportionally enormous. Most dishes, including the *enchilados,* require that you cut the tails into smaller chunks. The way the meat curls when you cook it, they end up looking and tasting like a sweeter, more delicate version of shrimp. I kept wondering what we were going to do with those claws. Little did I know the sweetness they contained.

We got back in the car right away and drove home as quickly as we could.

It was around six P.M. when we got back. Manuela was ready and waiting with a pot of sauce simmering on a back burner. She had sautéed chopped onions, garlic, and green pepper, added a few pinches of saffron and oregano, a drop of wine, and a little tomato sauce. She was ready for the lobster. "But we need more wine," she said. "I used the last of it in the sauce."

Oscar took the lobsters out. He dropped the bag of lobsters on the table and took off for the liquor store.

Manuela was horrified at the sight of the enormous lobsters.

"What are these?" she asked, wide eyed.

"The sign said lobsters," I said with a shrug.

"They're so big!" she exclaimed, but she was on a mission.

Even though she had never prepared Maine lobsters before, my grandmother instinctively knew what to do. She attacked the creatures with a giant knife, quickly decapitating them. She knew, too, to save the claw meat, cracking the largest part in half and sectioning the joints off into little meat-filled knuckles. She sectioned the tails into four or five pieces, then pushed the meat out and collected it in a bowl. Then she made the rice.

It was another hour before everyone was ready for dinner, but the rest was easy. Manuela just dropped the lobster pieces into the simmering tomato sauce and a minute later we were ready to eat the fragrant stew over the fluffy white rice.

"Oh, my. I had no idea," Diane kept repeating. My mother smiled at her. My father laughed.

"It's good not being a vegetarian," he said. "We Cubans know how to live, right, Diane?"

"You bet, Othon! Hugo's teaching me everything!" Diane replied.

"Everything?" My dad's voice turned seductive.

"Everything," Hugo barked back.

"What are they saying?" my grandmother asked me in Spanish.

"Nothing, Mama, just that this food is genius," my father quickly answered.

It *was* genius. The texture was completely different from Caribbean lobster. It was so powerfully sweet and succulent, it matched perfectly with the saffron and wine in the light tomato sauce. I especially loved sucking meat out of the claw joints. The claws themselves were like creatures from another planet, but I loved those, too. They were so plump, and I liked the slightly waxy texture of the pincer portion. It was both creamy and dense next to the juiciness of the palm.

Oscar started telling stories of how he used to set lobster traps in Cojimar. Hugo remembered going with him to help. Othin listened to the tales of his childhood. He even said he remembered setting the traps himself, even though he was far to young at the time. Jeanette and Didi had tiny cups of wine my mother would encourage them to sip from. "Or else you'll get a tummy ache," she warned.

It was an evening rich with food and family. If we had had some sweet plantains it would have been perfect. Although we hadn't arrived completely, that lobster feast was a mile marker on our road to belonging. We had made it this far; we could keep going for sure.

Another mile marker was Valentine's Day that year. In a house full of people, there's not much room for romance, but Mother decided she wanted Valentine's Day to be extra-special. So she cooked. The meal was familiar, grilled steaks and mashed yams (the orange ones), white rice and black beans. She had to feed the family, and we'd eat whatever she made. The surprise came when dinner was over.

"That was delicious," said my father.

"It's not over yet," said Mom. "It's Valentine's Day."

"I know that," said Dad. "I got you flowers."

He presented her with a bouquet of red carnations and kissed her strong on the mouth.

"Manuela," my grandfather said, "your present is waiting for you in our room." Manuela smacked him playfully.

My mother disappeared into the kitchen and returned a moment later with her present. It was a heart-shaped *flan* she had prepared with extra yolks to make it rich and bright yellow. She had frosted the *flan* with a pure white meringue, then used more meringue tinted pink with red food coloring to write "Gilda and Othon" in curlicue script.

We all looked at the cake in a reverent silence. A tear rolled down my father's cheek. He kissed her again.

"Let's have some *flan*," Mother said, preparing to slice into the heart.

"Wait, Mami," I begged. "Let us look at it for another minute. It's so beautiful."

She was overcome with pride. She waited to cut into it. As I stared deeply into the heart of fluffy white, I felt a pang that was familiar by now. It was loss, longing, but there was more in this feeling. Something had been missing all this time. As castaways, uprooted in America, we had been in survival mode for several years. Survival can make you tough, hard even, but the heart-shaped *flan* with mother's perfect pink penmanship seemed to recall a more innocent time. It brought back a moment from the past, when things were simpler, and it was so much easier to be delicate and sweet.

▌ *Cuban Enchiladas* ▌

This dish is true Cuban-American fusion, born out of necessity and longing and stubbornness. My mother made us these enchiladas to remind us of Cuba, but today it feels, like, totally Californian. With all the ingredients and labor-intensive steps, it may seem complicated to prepare, but it tastes like nothing else in the world. If you've got time beforehand, you can prepare and assemble everything, then refrigerate it until you're ready to bake. Just add five or ten minutes to the baking time to give the filling and cheese a chance to get nice and hot. Kids love it, adults love it, and if Terri was alive to say anything about the matter, I'm sure he'd bark his approval, too.

For the Cuban tomato sauce:
½ cup olive oil
1 Spanish onion, peeled and cut into ¼-inch dice
1 green pepper, stem and seeds removed, cut into ¼-inch dice
6 garlic cloves, peeled and finely chopped
One 14.5-ounce can diced tomatoes

Four 8-ounce cans Goya tomato sauce
¼ cup capers, drained
½ cup manzanilla olives,* coarsely chopped
½ cup raisins
½ teaspoon salt
½ teaspoon ground black pepper
1 tablespoon sugar
1 teaspoon dried oregano
¼ teaspoon ground cumin
1 cup water

For the filling:
1 teaspoon olive oil
1½ pounds ground sirloin
¼ cup manzanilla olives,* coarsely chopped
¼ cup raisins
1 teaspoon salt
½ teaspoon ground black pepper
¼ teaspoon cayenne pepper
½ teaspoon ground cumin
1 tablespoon distilled white vinegar

To finish:
12 corn tortillas
8 ounces shredded cheese (Jack, cheddar, or a combination)

*Manzanilla olives are small, green pitted olives stuffed with a tiny piece of sweet red pepper.

Prepare the Cuban tomato sauce:

1. In a 6-quart pot, heat the olive oil over medium-high heat until hot but not smoking. Add the onions and peppers and cook, stirring,

until softened slightly, 3 minutes. Add the garlic and cook, stirring, 1 minute more.

2. Add the remaining sauce ingredients and stir. Bring to a boil. Reduce the heat to low and simmer, covered, 30 minutes, until the flavors have blended.

Meanwhile, prepare the filling:

1. Heat the olive oil in a large skillet over high heat until it begins to smoke. Add the ground sirloin and brown, breaking the meat into smaller pieces, 5 minutes.

2. Add the remaining filling ingredients, along with 2 cups of the simmering Cuban tomato sauce. Cook until all the liquid has evaporated, 2 to 3 minutes more. Turn off the heat and set aside to cool.

To finish:

1. Preheat the oven to 375°F. Spread 1 cup Cuban tomato sauce over the bottom of a 9 × 13-inch baking dish. If your tortillas aren't fresh enough to roll without breaking, wrap them 6 at a time in a clean kitchen towel and microwave for 1 minute on High.

2. On a clean working surface, place ⅓ cup filling on a tortilla near the edge closest to you. Roll the tortilla tightly away from you, then transfer the bundle to the baking dish. If a little filling falls out, just stuff it in the open end of the tortilla. Repeat with the remaining tortillas, arranging them in a long row so they fit snugly in the pan. You'll need to put the last four bundles in perpendicular to the first row.

3. Pour the remaining Cuban tomato sauce over the enchiladas. Sprinkle the cheese evenly over the top. Bake in the upper third of the oven until the cheese is melted and bubbling around the edges, 20 minutes. Serve immediately.

Makes 6 servings

❘ Communal Croquetas ❘

Even though she would have done all the work gladly, my mother always made these with friends. The irony of the socialist-sounding name does not escape me. Do yourself the favor of inviting your compañeros over to help. The incentive? They get to bring a share of the goodies home, because there are plenty to go around. You could even double the recipe and have a really good time. Once you prepare the base, set up an assembly line where one person rolls the cylinders and the other does the dipping. If you've got an extra set of hands, put them in charge of frying or packing if you plan to divvy up the treats and freeze them for later.

4 cups milk
2 sticks salted butter
3 cups all-purpose flour
1 pound cooked ham, very finely chopped
2 teaspoons salt
½ teaspoon ground black pepper
⅛ teaspoon ground nutmeg
2 tablespoons distilled white vinegar
¼ cup finely chopped flat-leaf parsley
2 cups breadcrumbs*
3 large eggs
4 cups vegetable oil

*Store bought is fine, but make sure they are plain, not seasoned with Italian or other spices.

Prepare the base:

1. Heat the milk in a saucepan until it just starts to boil. Turn off the heat and set aside.

2. Melt the butter in a large skillet over medium heat, swirling the pan occasionally. When the butter is hot enough that it bubbles

then foams, add the flour and cook for 2 minutes, stirring constantly with a wooden spoon. At this point, the mixture should be crumbly.

3. Add the milk, 1 cup at a time, stirring constantly until you have a smooth, thick paste, 2 to 3 minutes total.

4. Remove the pan from the heat. Add the ham, salt, pepper, nutmeg, vinegar, and parsley. Return to the stove and cook, stirring constantly, 2 minutes more.

5. Turn off the heat and transfer the mixture to a baking dish or large plate. Set aside until cool enough to handle.

Prepare the croquetas:

1. Place the breadcrumbs into a pie plate or dish with raised edges. Crack the eggs into a separate pie plate or dish with raised edges and mix with a fork until well blended. Shape a heaping teaspoon of the *croqueta* base into a small cylinder by rolling it between your palms, then gently flattening the edges. The *croqueta* should be about 1½ inches long with a ¾ inch diameter.

2. Dip the cylinder in the beaten egg, then roll it in the breadcrumbs. Transfer to a parchment lined baking sheet. Repeat with the remaining base. Note: At this point the *croquetas* should be refrigerated until ready to fry, at least ½ hour or overnight. They can also be frozen in a single layer, then packed and sealed to keep indefinitely. If you freeze them, just defrost to room temperature, then proceed with the recipe.

Fry the croquetas:

Heat the vegetable oil in a 10- to 12-inch skillet with raised edges over medium-high heat until very hot (about 375°F). Fry the *cro-*

quetas, 6 at a time, turning with a slotted spoon until golden on all sides, 2 minutes total. Make sure the oil has time to heat up again after each batch, otherwise the *croquetas* will be greasy. As they're done, transfer the *croquetas* to a plate lined with paper towels to collect excess oil. Serve immediately, or keep warm in a low oven until ready. Serve on their own, with Cuban crackers and slices of Swiss cheese, or as a sandwich squished between two slices of Cuban toast with lettuce, tomato, and mustard.

Makes about 90 *croquetas*

▌ *Lobster Enchilados* ▐

Enchilado, the masculine form of *enchilada*, translates as "spicy" in terms of both flavor and heat. While the rich and flavorful Creole tomato sauce used here is delicious on its own, it is the fiery jalapeño pepper that makes this a true *enchilados*. When I ate this dish in Granada Hills, we used Maine lobster. It was scrumptious, and it was fun to eat the claw meat, but not quite practical for everyday fare. In Cuba we always used spiny, or Caribbean, lobster tails. They were inexpensive and their meat was sweet, but I find that the price and flavor of U.S. lobsters is not comparable unless you're in the southern part of the country. I recommend using slipper lobster tails, the smaller relatives of the spiny lobster, instead, usually available in your grocer's seafood or freezer section. While the preparation is still labor intensive, the work before makes the meal extra-special.

3 pounds frozen lobster tails, thawed
½ cup olive oil
½ Spanish onion, peeled and cut into ¼-inch dice
½ green pepper, stem and seeds removed, cut into ¼-inch dice

8 garlic cloves, peeled and finely chopped

1 jalapeño pepper, stem removed, cut into ¼-inch dice*

1 teaspoon salt

½ teaspoon ground black pepper

¼ teaspoon cumin

½ gram saffron (about 2 big pinches)

1 cup white wine

Two 8-ounce cans Goya tomato sauce

1 tablespoon ketchup

1 teaspoon fresh lime juice

¼ cup finely chopped flat-leaf parsley

*Don't forget to wash your hands after handling the pepper. If you want to reduce the spiciness of the jalapeño, remove the seeds and inner membrane (which contain all the heat), using only the green flesh. Also, you may omit the jalapeño entirely.

1. Using a sharp knife, cut each lobster tail into bite-size pieces: With the hard part of the shell facing the cutting board, remove the very tip of the tail and discard. Flip the shell so it's facing upward and cut into 2 or 3 sections by wedging the knife between the joints of the tail. Push the meat out of the shell using your finger or a chopstick. If you see any dark veins running down the center of the pieces, try to pull them out or give them a quick rinse. Reserve the meat in a separate container. Refrigerate until ready to use.

2. Heat the olive oil in a large pot or Dutch oven over medium-high heat. Add the onion and green pepper and cook, stirring, until softened slightly, 3 minutes. Add the garlic, jalapeño, salt, black pepper, cumin, and saffron. Cook, stirring, 1 minute more. Add the white wine and cook until the alcohol has evaporated, 3 minutes.

3. Add the tomato sauce and ketchup. Stir to combine and continue cooking to reduce slightly, 4 minutes.

Eduardo Machado & Michael Domitrovich

4. Add all the lobster to the pot at once. Cook, uncovered, stirring occasionally until just cooked through, 5 to 6 minutes.

5. Turn off the heat, add the lime juice, and stir. Transfer to a serving dish, garnish with parsley, and serve immediately with white rice.

Makes 6 servings

Seven

Lost and Found

Desi Arnaz helped me make it through adolescence. I didn't know him personally, his children didn't go to my school, but he helped me nonetheless. Barely thirteen, my dark looks and Cuban accent should have set me apart from all the showbiz kids, but all it took was one person to say, "Hey! You sound just like Desi Arnaz!" and I was in.

"Do Desi!" they'd say, and I'd respond suavely.

"Luuuuucy, I'm hoooooome!"

Mind you, my English had vastly improved. Singing all those show tunes was like linguistics training in itself. I had also started reading scripts I found in Mrs. Davidson's music room. I knew the songs from *Carousel* and *South Pacific*, but reading the books of the Rodgers and Hammerstein canon revealed deeper and more intricate uses of dramatic text as language coach. Beyond the practical uses of musicals I was digging deeper and deeper into all kinds of plays.

I hated novels. I hated all the reading we got in school, but I was obsessed with Shakespeare. After *The Tempest* I read all his plays in less than a year, one of the complete works (sonnets included) from cover to cover. After that I discovered Tennessee Williams, then Ibsen. I say discovered because there was some sequence of absorbing and processing the plays, but it might be more accurate to say that once I discovered Williams and Ibsen, I devoured their plays like a long line of *Media Noches*. They never stood a chance.

I liked that I could get from the beginning to the end of a play

Eduardo Machado & Michael Domitrovich

in one sitting. Most of all I liked disappearing into the world of the characters. People talk about getting lost in novels, feeling the world around you. Great theater can make you get lost in the world of the stage. But reading plays alone in your room is a different animal. It's voices you hear, but it's the people you get lost in.

As I read each new play out loud, I felt safe inside the characters. The dialogue saved me from my isolation and loneliness. I may have been having imaginary conversations, but it was like watching myself reflected back to me in a hundred different ways.

Maybe that's what happened when people's eyes lit up when I would "do Desi." I was just speaking in my own voice—I barely had to exaggerate—but I was someone else, someone none of us knew but we all understood. Even if it wasn't me, it was an identity that made me accessible, and that was enough to feel like I belonged. If only I had known how to play the bongos.

For my thirteenth birthday I convinced my dad to take me to the Dorothy Chandler Pavilion in downtown Los Angeles to see the musical *Mame*, the same show in which I had made my stage debut. I wasn't into reading glossies or trade mags and I definitely didn't follow the industry the way most folks in L.A. did, but I owned the soundtrack, memorized the liner notes, and was beside myself knowing that I was going to see Angela Lansbury and Bea Arthur live onstage.

What a night it was. The grand dames were unstoppable. Remember, this was the first time I had ever seen a real pro do their stuff onstage. I prayed that I could be like them. I even thought I had a chance. After all, my math teacher had told me I had that rare thing called charisma. Maybe he was right. I repeated to myself, "You do have pizzazz."

My grandfather Oscar refused to believe we had gone to see *Mame*.

"Who ever heard of taking a thirteen-year-old boy to see a musical?" he wondered aloud. He was sure we had gone to a whorehouse, my father reenacting the age-old Latin ritual of paying to pop his son's cherry.

Oscar kept winking at me and asking how the show was. He was very disappointed when I showed him the program and told him my favorite song. He preferred to believe I'd had sex with a whore.

My choir teacher, Mrs. Davidson, had noticed my talent. She convinced me to take all my required classes in junior high early so that in the last semester I could study voice at Juilliard. I wasn't sure how that was supposed to work out. I'm still amazed that it was even a possibility, but I didn't stop to think. I just dreamed of New York and pored over the subway maps in the library every day. My aunt Chichi was living in Jackson Heights, and I knew I'd be staying with her if I did make it to the big city. Jackson Heights wasn't that far away from Broadway. All I'd have to do was take the 7 train to Times Square.

It's funny that even though I lived minutes away from Hollywood, all my dreams were in New York. But then I was used to longing for something just out of reach.

That summer we all took a roadtrip to Miami. Well, not all. All, by now, was such a big word. It was the nuclear family, Mom, Dad, my brother, my two sisters, and me. We left at five o'clock on a Friday morning, buzzing with excitement over driving to the new promised land, Miami.

"It's different now," said Dad, "more Cubans." Like that was a good thing.

"It's still Miami," my mother said. "Last time I was there all I wanted to do was leave." I knew the feeling.

My father had decided to make the trip in five days and four nights, and nothing was going to stop him; not crying children, speed limits, or tourist sights. He was ready to drive us through the country, but it was going to be on his terms.

I finally got to see the desert I missed the last time Dad drove to Miami. Zooming through the barren land, I kept touching the window, amazed by the heat, the dryness, the relentless sun. The air-conditioning was on full blast, but the glass was still like a griddle.

I thought Los Angeles was supposed to be a desert. Palm Springs was more like what I imagined, but it paled in comparison to the parched plains of the Mojave. Dad made me his copilot, so I got to sit in the front seat, taking in the stretches of sand. When the vast dryness bored me I would read all the booklets given to us by Triple A. "So much country," I mused, imagining desert going on forever. Our pilgrimage had only just begun.

On the first day my father drove more than fifteen hours. At around eight P.M. we finally stopped when we crossed the border to New Mexico. We found a Holiday Inn, and the minute Dad shifted into park we all ran out of the car, jumping around with excitement and pent-up energy. We had stopped twice the entire day—once for the bathroom, once for gas. Mother had fed us sandwiches she had made the night before, tuna mixed with cream cheese on egg bread with the crusts cut off, of course, a Cuban delicacy in my tummy. To drink we had our choice of Coke or water that was wedged under my feet in the front seat. My mother was in the back with Didi, Jeanette, and Othin. Without the luxury of car seats, she spent most of the trip wrangling the little ones to sit still. When we finally got out of the car we were so happy to be let loose, we were like wild animals. Then my dad spotted a pool in the backyard of the Holiday Inn, and even though the sun was beginning to set, we all jumped in and swam past dark.

Every time I came up to breathe I was overwhelmed by the scent of unfiltered desert air. Without air-conditioning and rolled up windows there was nothing to get in the way of the smell. It was like dry leaves smoldering but still so pure and clean. "Breathe in," I told myself, "all of this is new."

We decided to have dinner in a diner across the street from the Holiday Inn. I ordered a cheeseburger, well done. I'm not sure if it's a thing with all Cubans, but my family cannot stand the sight of blood on anything. We do not care what the ideal texture or temperature is for a certain cut. Filet mignon, well done, roast beef, well done, lamb chops, well done, thank you very much.

The burger came with a choice of fries or onion rings. I had eaten french fries, *papas fritas*, in Cuba, but onion rings sounded exciting and new. I got a Coca-Cola to wash it all down.

We all drank as we waited for the meal. Dad was immersed in the road maps until he finally announced, "We have to get to Texas tomorrow." He sounded tense.

"Yes, sir!" I answered with a military salute. I was his copilot after all.

The waitress arrived with our dinners. The moment she set my burger down in front of me, my jaw dropped. I was transfixed.

"Well, for you, right?" she announced.

I nodded my head yes but continued to silently take in the all-American feast before me. What a burger.

It was almost two inches thick, cooked well done but still juicy on the inside. There was a sweet red tomato and thinly sliced raw onions on the bun, but I couldn't take my eyes off the cheddar cheese. It certainly was a slab, directly on top of the burger, the rectangle shape of the block it had been cut from still visible. But it had given in to its fate, oozing over the little bumps of meat, blanketing the burger in greasy goodness. I licked my chin after my first bite, trying to slurp up all the juices. Then I moved on to the onion rings.

They were bathed in hot oil, the crispy batter of flour and eggs blanketing the slippery onion in its protective coating. I wasn't prepared for the burst of steam that burnt the roof of my mouth, or the way the onion slid out of its golden shell so that all I was left with was a crunchy hook. The crunchy hook was even better than the onion ring. I was fascinated.

"Hey, honey, why don't you try dipping 'em in ketchup?" the waitress said in passing. I was a little offended that she interrupted my moment, but I took her advice.

The ketchup was ideal as a topping to the crunchy hook. It was not quite right on the first bite when the onion was still a ring—it needed the end point to dip. But I took bite after bite, sweet and salty, hot and cold, soft and crunchy. It was an adventure that made me love America with all my heart, or at least my stomach. What new flavors lay ahead on the open road?

On the way back to the Holiday Inn we stopped at a convenience store and filled the cooler with ice and Coca-Cola. Mother bought some sliced ham and cheese and a loaf of bread for sandwiches the next day.

We fell right asleep when we reached the Holiday Inn. We had a six A.M. departure scheduled, and Dad wasn't going to let a little extra sleep come between us and Miami. I noticed everything we'd miss on the Triple A maps and I begged him to make at least one stop, but he refused. No Grand Canyon, no Monument Valley, no Rocky Mountains for us.

"What do you need all those places for?" he said. "We're going to Miami, and there you can go to the beach."

Why cross the whole country just so we could feel like we were in Cuba? Florida was not and would never be Cuba. Did they need to feel at home that badly? Looking out the window at the desert, I remember thinking, "Where is home? Why not here? I could feel at home in the Southwest. Just as much as I could in Florida." But Dad was a man with a plan, so I kept my thoughts to myself.

We crossed New Mexico in a flash. Cacti and small towns whizzed by. We only saw the gas stations. Making sandwiches in the car as it went sixty miles an hour was not easy for Mother, but Dad wouldn't slow down. He had to get to Texas by nightfall.

And he did. We stopped just outside El Paso at another Holiday Inn. As we looked out the car window, we could all see that the town was poor, dirt poor. There were Mexicans all around us, walking down the streets, waiting for buses, in old cars, on bicycles. Some were pumping gas, some selling fruit. I knew if there were this many Mexicans in town, there had to be a taco stand somewhere nearby.

"Let's have Mexican food tonight!" I yelled.

But my father was afraid to drive too far from the security of the Holiday Inn. This time the restaurant across the street was a barbecue shack. There was no other choice.

"But we have barbecue every weekend!" I whined.

"Don't start complaining," my mother warned me.

Once again, I had a totally eye-opening experience.

American barbecued chicken was like *Pollo Frito*'s slutty cousin. Its rich tomato sauce, deep brown and sugary, was tinged with the deeply satisfying smell of hickory. The charred taste, chewy skin, and juicy flesh converted me to a Southern boy proud of his culinary heritage, if only for one night. We stocked up with ice and more Cokes that Dad bought from a vending machine, then it was off to dreamland.

By five-thirty the next day we were on the road again. About a hundred miles past El Paso, Texas began to live up to its reputation. The roads were huge, not just two or three lanes but five lanes and completely flat. There were no curbs along the side—you could go a hundred miles an hour if you felt like it. The cars that drove past us were stunning, souped-up trucks and convertibles with shiny paint in every sparkling color of the rainbow. They all seemed to have music blaring from the radio, country or rock and roll. Some of the truck drivers even wore cowboy hats. "But where are the Indians?" I wondered. Off the main road like everything else. A green Lincoln Continental sped past us.

"This is America!" Dad said proudly.

"Where are the towns?" my mother asked.

"Away from the highway," my father snapped back.

There really wasn't one town in sight, only exits leading to roads that probably led to towns. My father smiled as he burned road beneath him, doing nearly eighty.

"The only town we want is Miami!" Othin shouted out of nowhere.

My mother laughed, and Dad beamed proudly. Didi and Jeanette giggled, too, but I just buried my head in the map. I was busy dissecting my brother's statement.

Little brothers are always annoying. I know that, but I heard something in his voice. The way he said Miami sounded just like the way he used to say Cuba. It was full of passion, maybe too much for a little boy ... but it wouldn't have been if he were saying Cuba. But this wasn't Cuba, this was Miami. It made me hate the thought of our final destination even more.

We made it to the outskirts of Dallas around seven o'clock that night. Unlike El Paso, it was a clean, wealthy looking town, not unlike Granada Hills. We stopped at a local hotel that had vacancies, but Dad returned from the office moments after entering to inquire about a room.

"Funny," he said, "the sign said they had rooms."

"Maybe they thought you were a Mexican," my mother said.

"What difference would that make?" my father asked, maybe already knowing the answer.

"They're prejudiced against Mexicans in Texas," she announced.

"Why?" Othin and Jeanette wanted to know.

Didi repeated, "Why?"

"Because they stole Texas from the Mexicans," my mother whispered to us.

"Why?" This time I asked the question.

"Because Americans want everything." Her voice sounded hurt when she said that.

Then we drove in silence. The air was tense. Finally my father snapped.

"I don't look Mexican!" he yelled.

"You're tan," my mother said sweetly.

"So?" my father demanded.

"You look Mexican to them."

My father did not have an answer for her. He looked at himself in the rearview mirror, and the silence came again. For the next ten miles no one spoke.

As we drove past Dallas, I could see the lights of the city from the highway. We drove till nine o'clock, then stopped at a roadside motel. We ate burritos and tacos from a shack next door. The stand was owned by Mexicans who spoke Spanish to us and gave us a free Coca-Cola.

The motel was not anywhere nearly as nice as a Holiday Inn. There was no pool. My father triple-locked the door, even placing a chair against it.

The next morning he said, "Let's just get the hell out of Texas."

"Really?" my mother said in a very sarcastic tone.

"You were right. Even the Mexicans think we are Mexicans."

"Wetbacks!" Mother exclaimed. She was angry.

"Texas might be clean and big and flashy, but if they don't want us, the best thing is to move on," my father declared.

We all cheered as we motored out of Texas the next day. We crossed the state line to Louisiana around noon. If we had known the full implications of that simple border, we probably would have zoomed right on through. We hated Texas so much that we figured anything would be better. But this was the Deep South, a lot more fun, and a lot more dangerous.

After three days with the hot desert sun hitting the windshield, Dad's arms and face were tanned a deep brown. With his thick snarl of unwashed kinky hair, he almost looked like a mulatto. My mother was bleached blonde at the time, and still very white. She had put a cloth up on the side of her window to keep her and Didi and Jeanette from getting too much sun. It was 1966, and suddenly I was entering Louisiana as the progeny of what looked to be an interracial marriage.

Me, Didi, Dad, Jeanette, Mom, and Michelle
on one of our road trips

We stopped that evening somewhere around Alexandria, and of course the first hotel had no room for us. They directed us to a hotel just outside of town. It was a motel made up of a long line of about thirty cabins, small but welcoming wooden structures painted brick red. Inside were two tiny bedrooms and a kitchen. There was no air-conditioning, just ceiling fans, but each cabin had a small porch out front where families could gather.

In the middle of the motel was a big square swimming pool. We changed into suits and went for a swim right away. Everyone else in the motel had finished their day of swimming and was sitting out on their porches. Some kids played ball on the dirt road in front of the cabins. Others were loading into cars all dressed up for dinner. Standing on the edge of the pool I noticed, all at once, that all the families were black.

My head was flooded by a rush of recollection as I remembered the gas station we stopped at right after crossing the Louisiana border. The bathroom signs said WHITES ONLY and there was a long line of black customers waiting to use a ramshackle outhouse way in back. My father had gotten on that long line. I just looked away, unable to believe what I was seeing.

As we swam, my father kept saying, "This is beautiful, it reminds me of Cuba." But there was a glimmer of fear in his eyes, and I knew he was lying.

All the families said hello to us and welcomed us. In one of the cabins jazz music was playing. We swam until dark with the heavy humidity wrapped around us.

As we finished dressing for dinner, my father took Othin, Jeanette, and Didi into the car. I watched my mother put on the final touches of lipstick.

"Isn't it beautiful?" my mother whispered to me.

"What?" I asked.

"To be so near home, a hundred miles away is the Gulf of Mexico, and across the Gulf is Cuba, and in Cuba there is La Habana, and next to La Habana there is Cojimar, and in Cojimar is our house." She started to cry. She said "La Habana." She was going home in her head.

My father was honking the horn, and we hurried into the car. When Mother stepped in, she looked at my dad and smiled. He purred at her and in Spanish said the word *sexy*. She was at her most beautiful that summer, wrapped in the heat of Louisiana, so close to home.

We had dinner a few miles down the road at a tiny restaurant in a house surrounded by a parking lot. There was nothing else for miles around. When we walked in, I noticed that all the customers were white. Where were our friends from the pool eating, I wondered? As we sat, the place got quiet and they stared at us when we spoke Spanish to one another. The waitress, a plump blonde in her late twenties, nervously took our order.

I ordered fried chicken. Honest to goodness crackly southern fried chicken with a thick crust of spicy breading (which I was starting to get used to). As I bit into the juicy, well-seasoned meat, I noticed that the customers were complaining to the waitress, who kept nodding her head and saying things like "No, they're not mixed, they're Spanish," and "What am I supposed to do about it?" Then she'd flash a fake smile.

My father and mother kept looking around as they ate their dinner, fried catfish for my dad and pot roast for my mother. Othin had also ordered fried chicken, and Jeanette and Didi were sharing a hamburger and fries.

"Why are they looking at us, Mami?" Othin asked loudly enough so everyone heard him.

"Quiet!" my father shushed him.

As we were finishing our meal, the waitress came up to us and smiled without showing her teeth. "If you want dessert, why don't you take it to go?" she said politely.

My father was angry now. He snapped, "Why?"

She quietly replied, "It's just a good idea, sir."

For a moment my father felt sorry for her and thanked her. He ordered two pieces of pecan pie and two pieces of peach to go.

As my father was paying the bill, the waitress asked sweetly, "Where exactly are you from?"

"Cuba." My dad was now beside himself, a jumble of fear, anger, and resentment.

"I see," she muttered dismissively.

My dad walked back to the table. It was clear that we were not welcome here, that we were not good enough to sit in this shitty little restaurant in some backward town in the middle of Louisiana. My mother took my dad's hand and told him in Spanish, "Leave a very big tip. So they know that this was beneath us."

She gave me a long look.

Without arguing, Dad left twenty dollars on the table. The waitress handed us the pies without looking at the money. As we were leaving, we could hear her say, "They're Cubans."

"That's the same thing as being a Negro," said someone else.

That night we felt much safer in the security of our own little porch in the long row of cabins. It's easy to forget injustice as you feast on the glorious flavors of homemade peach and pecan pie. Maybe that's why pies are so popular in the South. They're good when your soul hurts.

Dad wasn't one to stay calm for long, though, and as the gooey coating around the pecans dissolved into salty snaps, he proclaimed, "No matter how long it takes, tomorrow we are driving all the way to Miami!"

I nodded in agreement but didn't say anything. I took a bite of peach pie. The peaches were sweet themselves, the thick syrup surrounding them elevating all their floral flavors. I knew, even then, that these pies were special because the crust was made extra-rich and flaky with gobs of lard. The bigots knew better than to use vegetable shortening. How could people who make such delicious desserts be so mean and stupid?

We drove out of Louisiana before dawn. None of us slept well that night. We reached Florida by noon, stopping for gas soon after we crossed the state line. A few hours later we had lunch at a Howard Johnson's.

I feel the need to take a moment to pay homage to Howard Johnson's fried clams with tartar sauce. The texture of the clams, at once chewy and tender, encased lovingly in crispy batter, so perfectly golden, never overdone. The little cup of tartar sauce, sweet and creamy, matching perfectly with the even sweeter coleslaw. Any fried food is fine by me, but few dishes in memory hold a candle to this Howard Johnson's masterpiece.

We then drove for what seemed like an eternity. The panhandle of Florida is still the Deep South, and we thought it best to get it over with as quickly as possible. We subsisted on juice, Cokes, and donuts purchased as we passed through another couple of gas stations.

We reached my aunt Maria's house, honking the horn to announce our arrival just after ten-thirty. I have never been as happy to see Hialeah as I was on that night.

By 1966 Miami had become a Cuban city. Spanish was spoken everywhere and Cubans had begun to replace the snowbirds from the north. Miami Beach was still a very sexy kind of Israel, but the city of Miami belonged to us.

The first day we all wanted to go to the beach, so after my dad spent the morning with his parents, off we went. My aunt Maria followed in her new car with my cousins. We found parking and then spotted a Cuban lunch counter.

The Cuban lunch counter is an archetype of Florida dining. There is no focus on decor, usually just wood-paneled walls and bad overhead lighting. The room need only be clean, and sometimes not even that. What's most important is that there are enough stools at the counter (or enough space behind the stools) to fit all the hungry customers.

In every stand you will find two things, guaranteed. First, a grill press: two heavy heated metal plates, wrapped in aluminum foil with a large handle on the upper portion. This contraption is used to weight and heat sandwiches, pressing the air out of fluffy Cuban bread until it gets crispy on the outside and spongy in the middle, warming whatever's inside. Second is the coffee machine: usually a shiny metal contraption, all polished chrome and copper pipes. If you see both of these implements, chances are you're going to get something good, or at least something authentic.

We lined up at the counter, Mom, Dad, Othin, Maria, and me, all ordering double shots of espresso. The coffee dribbled out in a viscous stream as steam hummed out of a little pipe in the back. It was so thick and black, nearly red, just as it should be. We drank the brew out of little paper cups with lots of sugar added and just a drop of milk.

As we sipped, the man behind the counter brought toast without our even having to ask. The toast had never seen a toaster coil; it had simply been squeezed in the sandwich press until the edges were crispy and the bread slightly deflated. I smeared butter on mine and dipped it in the coffee. The pools of oil collected on the surface and I got lost for a moment in their shine.

In that space where time stopped I thought that maybe I understood my brother when he said, "We only want Miami." Maybe Othin was right. Maybe this was the new Cuba.

I came back to earth as I heard my father order a dozen *pasteles*, half meat and half *guayaba*. As the man who made our coffee filled a box with flaky pastries, I forgot all about the beach. I could have spent the whole day at that counter enjoying its simple Cuban pleasures, but I realized all the kids were gone and I soon remembered how much I wanted to swim in the salt water. I took off toward the ocean, my dad following with our box lunch behind me.

We were definitely the only family of Cubans on South Beach that day. Everybody else was pasty white and over fifty. They wore the standard South Beach uniform of the time, Bermudas with black socks for the men, printed house dresses for the women. We got funny looks from all as we sat in the sand munching our lunch of meat and guava pastries. They never would have entered the lunch counter, much less eaten something from it.

After lunch I was thirsty, but I didn't want Coca-Cola. I had a craving for a long-lost flavor. My tongue scraped the roof of my mouth as I searched for the taste. Then it hit me. *Guarapo*. Sugar cane juice like they served on the beach in Varadero. I remembered my trips with Grandpa Oscar and thought if I could only find a *guarapo* stand I would never need to drink a Coke again.

It became an obsession with me on that trip to Miami. I asked at every stand and counter, any place that even had a Cuban standing near it. But in Miami there was not a single piece of sugar cane to be found, much less one of those arcane juicers with the winch and press so common in Cuba. Some things really do get lost in translation.

The flavors I encountered on the rest of that trip were disappointing to say the least. We ate only Cuban food, and that should have been enough, but, of course, it wasn't.

This was before Café Versailles opened in 1971, when it became the standard of Cuban cafes in Miami. The restaurant would later serve traditional Cuban fare with faux-French pretensions, quickly making it a favorite among the city's exile community. At that time there was nothing quite so polished, but still there were plenty of Cuban diners and the ubiquitous lunch counters.

The food did remind me of Cuba, but it didn't feel authentic. How can I explain? It was crude. It lacked subtlety. I ate *Ropa Vieja* in one diner. The meat was tender and stringy, just as it should be, but the tomato sauce it was bathed in gave me pains at the base of my jaw. It made me pucker my lips. Cuban tomato sauce is the most basic base we have to cook with. It's a blend of sweet, salty, sour, spicy, and bitter flavors. Every component has a voice—tomato, garlic, onions, peppers, capers, olives, and raisins—separate if you look for them, but unified and balanced.

The *Ropa Vieja* was insulting in its obviousness. Worse still, whenever I finished a meal in a café in Miami, I got a headache. Sometimes I got nauseous, too. Othin and I would drink gallons of water to wash down the salty pain the food caused us. It would take years to figure out the source of all this unpleasantness. *Accent. Sazón.* Seasoning blends containing or made entirely of MSG, before any of us knew how awful it could make you feel if you were particularly sensitive. And as you must know by now, we were, and are, a very sensitive family.

The only sure thing were the Cuban *pastelitos*, always flaky, and stuffed with a blessedly underseasoned *picadillo*, or a guava jelly waiting to burst out from inside.

As the trip drew to a close, Grandpa Fernando had a surprise for us. He was cooking a big dinner for the family that Saturday. He was going to make *Arroz con Pollo* with what he claimed was a new secret recipe.

"It will taste just like Cuba," he said.

It was a big promise, but one we didn't think to question. How do you make a meal taste like a place? I should have asked him directly. Instead, I spent the rest of my life looking for the answer.

No one was allowed in the kitchen while he cooked. He kept all his ingredients hidden in brown paper bags in case anyone tried to sneak a peek. The great divide of dining between husband and wife was still in effect, my grandmother Cuca saying, "Whatever he's putting in it will make you all sick." We played baseball, which I was very bad at, while waiting for Fernando's *Arroz con Pollo*.

When he finished adding the last of the ingredients, covering the pot until the rice was finished cooking, he allowed my mother into the kitchen to fry plantains. He had already made an avocado salad with sweet onions and a vinaigrette dressing.

As my mother fried the plantains, my aunt Maria and I set the table. Cuca and Fernando got into a fight over what to set the table with. She wanted paper plates; he insisted on proper dishes and cutlery. The fact that Fernando had cooked trumped his wife's passive aggression. Cuca remained in some sort of control, though, when she refused to eat the meal he had prepared.

Fernando took a pan and hit a spoon against it, announcing that the food was ready. We all piled into the kitchen to serve ourselves. The air was heavy with fragrance. Beer, saffron, and asparagus were all detectable, but it was the full-bodied scent of simmering chicken in broth that overpowered them all. The red and green confetti of *pimientos* and *petit pois* added accents of color to the large pot of still-steaming yellow rice.

It was different from the stuff he served in Cuba, but there still was just the right ratio of liquid to rice, with thick bubbles of yellow popping up between the chicken parts. The broth was powerfully flavored, maybe more so than when he used to make it, and it had a new creaminess that I wasn't used to. I wasn't sure how much I liked it, though everybody else seemed to, especially mother, who badgered him to try to get the secret ingredient.

Fernando refused to budge, only explaining that "It makes the flavorless chicken they have in the United States taste like real chicken," meaning Cuban chicken.

We played music after dinner, like the old days when we ate in

Fernando's dining room. Benny Moré, the crooner who sounds just a little bit like a trumpet. We had no Spanish wine, just beer. There were no maids serving us; instead, we served ourselves. But the feeling of family was familiar.

Cuca never even sat at the table, which made it feel even more like home. While we ate, she disappeared into the kitchen to make her famous brown meringues to surprise us for dessert.

"Here," she said to me. "These will help settle your stomach."

And she was right. I had a stomachache, even a mild headache. What was the secret addition? It turns out it was more elusive than *Accent* or *sazón*, an ingredient whose identity it would take me even longer to discover.

The day we were leaving we bought bags full of pastries to share with the family in L.A. Needless to say, they were long gone before we reached California. There was a shared moment in the car, just as we were passing by Palm Springs, when the whole family yearned for more *pastelitos* so strongly that it felt like maybe we should have stayed in Miami.

What we didn't know, and what would have erased that longing immediately, was that Grandpa Oscar had a surprise waiting for us when we got home to Granada Hills.

My grandmother greeted us at the door with a silver serving tray full of pale circles with vibrant orange rectangles on top of creamy white smears. My mother stopped short as she saw the treats.

"What's this?" my mother asked.

"Guayaba," said Manuela.

"Galletas?" said Mother. She took a bite of a Cuban cracker topped with cream cheese and guava paste. The rest of us stood outside but pushed through when we heard Oscar calling us.

"Come into the kitchen!" my grandfather shouted mischievously.

To our amazement, the counters were overflowing with plantains, *malangas*, *boniatos*, and *yuca*. The freezer was full of *tamales* in corn husks. The cupboards had *galletas* and a dark roast coffee called Bustelo.

Mother opened the refrigerator. It was like Christmas. Brisket cut perfectly for *boliche*. Hunks of pork shoulder for *lechón*. Round nubs of *rabo*, oxtails (really cowtails), Manuela's favorite. Mother clutched her throat. On the bottom of the fridge, piled high in parchment paper, she saw the thinly sliced steaks and almost fell over.

"Are these *palomilla?*" she asked.

"Top sirloin," said Oscar.

"How?" asked my father.

"Did someone mail them to us?" I asked.

"There is a Cuban store now in Glendale. They have everything. And right next door there is a bakery. I heard about them at the garage," he explained.

A Cuban bakery, with sandwiches and meat pies, I kept repeating to myself! *Pastelitos! Croquetas!*

"*Galletas*," Mother sighed with relief. "Tonight I am making *Bistec Empanizado*." She never had to face the butcher with fear again. Her father had taken care of it for her.

There was no pounding necessary. The butcher at the store had taken care of that. She marinated the steaks quickly to tenderize them a little more, then filled a bag with *galletas* and crushed them with a rolling pin until they were a powdery meal. She seasoned the cracker crumbs, whisked a couple eggs, and voilà! She was ready to go.

Crumbs. Egg. Crumbs. And into the pan.

This was easy.

As I watched her cook, I understood just how hard it must have been to make *Bistec Empanizado* when we first arrived. Even though her previous failure had prevented her from attempting the dish for years after, she now moved through the kitchen with a newfound confidence. She knew where she was. She knew what she was doing. Her hands were busy, full. She didn't falter. It was balletic. I hadn't seen her move that way in a long time. The ingredients were everything; without them she was lost.

The steaks were tender on the inside and crispy on the outside. We ate them with white rice and fried plantains. Plantains! And, for once, I didn't have a single issue with the meal. This tasted just like home.

❚ *Southern Pecan Pie* ❚

Some people like their pecan pie on the lighter side, but this Deep South version is full of bittersweet molasses flavor and color. I guess even pie can get caught up in an age-old conflict. Don't worry, though—for all the tension that surrounded us when I first tried pecan pie like this, it was still sweet and sexy, just like the South. And no matter how you cut it, you're still going to get a serious sugar high.

1 cup firmly packed dark brown sugar
1 cup dark corn syrup
1 teaspoon salt
8 tablespoons (1 stick) salted butter, chilled and cut into small pieces
1 teaspoon vanilla extract
2 tablespoons bourbon
3 large eggs
2 cups coarsely chopped pecans
One 9-inch deep dish pie crust (store-bought is okay), unbaked

1. Preheat the oven to 300°F. Combine the brown sugar, dark corn syrup, and salt in a saucepan. Cook over medium-high heat, stirring occasionally, until the mixture boils gently and the brown sugar and salt dissolve, 5 minutes.

2. Turn off the heat and add the butter, vanilla, and bourbon. Stir carefully until the butter melts.

3. In a separate bowl, whisk the eggs until frothy. Add the sugar mixture to the eggs a little at a time, whisking after each addition. Stir in the pecans. Pour the mixture into the unbaked pie shell.

4. Bake the pie on a foil-lined baking sheet in the center of the oven, 1 hour, until the center is set. Transfer to a rack and cool to room temperature. Refrigerate until chilled completely. Slice and serve with a dollop of whipped cream.

Makes 8 servings

Eduardo Machado & Michael Domitrovich

⟦ Galletas with Guava and Cream Cheese ⟧

This is a yummy little snack that uses intensely traditional Cuban flavors. Sweet, sour, and satisfying on their own, the cream cheese and guava paste become an elegant hors d'oeuvre when served atop savory Cuban *galletas*. I like to use the guava paste that comes in a long block wrapped in cellophane rather than the kind that comes in a tin. The rectangular shape makes it much easier to portion out into pretty little cubes. Many Cuban children like to eat this as an after-school snack. Even after all these years, it is still a treat I love coming home to.

8 ounces cream cheese, chilled
8 ounces guava paste (half of a 16-ounce block)
32 small *galletas**

*Saltines or water crackers can be substituted if you can't find small Cuban *galletas*.

1. Slice the cream cheese in half lengthwise, then again crosswise so you have 4 rectangles. Slice each rectangle into 8 pieces so you have 32 little pieces of cream cheese in all.

2. Slice the guava paste in half lengthwise, then again crosswise so you have 4 rectangles. Slice each rectangle into 8 pieces so you have 32 little pieces of guava paste.

3. Place one piece of cream cheese on each *galleta*, then top with a piece of guava paste. Transfer the *galletas* to a platter lined with a decorative doily and serve.

Makes 32 individual servings

❙ Bistec Empanizado ❙

It took my mother years to find *palomilla* steaks, but today they're available in the butcher section of larger grocery stores, especially in cities with Hispanic communities. Three pieces of *palomilla* steak should weigh between 1 and 1½ pounds. If you can't find thinly sliced steak, just buy a top sirloin London broil, cut it in half lengthwise, then cut each half crosswise into three equal pieces. You will have to pound the meat a little more, but don't worry, you'll get there.

1 to 1½ pounds *palomilla* steak (thinly sliced top sirloin), about 3 big
    pieces
2 garlic cloves, peeled and finely chopped
2 tablespoons lime juice
1 tablespoon salt
1½ teaspoons ground black pepper
1½ cups finely ground *galleta* (Cuban cracker) crumbs*
3 large eggs
½ cup vegetable oil
1 lime, cut into 6 wedges, for garnish

*If you can't find *galleta* crumbs, you can substitute regular cracker crumbs, or you can make your own: For 1½ cups *galleta* crumbs, pulse 15 or so large *galletas* (more if using small galletas) in the bowl of a food processor until they make a fine meal. If you don't have a food processor, just put the *galletas* in a big zip-top bag and squeeze all the air out before you seal it. Crush the *galletas* using a rolling pin, breaking up any big pieces and rolling over the smaller ones until they make a fine meal.

1. Cut the steak so that you have 6 equal pieces. If necessary, pound
    each steak between 2 pieces of plastic wrap using a meat tenderizer,

until they are between ¼ and ⅛ inch thick. Transfer to a bowl big enough to hold all 6 steaks.

2. Combine the garlic, lime juice, 1 teaspoon of the salt, and ½ teaspoon of the black pepper. Pour the marinade over the steaks and toss so they are coated evenly. Cover with plastic wrap and marinate in the refrigerator, 1 hour.

3. Place the *galleta* crumbs in a pie plate or dish with raised edges and season with 1 teaspoon of the remaining salt and ½ teaspoon of the remaining black pepper. Mix with a fork. Crack the eggs into a separate pie plate or dish with raised edges and season with the remaining 1 teaspoon salt and ½ teaspoon black pepper. Mix with a fork until well blended. Remove a steak from the marinade and dip both sides in the *galleta* crumbs, shaking off any excess. Dip both sides of the steak in egg, then again in *galletas*. Transfer to a plate until ready to fry. Repeat with the remaining steaks.

4. Heat ¼ cup of the vegetable oil in a 12-inch skillet with raised edges over medium-high heat until shimmering and very hot. Fry 3 of the steaks in the hot oil until golden brown, 2 minutes per side. Transfer to a paper towel–lined plate when cooked. Add the remaining ¼ cup vegetable oil to the pan and let it return to frying temperature. Fry the remaining 3 steaks and transfer to a paper towel–lined plate when cooked. Garnish each steak with a lime wedge and serve immediately with rice, beans, and fried plantains.

Makes 6 servings

Eight

The Shy Stud

I was now fifteen, and in my last semester at Porter Junior High. I had taken all my required classes and was set to spend the end of the school year singing at Juilliard. Cuba got in the way once more, and history interfered. Or maybe history just happened and it was, as always, my father who interfered. There were more planes hijacked and taken to Cuba in 1969 than any year before or since. That was enough for my dad to veto any air travel I wanted to do that summer. I think it gave him extra satisfaction that he was preventing me from attending Juilliard.

So instead I sat at home reading Shakespeare. The more I would speak the speech out loud, the more worried my mother and grandmother looked. Then about a month after Juilliard's final registration date, for no observable reason my father announced that it was safe to go to New York.

It turned out that waiting for me in New York was the next nightmare of my childhood. Rather than supporting my singing, my parents and grandparents had once again decided that something was fundamentally wrong with me. My father made it clear that in his book, singing was something only "fags" did. He believed the only possible explanation for my desire to be in show business was that I had mental issues. My grandmother Manuela suggested I become a television repairman, as if it would somehow satisfy my growing creative needs.

Their proposed solution: send me to the same psychiatrist I had in

Cuba, who was now practicing in Elmhurst, New York, a few minutes away from Jackson Heights, where my aunt Chichi lived. That would get the singing fag right out of me.

After the first session, the shrink told my aunt that I should get a job.

"There is nothing wrong here that a few months of hard work can't cure." He was smug in that macho Cuban manner I had grown to despise. Then he wrote out a prescription for massive dosages of tranquilizers. Valium, three times a day.

My aunt's fervor was ignited, and she went on an all-out mission to save me from the decadence of showbiz. She and her husband came up with a plan. Somehow they changed the date on my birth certificate to make me sixteen, old enough to get me a social security card. And so I was eligible to work.

What followed was a series of jobs, first at a cleaners where the owner and I shared a love for Barbra Streisand. She fired me because I was notoriously bad at keeping orders organized. I worked as a cashier at a grocery store, bagging haphazardly and always giving people the wrong change. I moved on quickly to a job as a stockboy at a hardware store on Roosevelt Avenue. In a supremely sedated state induced by three Valiums daily, I embraced the world of pricing items while listening to the rumble of the 7 train as it carried people to the promised land of Manhattan.

I don't know why parents think they have the right to discourage their children from who they want to be. It wastes so much time. Overnight, and because of some doctor who idolized my father, my life became a fogged haze of Valium, work, and putting up with my aunt, her critical husband, and his mean parents.

The funny thing is they all thought they could conspire to keep me away from the theater. But why send me to New York then? New York City! I made it my mission to see as many plays and musicals as I could. Nothing could stop me from doing that.

Twice a week I would pretend I was going to the library or a party with coworkers. Instead I would ride the 7 train to Times Square and buy a ticket to a show. I entered dozens of theaters and saw people like

Gwen Verdon, Leslie Uggams, Lauren Bacall, Jason Robards, and Angela Lansbury all do their stuff. I would watch and then wait by the stage door for one of them to say hello to me or wave in my general direction. If any of them so much as acknowledged me (and being real stars they were always polite to their fans), it made me believe that I could be one of them.

My math teacher thought it was possible, my family thought it was ridiculous, and I was left staring up in the dark. My aunt and uncle and my psychiatrist kept telling me that I was wrong, that I was clumsy, that I didn't have the looks or the talent, to forget it. They said I should look to something else, that I was stuck in a fantasy, a daydream. But I didn't give up.

One day I went to see Pearl Bailey in *Hello, Dolly!* The ticket agent assured me that I had been given a great seat. It was in the balcony, of course, but when the usher sat me I was surprised to find that I had nearly a whole row to myself, with no one on either side of me for three or four seats.

As I sat alone in the dark while the overture surged, I began to cry. I am alone, I thought, even at the theater I am alone. I tried to control myself when the show began, but the tears kept silently rolling down my face. I had finally cracked from the pressure of my drugged-out trip to New York. Then Miss Bailey came out and started to sing. After her first song, she paused for applause and then waved up to the balcony. Who was she waving at? Then she looked exactly in my direction, waved again, and called out, "I'm going to the end of this song again for you."

The audience applauded joyfully, but I barely heard it. I was alone in the theater with Pearl Bailey, and she was singing just for me.

Now, Miss Bailey was known to stop the show and do asides to the audience, so maybe it was a plural "you" she was singing to, but it felt like the entire show was being played for me that day. It gave me hope.

I waited for Miss Bailey at the stage door, and as she was getting into her car, she stopped and hugged me.

She whispered, "Good luck, honey," as her chauffeur opened the car door. In she went, driving away.

That night was my baptism into the theater. If I had ever doubted it, I knew then for certain that from that moment on and for the rest of my life I would be a part of that world. I would be in the theater, and no one was going to stop me.

I left before the summer was over, impatient to break the spell of New York. Even if I wanted to be in the theater, my home was in California. Fortunately I experienced a little piece of the East Coast that would always make me want to return.

It happened one day, on a trip to the "library," when I got off the 7 train with time to kill before any of the plays started on Broadway. Instead of walking uptown, I decided to go the other way on Fifth Avenue. The Valium was working hard, and I got caught up in the drift of the city until I was miles away from Times Square at the north edge of Washington Square Park.

What in God's name was going on?

There were hippies everywhere, drugs and music, and bodies sprawling on grass. In one part of the park there was a high-end fashion shoot with models in evening gowns posing like goddesses while a sleek-looking European snapped their pictures. Commercial culture clashing with counterculture, high art, and deadbeats, all surrounded by music and city and fantasy.

This is the real me, I thought to myself. I am not a stranger here. These people understand me. I understand them. I will survive my family. I will leave Los Angeles someday and move here to Greenwich Village and find peace.

And so, back in L.A., I had plenty to remember, plenty to dream about. There was a whole different world, two thousand miles away from Los Angeles, in a different direction than Cuba, a world where my family didn't matter. There couldn't have been a better time to learn that lesson, because when I got back to L.A., the family drama kicked into high gear and everything started to unravel. My dreams would prove invaluable.

For starters, Hugo had married Diane, and they were now living on their own. My mother was pregnant all over again, and a few months after I returned my sister Michelle was born. After she came home from the hospital, complications caused my mother to blow up like a balloon. She was rushed right back to the hospital. Because she looked so bad when she left, I thought for sure she was going to die. During the few days she was gone, we all took care of Michelle. She was so tiny, pale, and sweet, and, thankfully, she slept a lot. My mother came back alive.

Dad was doing better and better in his career, but rather than enjoying it, he decided we had to move again. This time he bought a house in Woodland Hills, the town Mr. Anderson lived in. The fights between my father and me got worse after we moved.

"You will not be an actor!" he would yell.

"Yes, I will!" I'd snap back.

"Not while I'm supporting you!" He pounded his fist on a table.

"I don't care!" I was vehement.

I'd go to my room and slam the door behind me. This happened at least twice a week.

We had a calm patch when I helped him furnish the new five-bedroom house. We bonded over picking fabric swatches and cabinet hardware, wood stains and wallpaper, and we had a glorious moment of union over his decision to build a pool in the backyard.

Jeanette, Michelle, Mom, Dad, Didi, Othin, and me inside the house in Woodland Hills, 1971

Then one day as the bulldozers were digging the hole for the pool, he told me again that he would not allow me to study drama when I started school at Camino Real Senior High. I told him I would study drama whether he liked it or not.

"Not while you are living in my house," he told me again.

"Then I won't live with you," I said coldly.

"How can you live without your parents?" my mother butted in, unable to control herself.

"I've done it before!" I was glowing with anger.

I had to come up with a plan, so I called Hugo and asked if I could stay on the couch in the apartment he had with Diane in Van Nuys. He said of course and picked me up that night.

The next day I enrolled in Van Nuys High School.

My dad could not believe what I had done, but he gave me an allowance anyway. Guilt money, he called it. We didn't talk for days at a time, but I would see him if I had dinner with the family on Sunday nights. Sometimes I'd feel a soft spot for him and so I'd show up at his offices on Van Nuys Boulevard. We'd drive home together, try to have a conversation, sometimes we'd stop for a bite to eat. If things between Dad and me were smooth, I'd stay in my room at home. Everything would be fine for a while, and then we'd have another fight. Hugo's couch was always open.

Dad at work in his office, 1971

I was somewhere between adolescence and adulthood. I was making the decisions that would set the course of the rest of my life, but I was still just sixteen. One thing was certain, though, I knew I could never depend on my parents for anything. Of all the myths in my life, that one was definitely over.

Meanwhile there was a whole different world right in Los Angeles just waiting to be discovered by me. Van Nuys High was not only Sandy Koufax's alma mater, but Marilyn Monroe's, too. It was a very mixed school, filled with poor kids from Van Nuys and rich kids from the suburb of Encino. The school itself was nothing fancy, especially when compared to Camino Real, the school I would have attended in Woodland Hills. There was a lot to be desired at Van Nuys High, but they had what I deemed most important: a top-notch drama department. I took drama classes, joined the Thespian Club, and spent all my time in the performing arts wing of the school. I even won an award for my rendition of *The Road to Rome* by Robert E. Sherwood. I joined the debate team, too, and learned how to argue both sides of any subject, something I knew would come in handy in showbiz.

When I was sixteen, I had my first real crush, Gena Franz. She was the daughter of Eduard Franz, a blacklisted actor, and she dressed like a hippie in long skirts and flowy blouses. She had long straight hair parted down the middle. She was thin and androgynous, the first boy/girl I had ever known. I remember seeing her rehearsing a monologue from *Romeo and Juliet* for a drama competition. A few moments after beginning, she picked up an apple and munched it through the rest of the piece. The way she used the apple was inspiring. She didn't draw attention to it; she simply let it be there, and by eating it while acting, she made the scene feel so real. It was one of the finest pieces of acting I had ever seen, so naturally I fell for her.

I didn't get up the courage to ask her out, but I saw her often around school and in the drama department, so we became friends. I also made two close male friends, Sandor and Charles. Sandor was from Hungary with an engineer dad and a homemaking mom. Charles was an Italian-American whose father was a Reichian therapist. I had no idea what that was, but I didn't care. I had two best friends. And although we had our differences, it was our similarities that brought us together. Actually, it was one similarity in particular: we all had foreskins.

We noticed this one day in the showers during gym. We didn't speak about it out loud. No comments were exchanged on each other's original packaging. But it was that little piece of skin that broke the ice with all of us. It also helped that Charles had a car, a blue Jaguar that he liked to drive his twenty-seven-year-old girlfriend around in.

After we had known Charles for about a month, he invited Sandor and me to his house for a Sunday lunch. I had my grandfather drop me off. As I walked through the high iron gates of a two-acre mansion, I was filled with the sense of something very familiar. There were many cars in the driveway, and I could hear voices and music in the back. I walked toward the noise. In the backyard of the estate was an enormous pool full of people in their late twenties wearing bikinis and Speedos. Charles ran up to me and hugged me.

"Where's your suit?" he asked

"Didn't bring one," I muttered.

His girlfriend, Holly, joined us. She had short hair and a very round figure. She was the daughter of blacklisted writers and one of Charles's dad's patients, I would soon learn. She was ten years older than Charles, and she had been a child actress. She now taught at a private school.

"Swim in your underwear," Holly commanded.

And so I stripped to my underwear and jumped in the pool. Sandor joined us a few minutes later in his underwear, and for the first time I noticed how musclebound he was. Charles jumped in, and I was a little disturbed by his lean, dark Italian body. Disturbed and confused by the sensuality of it all.

The party guests left one by one until it was just Charles, Sandor, and me swimming and confessing secrets we had never discussed at school.

Charles wanted to be a photographer, but his father opposed him because he wanted Charles to be a chiropractor and later a Reichian therapist, like himself.

"A Reichian what?" I had to ask.

"My father is a famous analyst. Well, not quite an analyst, but like an analyst. You know what a shrink is, right?" Charles asked.

"A jailor!" I said. Then I told my two new friends about my psychiatrist in New York and how I was still on sedatives and how my father didn't want me to become an actor. "He says acting is only for homosexuals."

They hugged me and told me they were there for me.

Sandor didn't know what he wanted, but he knew it was something different from what his parents expected.

"They don't understand me. Sometimes I feel like they don't even know me." We could all relate.

We all swore to be the best of friends. We said we would be there through thick and thin, and we sealed our oath by diving under water and holding our breath.

Then I heard something deep and gruff but warm at the same time. It sounded like bubbles gurgling under water, but I soon realized it was a voice.

"Come in boys. Stop dreaming. It's time to eat spaghetti."

As my head came out of the water, I found myself face to face with Philip Curcuruto, Charles's dad. In stature he was a perfect combination of my grandfathers Oscar and Fernando. Short and immaculately dressed in linen like Fernando, muscular and streetwise just like Oscar. From the minute I laid eyes on him, I thought, "This man will save me!"

But first there was his famous spaghetti sauce to be tasted. Charles told me it took two days to cook.

The inside of Charles's house was just as beautiful as the backyard. The focus was the great room, a huge sprawl of living room, dining room, and kitchen with an adjoining sunroom.

Charles's mother was there, surprisingly bland, very American, blonde and short and a little matronly. She had an expensive set of pearls dangling from her neck. Charles's sister was also there. She looked like Charles, with dark lean features and long black hair, and although she was not striking, she was pretty and a little exotic. The surprise guests at dinner were Mr. Cururuto's patients, several of whom were already eating and complimenting Mr. Cururuto on the sauce. The one who absorbed my attention completely was named Debra. She looked like a mixture of Anne Bancroft and Sophia Loren. She was smoking and eating at the same time and she wore a sheer blouse that showed off her braless breasts. They were enormous. And if that weren't enough, one of them was leaking breast milk, and I couldn't take my eyes off it. Just as I became transfixed, her two-year-old daughter grabbed at her breast and began to suck.

"No biting," Debra commanded, smiling at me as I stared.

"If she bites, she bites. You just have a fear of pleasure, Debra!" Mr. Curcuruto interrupted.

"Do I, Phil?" she purred seductively.

"Hey, guys, grab the pasta before it's gone," Charles nervously said as he pushed us toward the dining room table.

The room was filled with the smell of homemade meat sauce. It was such a rich smell, such a thick smell, you knew it was the kind that took ages to make. The kind that uses browned bones for extra flavor, tons of garlic and tomatoes, herbs and spices. As the smell filled my nostrils, all basil and beef and tomatoes, I really could have shouted "Mama mia!"

Phil (as Mr. Curcuruto insisted I call him) took a plate for me and filled it with pasta and salad. "Here you go, stud," he said as he handed it to me, laughing at his own joke.

Sandor, Charles, and I retreated to a corner of the house to eat and talk. The pasta was al dente and bathed in rich, peppery sauce. It was a complete taste, a round taste, full of heft and body. This was meat sauce that would truly stick to your ribs.

I noticed that Charles's girlfriend, Holly, was hanging around Debra the whole night, and I wondered what that was about. Charles explained that they were best friends and that they shared a house down the street.

That night, when Charles drove me home to Woodland Hills, we dropped Holly off first at Debra's, a house almost as large as Phil's. These must be rich people, I thought.

As we drove to my house, Charles talked about how he started dating Holly when he was thirteen and she twenty-three because his father had encouraged it.

"He told me he didn't want me to spend my teenage years masturbating all the time." The thought that his father would talk so openly about masturbation made me want him as a shrink, so I pressed Charles for more information. He explained that Wilhelm Reich, who was a follower of Freud, believed that neuroses were contained as blockages in the patient's physical body as well as in the mind. Reich devised a therapy to break through these blocks using a combination of psycho-analysis and body work similar to Chinese accupressure. One of the goals in the therapy was to have a true orgasm so powerful that it would help you discharge all your neuroses. I told Charles that it sounded fascinating. He admitted that his father was brilliant, and that he loved him very much, but that his family was not normal.

"Neither is mine," I said.

"I knew you'd understand," he whispered.

When we got to my house, we sat in the driveway and put our arms around each other's shoulders while listening to the radio.

I turned to look Charles straight in the eyes and I began my own confession.

"My family is not normal either. There is something really wrong with them, especially my dad's family. I do not know how to say it, but it is something that scares me and something that I have never been able to understand."

"I understand. We understand each other," said Charles, his voice filled with emotion.

"I need to get off these Valiums!" I blurted without even thinking. "I'm hooked. I think your father can help me. Please. Ask him if he will see me?"

"Of course I will," Charles assured me.

"Thank you," I replied.

As I was getting out of the Jaguar, he grabbed my hand.

"You'll still be friends with me, right? Even if you are my dad's patient?"

"Of course," I smiled.

"I knew you'd understand my family," he said again.

"How could I not? It's so much like mine."

When I got into my house, my mother was waiting for me.

"Did you have a good time?" she asked.

"Yes," I muttered.

"I just made some café, do you want some?"

I nodded yes. She went to get my café and I got dizzy for a second. I felt, for the first time, like an adult, a person with my own private life.

My mother appeared with the café.

"What did you eat?" She seemed nervous.

"Spaghetti in meat sauce," I answered. I drank my café.

"They're Italians?" She had so many questions tonight.

"The father is, not the mother," I explained.

"Was it good? The spaghetti?" Yet another question.

"Almost as good as your lasagna." I winked at her.

She smiled at me and went off to bed. She knew something was different, but I convinced her otherwise. Maybe my math teacher was right. Maybe charm was all you needed to make the world go your own way.

From that moment on I spent most of my time with Charles and his family. Phil took me as his patient, and I joined an acting group that Holly had started. Charles was always taking pictures and we were always doing scene work and little shows. It didn't matter that at Van Nuys High the only part I got in the school play *David and Lisa* was not the lead, David, not even the supporting role of the French student. No, they had given the Cuban the special part of the handicapped boy in a wheelchair. What else were they supposed to do with my accent? Even working-class schools have elitism bred into them.

Anyway, it didn't matter because at Holly's acting group I was playing Valentino both onstage and off. It was the seventies and all around us people were being sexually awakened, certainly in the microcosm surrounding a Reichian therapist. So I was shy at Van Nuys High, a stud everywhere else.

Debra liked to give parties almost as much as Phil did. She had followers of her own, having started a popular school based on the Summerhill School in England. Summerhill's founder, A. S. Neill, believed that children should be autonomous, and so he created an institution in which lessons were optional and students had an equal say in their day-to-day lives at the school. A perfect model for California in the seventies.

So there were no issues with parents, teachers, or students fraternizing outside of school. The mix of people was always fascinating, and oftentimes I'd end up as the center of someone's attention. Apparently I, too, was interesting. Finally being Cuban was working for me the way it did for my dad—it made me exotic and desirable. Gracias, Desi Arnaz.

It was at one of Debra's parties, sometime in 1970, that I met Hariette. Gena Franz never stood a chance, and Hariette quickly replaced her as my number-one crush. They both had a similar air of Jewish aristocracy that I must have been drawn to, but any similarities ended there.

Gena was a girl and Hariette was a woman. Gena was an artist, Hariette was an anarchist. Gena was pretty and Hariette was tear-your-heart-out gorgeous. She had long straight hair and perfect skin. She wore miniskirts with cowboy boots, black pantyhose without underwear, and talked socialism constantly. She looked like she was in her early twenties but in fact she was forty and had eight daughters. Eight daughters from two marriages that had both ended. All her kids went to Debra's Summerhill School, and she was also a patient of Phil's.

Debra introduced me to Hariette as if we were fated for each other. I was seventeen now. I had stopped taking Valium and was filled with an endless supply of energy that shocked everyone, including myself. I had grown up enough to be quite good-looking and though I pretended I didn't know it, I was confident enough to say to myself that, no matter what, I was going to go to bed with this forty-year-old woman. Twenty-three years older than me. I tried to be seductive that night. I even asked her to dance, but she said I'd be better off with her seventeen-year-old daughter. My mind was made up, and though it didn't happen that night, I knew it would only be a matter of time till I got my hands on her.

So I gave her long looks during functions at Debra's school. I talked to her about poetry at parties. I made my appointment with Phil right after hers and hugged her when she was crying between our sessions. I told Phil about my fixation on Hariette, and after a few moments of consideration he told me he thought my desires were very natural and a wonderful idea. And then he told Hariette.

On Valentine's Day of my seventeenth year, I went to a hotel in Burbank with Hariette and made all my dreams come true. I felt like the luckiest seventeen-year-old on the planet.

Hariette was a true bohemian. She did a little bit of everything and nothing at all. She worked constantly but lived and supported her family with regular checks from her father's haberdashery, Louis the Hatter, in her hometown of Detroit. Because of her father's money, Hariette was free to live the life her mother longed for as a young girl when she dreamed of running off to dance with Isadora Duncan. Her mother wasn't even a dancer, but it was the life she dreamed of, the life her daughter was living when I met her.

Hariette on Venice Beach, 1971

Both Hariette's parents were Russian. Her mother's family had been socialists and her father's capitalists. Although they had completely different ideologies, both families were victims of a revolution. Different times, different ideas, different revolutions, but we were all the same kind of victim.

Hariette was born in America, though, and her parents' ideologies blended nicely in the melting pot. She was a socialist funded by a capitalist. Doesn't it just make your heart melt?

Hariette had a gorgeous house paid for by her father. It was a one-acre ranch in Northridge with a guesthouse and a huge pool. There were empty horse stalls out back and patios lining the perimeter of the house. The interior was furnished with numerous chairs and thick mattresses, cushions abounding, and a very large wooden table surrounded by still more chairs.

It was basically one big hippie pad. People hitchhiking cross-country were always crashing on the floor and swimming naked in the pool. While Debra's and Phil's places were strange but familiar, Hariette's was nothing at all like home.

The brave new world extended to the food Hariette made for the five daughters living with her and the minimum four guests she always seemed to have. Where my family probably would have roasted a whole animal of some sort, Hariette liked to make huge salads.

Salads?

Cubans don't eat salads. The only thing more foreign to us than blood in beef is fresh vegetables. Hariette liked both. She'd fill huge wooden bowls full of bright green lettuce and spinach, carrots, watercress, cucumbers, mushrooms, string beans, or zucchini. She'd throw anything in and cover it with homemade dressings using ginger and sesame oil, soy sauce, citrus, homemade flavored vinegars or fruity extra virgin olive oil. And though she rarely served chicken or fish, Hariette had a deep love for London broil. Maybe there was something familiar in this leafy green land after all. I panicked the first time I saw her cut into a steak. Medium rare and bloody. Yuck.

For the first few months I knew Hariette, I couldn't bring myself to have a meal with her. It was all a little too foreign, and besides, the idea of partaking felt almost treasonous at the time. It wasn't just that I was scared of salad. I recalled my mother, terrified on the way to Los Angeles. What if, by eating at this woman's table, I was making a decision I didn't understand? What if I ate fresh salad and medium-rare steak? Would I get lost? Would I recognize myself?

I think the dynamics here were operating on an even deeper level. The prized role of the most important woman in my life was about to be played by someone new. Someone not my mother. No wonder the thought of salad felt like betrayal.

I spent more and more time at Hariette's than at home. I told my parents I was having an affair with one of her daughters, and whether or not they believed me, they knew I was no longer theirs.

If I was alone, I lived on McDonald's french fries. If I was with Hariette, I waited for the morning, after all her kids had left for school. Then she'd make me eggs.

My grandmother Manuela used to make omelettes with still-warm eggs from the inside of a freshly killed hen. I didn't think it got any earthier than that. But somehow in the morning, when she and I were alone reading the paper, Hariette's scrambled eggs took on a primal deliciousness. She made them just for me, scrambled with Jack cheese and toast, served with the best American coffee I had ever tasted. Maybe it was the drop of raw milk she added. Raw milk. Just like Manuela.

So now my life was ruled by sex, salad, and coffee with raw milk. I'd say it felt familiar, but I honestly didn't know what familiar was anymore. Also, I was getting laid too much to care. Remember, I was seventeen and had the hormones to prove it.

Hariette and I lived in sin for two years, during which time I graduated from Van Nuys High. I didn't attend the commencement ceremonies, preferring to stay home and swim the day away.

When I was nineteen, without my parents knowing, Hariette and I decided to get married at City Hall. We moved to a smaller house in Tarzana after the ranch house burned down one night because of faulty wiring. The Tarzana house was not as big as the ranch, but it still had a pool. There were beautiful wood floors and a big black Swedish fireplace. I was busy going to acting classes and selling suits at Bullock's, a department store in Sherman Oaks. I was waiting for my big break, but there was business in the house that I saw to on a daily basis.

The Tarzana house had great light, and so, on a whim, I brought home scads of houseplants over several months. We planted gardens outside, with low crawling shrubs and bright flowers scattered here and there. But it was the indoor houseplants that I cared for the most. I watered them and talked to them and sang to them every day. Those plants were me, my presence in that house, slowly growing, changing, reaching for the sun.

When my parents finally found out that I was married to Hariette, my father asked me out to lunch.

Me, Los Angeles, 1973

My mother pretended to understand and, as usual, made very few demands. I still went to her house most Sundays and ate Cuban food. Sometimes I brought Hariette and her kids; sometimes I went alone. My sisters loved spending the weekend with me in Tarzana, and my brother visited when he wasn't busy being a teenager.

It was only my father who treated me differently. "You are the biggest disappointment of my life," he told me. Thanks, Dad. Thanks for being there.

I decided I wouldn't let it get to me. He couldn't hurt me. I had my own house now. I even had children. A lot of children who were less than thrilled that their mother had married someone young enough to be their brother. I decided to make peace offerings through food. And so, as I settled into a long stretch of domestic life, I started to cook.

First, I learned how to make stir-fries, the pinnacle of which was chicken and string beans with soy sauce and brown sugar. Then one day I was watching television and found a channel with Julia Child making a roast chicken. As she placed each ingredient carefully on the fowl, I thought, this is it! I will become a French chef! That will be my hobby while I wait for an acting job.

So I began to cook French. Now, I know Julia is the one who is supposed to have made French cooking accessible, but her recipes are a pain in the ass to say the very least. Maybe I should have started with a different recipe, but I got it into my head that I would best start by mastering *Boeuf Bourguignon*.

I browned the meat. I made the bouquet of herbs and put them in cheesecloth. I peeled every baby onion, two dozen in all. I cooked the whole thing slowly, boiled the egg noodles, and served the steaming dish hours later to a table full of hungry women and guests. Everyone agreed it was a success. And so I repeated the process time and again.

I tried other dishes, too. I loved to make soufflés. I bought all the right whisks and pots and ramekins. I learned how to whip the whites and cook the yolks, and how to mix the whole mess together and bake it in a water bath. So, even if I never became a bona fide chef de cuisine, I could make a mean soufflé, and that was more than enough.

One afternoon when I was making *Boeuf Bourguignon*, my grandfather Fernando came to visit with a bottle of wine and several cigars. By then I was twenty-one, so he shared everything freely with me, although it's not like he would have had a problem smoking and drinking with me at fifteen, either.

He was, of course, wearing a suit. Hariette was home, so she put on Beethoven and went swimming with her daughters in the pool. Fernando puffed on his cigar while I cooked and smoked nearby.

That day he talked to me, really talked to me, for the first and only time in his life. He told me how being part of the docks had allowed him to watch chefs from all over the world cook in their galleys. He told me how he had learned about fine wines, good cheese, crepes, Chinese food, bagels, lox, and *Boeuf Bourguignon*.

As the classical music played, he tapped his feet on the polished wood floors and sipped his wine. He leaned closer to me and whispered as I turned to look at him.

"You are why I did it," he said.

"Did what?" I asked.

"Struggled, got myself into a place of financial importance. I wanted one of my children or grandchildren to be you, to be an artist. To know the difference between what's great and what's common."

I looked away, embarrassed for all the people in my family. It was Fernando, the distant, the brutal, the coldest of them all; it was he who actually understood me.

Then he cleared his throat and said, "I am very proud of you. Thank you."

I stopped for a moment, frozen in the glow of acceptance.

"I want you to teach me how to cook," I blurted out.

I turned back to the onions I was peeling.

He laughed and said, "I'm making *Arroz con Pollo* this weekend at your mother's—come and cook with me."

That night the *Boeuf Bourguignon* tasted better than ever.

On Saturday I went to my mother's to watch Fernando make *Arroz con Pollo*.

It all seemed the same. Brown the chicken, make the *sofrito*, cook the rice. Fernando had begun to use *bijol* instead of saffron, but even that seemed normal. I was surprised when he added a can of beer to his recipe instead of wine, but I had heard of people using it in *paella*. What was the secret ingredient? After he added the beer he removed a small brown paper bag, folded over at the top to conceal what was inside.

"Now, Eduardo, the secret," he said, "the thing that makes these bland American chickens taste like they grew up roaming the fields eating Cuban grass. It's inside this bag. The reason my *Arroz con Pollo* is the best. Don't tell anybody."

"I won't," I stammered.

"Swear it to me!" he shouted.

"I swear," I said, and I did the sign of the cross.

"Fine," he whispered.

And out of the brown paper bag came a can of Campbell's Condensed Cream of Asparagus Soup, which he poured directly into the bubbling pot, mixing it into the chicken and rice. He took the can, put it back into the small brown paper bag, folded the top once more, and tossed it in the trash.

"It also keeps the rice moist," he added proudly. "You make it. You see."

So I became the newly crowned king of chicken and rice; at least I did at Hariette's house. It was requested by all the girls and any guests passing through. Fernando's recipe was a treat for my new family, a piece of tradition in this most unconventional of households.

I say I was king only at Hariette's because it was during that same visit that Fernando shared his secret recipe with my mother, too. I guess he was in a giving mood.

While working at Bullock's Sherman Oaks one day, one of the security agents, Kim Alexander, asked if I wanted to have lunch. She had heard that I wanted to be an actor and she wanted to let me know that her father was starting a new acting class at a school called the Academy of Stage and Screen. I said I was interested and met with her dad, David Alexander.

David was Jewish, from New York, smart and tough and kind and warm. He had been a part of the Actors Studio and had taught his interpretation of Stanislavski to Jack Lemmon, Nina Foch, Cliff Robertson and now, me.

He gave me a scholarship and extra responsibilities after my first year of study. My job was to help him go over scenes with other people. I was always expected to have matches close by to light his cigarettes. He taught me everything I know about the craft of acting. He sent me to a voice teacher named Godeane Eagle to get rid of most of my accent. Godeane put me through the complicated technical and emotional process of letting go of my speech.

"To let go of the speech you have to let go of your identity," she'd say, "Let go of your Spanish melody—it's what you have to do."

But what if I get lost? I wondered.

"It won't be gone forever; you'll be able to bring it back whenever you want. Now put your tongue between your teeth and go th ... thimble." And I did, over and over.

One day after class David confessed to me that he wanted more than anything to go to a traditional Cuban Christmas Eve. He even learned how to say it in Spanish, *Noche Buena*. He had two other Hispanic students, Yvonne Coll, a former Miss Puerto Rico, and Karmin

Murcello, a Cuban exile like me. They had told him what a great cook my mother was, and he had decided that we must all have dinner at my mother's. I told Mom this and Grandpa Oscar answered for her.

"We will have the biggest Noche Buena Los Angeles has ever seen."

So I invited a dozen of my closest friends from the acting school, along with all of Hariette's kids and a couple of her friends. My mother and father and grandparents invited their friends, and when all was said and done we had Noche Buena for sixty or more.

We had no caterers, no help even, just all of us working together for three days before the party. We rented tables, chairs, napkins, and silverware—no paper products that night. Even then I was terrified that all these Hollywood people would meet my parents and my cousins, and who knows what? Anything could go wrong.

But let me tell you, once you know how to give a party, you never forget. The *yuca*, black beans, and roast pork—perfection. The avocado and radishes and olives could have come from Spain. The *turrones* did come from Spain, and my mother made her famous *flan* that yielded no leftovers for Christmas Day. My brother took care of the music, Cuban and rock, and people danced and drank late into the night.

What a Christmas Eve. We did it, we had friends, we had Cuban food, we had money. It was the closest that we ever came to what it would have been like in Cuba. People still talk to me about that party. They remember my mother's cooking, but I remember it as the last time we were all together.

A few months later my grandfather Oscar came to my house to help me figure out why my green MG Midget was having trouble starting up in the mornings. Oscar had been depressed the previous few months, but I had no idea how badly until he opened the hood.

"I do not know if I want to live anymore," he said. "We are never going back. I know that now."

I stood silent as he fumbled with a spark plug. I wanted to say, don't talk like that. I wanted to shout, I need you! But all I could manage was "I love you." And he smiled.

A week later he got drunk with some other mechanics and had a stroke. He died that night.

The terrible thing is that I felt nothing. I faked tears, I screamed, but I felt nothing.

A year went by. My green MG Midget broke down and I had to push it home through the empty streets of Tarzana. As I trudged behind the car, my head toward the ground using all my strength to move the vehicle, I began to weep. I wept for Oscar Hernandez, the orphan who worked himself up from nothing and then lost it all to a revolution. I wept for the man who came here to the U.S.A., who worked as a mechanic till the day he died. I wept because he was gone forever and I missed him and I needed him to help me. But I knew that he was gone. So I wept, block by block, for a mile. They were not pretty tears, they were not appropriate. I cried sobs that tear out your guts, that make you shake so hard your body can still feel them a week later.

I made *Camarones Enchilados* as soon as I had the strength. I made *Pollo Frito* and ate hamburgers and tried to find Oscar in all of them. Fernando had given me his secret ingredient, but I never learned Oscar's. I know he had one somewhere up his sleeve, but it didn't matter if I ever discovered it. I felt closer to him just by trying.

A year later my mother and father divorced. My dad told me one day on the steps of our house in Woodland Hills. He wept and said he was leaving my mother for an Argentinian woman a few years older than me.

Mom and Dad (with tourists) at a cabaret in Spain, 1974

"I feel love for the first time in my life. I love her and she loves me," he whined. He tried to grab my hand, but I moved it away. I paused for a moment and then I asked the question I had wanted to ask him my whole life.

"How about us?" My voice was louder than I had intended.

"Us?"

"Your children! Didn't you love us?" I was screaming.

"I didn't know how," he said, looking away from me.

"Didn't know how?" I was angry. Then I thought, give him another chance. Maybe he didn't understand the question. I took his face in my hands and quietly asked, "Don't you love me? Don't you love us? Your children?"

And he shook his head no. He wept and pleaded for me to understand the tragedy of his failings and the possibility of new love. I spoke to him simply and without tears.

"I will never forgive you."

He cried on the steps as I walked inside the house and gave my mother a hug.

"What's going to happen to me?" she whispered.

"You'll be happier," I whispered back.

"Don't let your sisters know, not yet. They're young and they're girls, and he might change his mind."

I pushed her away gently, not knowing what to say. Finally I asked her for the one thing I was sure she could give me.

"Make me some café, Mama," I pleaded with the voice of a child who is no longer innocent.

She looked up and muttered, "He would never have the guts to do this if my father were still alive."

We heard my father's car drive off as she filled the espresso maker with café.

I Hippie Salad I

This is the quintessential California salad, like a trip to the salad bar that never seems to end. I've included my favorite vegetables here, but you can be laid-back about the ones you use, as long as there's lots of them. I use powdered garlic and ground ginger to flavor the dressing so as not to overpower the subtle freshness of all the vegetables. Feel free to use the fresh stuff for their holistic antibiotic properties. To add to the West Coast feel, go ahead and buy all organic produce. And if you're feeling really groovy, say "like" and "dude" when you tell your guests what's in the mix.

For the dressing:
¼ cup lemon juice
¼ cup tahini
1 tablespoon honey
1 teaspoon ground ginger
½ teaspoon garlic powder
1½ teaspoons salt
1 teaspoon ground black pepper
½ cup peanut oil

For the salad:
½ cup pumpkin seeds
1½ cups French beans (haricots verts)
1½ cups broccoli flowerets
1 large head romaine lettuce
1 beefsteak tomato
1 cucumber, peeled
2 carrots, peeled
½ red onion, peeled
1 red pepper, stem and seeds removed
1 cup sliced cooked beets
1 Hass avocado

1. First, prepare the dressing: Combine the lemon juice, tahini, honey, ginger, garlic powder, salt, and black pepper in a small mixing bowl. While whisking gently, drizzle in the peanut oil a little at a time until the mixture is emulsified. Chill until ready to serve.

2. Toast the pumpkin seeds in a dry pan over medium-high heat, swirling the pan to prevent scorching, 3 to 4 minutes. When the pumpkin seeds start to pop and brown slightly, transfer to a small bowl and set aside to cool.

3. Snap off the stems of the French beans and cut them in half cross-wise. Cut the broccoli into bite-size pieces. Blanch the French beans and broccoli in boiling water for 1 to 2 minutes, then trans-fer to an ice-water bath using a slotted spoon. Remove from the water and set aside to dry.

4. Shred the romaine lettuce into strips ½ to ¾ inch wide. Wash and dry well. Place the lettuce in a large serving bowl.

5. Slice the tomato into ¼-inch-thick half-circles. Slice the cucum-ber into ¼-inch-thick discs. Slice the carrots into ¼-inch-thick discs. Slice the onion into thin half-circles. Slice the red pepper into ¼-inch-thick strips, then cut the strips in half. Cut the beets into ¼ inch dice. Peel and remove the pit from the avocado and scoop out the flesh. Cut into ¼ inch strips.

6. Layer all the vegetables over the lettuce. Sprinkle with the pump-kin seeds. Drizzle with dressing and toss. Serve immediately, mak-ing sure to get some of all the veggies in each serving.

Makes 6 to 8 servings

⁅ *Fernando's Arroz con Pollo* ⁆

Every Cuban thinks their *Arroz con Pollo* is better than anyone else's. The arguments the topic can generate are endless. Beer or wine? Saf-fron or *bijol*? Wet or dry? Who is right? Does it even matter? Some-times I think the actual dish is just an afterthought. No Cuban could make *Arroz con Pollo* as often as they argue about it. No matter what I think about this version of the dish, I have learned to keep quiet. Of course I have feelings about *bijol* and condensed cream of asparagus soup, but this dish belongs to my grandfather Fernando, and so I partake of it with fondness.

One 3- to 4-pound chicken, cut into parts, skin removed
1 tablespoon salt
1 teaspoon ground black pepper
2 tablespoons lime juice
¼ cup vegetable oil
¼ cup olive oil
1 Spanish onion, peeled and cut into ¼-inch dice
½ green pepper, stem and seeds removed, cut into ¼-inch dice
3 garlic cloves, peeled and finely chopped
1 cup beer
½ cup Goya tomato sauce (from one 8-ounce can)
1½ teaspoons *bijol**
One 10.75-ounce can condensed cream of asparagus soup
2 cups Valencia (short-grain) rice
6 cups chicken broth
2 cups frozen peas, thawed
1 small (4- to 6-ounce) jar pimentos, drained and sliced into ¼-inch
    strips

*Look for *bijol*, or *bija suprema*, in the spice section of Latin grocery stores. Try to find the kind that has no MSG, or *sazón* in it. Check the ingredients. The best *bijol* has little more than annatto, spices, and trace amounts of starch or stabilizer.

1. Season the chicken parts with 2 teaspoons of the salt, ½ teaspoon of the black pepper, and the lime juice. Marinate for at least 1 hour or overnight.

2. Preheat the oven to 375°F. Heat the vegetable oil in a large pot or Dutch oven over high heat. Remove the chicken pieces from the marinade and pat dry with paper towels. Fry the chicken in 2 batches,

turning occasionally, until golden brown all over, 10 minutes for each batch. Transfer the cooked chicken to a plate and set aside.

3. Add the olive oil to the pot along with the onion and green pepper. Cook, stirring, until softened slightly, 3 minutes. Season with the remaining 1 teaspoon salt and ½ teaspoon black pepper. Add the garlic and cook, stirring, 1 minute more. Add the beer and cook until the alcohol has evaporated, scraping any caramelized bits off the bottom of the pot with a wooden spoon, 3 minutes. Add the tomato sauce, *bijol*, and condensed cream of asparagus soup. Stir to combine and continue cooking to thicken slightly, 1 minute.

4. Add the rice and broth, stirring gently. Return the chicken parts to the pot. Bring the whole thing to a boil, then transfer to the lower third of the oven and bake, uncovered, 30 minutes. If the liquid evaporates too quickly, just add a little more beer or broth.

5. Remove the pot from the oven and scatter the peas evenly over the surface. Garnish with pimentos. Return to the oven to warm through, 5 minutes more. Serve immediately.

Makes 4 servings

NOTE: If you want to make this recipe for a bigger group, just add a few more pieces of chicken to the pot. You can choose breasts, thighs, or drumsticks, but make sure they still have their bones. The only thing you have to do differently is season the chicken with extra salt, pepper, and lime, and make sure you don't crowd the pan in step 2. If you cook too much chicken at once, it won't brown sufficiently and the dish will lack that rounded chicken flavor.

Nine

Eating and Writing

After my father left, once the divorce was final, there was a new sense of freedom in my family. It was a limited freedom at first; familiar feelings hung around like specters. I felt guilty, like most kids do when a parent leaves. I wondered if Dad's inability to love us was my fault. I worried that Mother thought it was her doing, but I don't think she was concerned with blame or responsibility. She still refused to believe he had left for good.

The shock of Dad's departure was that it changed how we understood the very concept of family. It had always been drilled into us that family was everything, that you did anything you could to keep it together. Suddenly my suspicion that this was a lie was proven. Family was not everything; families did not stay together. And most importantly, the man, the one who was supposed to do all that extra work, the anything and everything to keep it going, was the one who failed. *He* couldn't keep it together.

Still, the family was there. The characters and relationships were all around me, but with one conspicuous empty place that seemed to rearrange the way we all fit together. All the rules changed. My sisters were suddenly allowed to date Americans without a chaperone. My brother stopped pretending that he had any desire whatsoever to become an accountant. I finally realized that there was nothing for me to live up to, no one person I had to please, because that one person had exposed himself as incapable of achieving the very standards he held me to.

And with that I no longer felt guilty about wanting to be an actor. Consciously, that is. There was still an underground river of self-criticism and doubt running deep within me, but I stopped questioning my desires and threw myself into the work.

I immersed myself completely in David Alexander's acting class. I went three times a week and always had a scene to show. There were more and more students coming to the school and many of them were actual working actors. We began performing one-act plays on weekends in the little theater where David taught.

I was particularly drawn to a one-act play by Bertolt Brecht called *The Beggar, or the Dead Dog*. I liked the piece for its blatant Marxist overtones. It gave me no small joy to embrace the very thing my parents claimed to have saved me from, especially after my father's departure. It felt appropriately rebellious, but the truth is I really just liked the part of the starving blind beggar who challenges an emperor.

I had wanted to play someone blind since high school. Van Nuys High had a school for the blind as one of their state-funded programs, and there were more than a dozen blind students enrolled. The only boy I had been friends with at school, besides Charles and Sandor, was a blind boy named Bill. He was lanky and awkward but with a mean sense of humor.

Bill was blind, and I knew him well. I would play Bill up there. But what to do about the character's starvation? I was plump. All that Cuban food. All those beans. And *croquetas*. I had to lose some weight fast.

I told Hariette I needed to lose weight if I was really going to become an actor. Hariette, ever the health fanatic, found a woman named Eileen Poole who had a private practice in Eagle Rock, a small, hilly town just outside of L.A.

Eileen touted a diet named after a doctor, Henry Bieler. Dr. Bieler believed that all the body's ailments could be healed through the foods we eat, and he wrote a manual on the subject called *Food Is Your Best Medicine*. Eileen had adapted this book to a West Coast lifestyle, and through consultations and visits to her office she'd prescribe exactly the foods you should eat to take care of whatever was bothering you. The common denominator was that everyone had to drink the same soup, at least twice a day, to cleanse the system and detoxify the blood. Bieler Soup was a bright green combination of zucchini, string beans, celery, parsley, and a little bit of fresh ginger to spice things up. Other than that it was a high-protein, low-salt, and no-carbohydrate diet with emphasis on green vegetables and bloody beef.

Eileen eventually became a go-to guru for a substratum of L.A. showbiz, but at that time her main claim to fame was that Gloria Swanson had been on the Bieler Diet for most of her adult life. If I could be even half as ready for a close-up as Ms. Swanson, I thought, then I would gladly eat whatever this woman told me to.

I made the soup in big batches, boiling all the vegetables to bring out their color, then pureeing it into a swampish porridge. I drank the Bieler Soup all day long. I'd have soft-boiled eggs for breakfast and rare steak at night. Caffeine wasn't allowed, so for a while my life was sorely lacking a regular intake of café, *con leche* or otherwise. I had no bread, no sweets. Almost nothing Cuban was allowed, especially if I really liked it.

The first three weeks I was on that diet I was tempted but never gave in. The biggest feat was when I visited my mom and refused to eat the food she offered. She clutched at her heart and my grandmother got angry.

"Not even café?" Manuela pleaded.

"No, thank you." I was practicing Zen, because I could smell the nutty roast as it bubbled on the stovetop. I had to turn away at the sight of the boiling milk.

"Have you become a vegetarian?" Manuela asked sagaciously.

"No. I eat steak," I said defiantly.

"Then let us make you *Bistec Empanizado!*"

"No, not breaded!" I said with fear.

"I give up!" Manuela shouted. I drove home soon after.

The truth is, Bieler Soup reminded me of Cuca's Newspaper Soup. Maybe just because it was pureed. Newspaper Soup was definitely

more flavorful, and the golden hue brought to mind sunsets, not creatures from the black lagoon. Perhaps the connection is that they both
had a tonic quality. Bieler Soup was such a bright green color, that it
looked alive, and it made me feel stronger to think that I could live on
it as the staple of my diet. It was like breaking an addiction at first,
especially giving up café. But over time the soup itself became an addiction, something my cells craved deeply. I was further bolstered by
the horror most people showed when I told them of my regimen.
Maybe my new addiction was actually a form of discipline. Maybe I
didn't need Cuban food to feel whole after all. I had given up Cuban
food for my art!

The results were miraculous. My skin got freakishly clear. I seemed
to both glow and shimmer, just like Gloria Swanson. I lost all the
weight I wanted, too, leaving my body toned and defined. My hair
seemed to get thicker and blacker, stronger and shinier. I noticed people stopping their cars to take a closer look at me when I crossed the
street in my short shorts and Mexican sandals. I was even beautiful to
myself. I was a star in the making, and, thanks to Brecht, a Marxist to
boot.

A few weeks later we readied ourselves for the first performance
of *The Beggar, or the Dead Dog.* I was possessed, having created a completely different person to inhabit. I wore a rag around my eyes for
weeks so I could feel the blindness. All the injustice in the world
seemed to filter through me as if I had been wronged personally on the
most fundamental level. The character's confrontational nature allowed me to let my anger out into the world. It was by no means a
complete release, but I let off some of the steam that had been boiling
inside for quite some time.

The television actor who played the part of the Emperor was so
intimidated by me that he began to stuff his crotch with socks.

"You might want to steal this play from me," he'd say, "but, buddy,
they are going to be looking at my legs in tights and my stuffed crotch.
Tom Jones does it. Why not me? All eyes will be on this." He pointed
to his crotch and laughed.

What an idiot.

Then I heard myself answer, "We'll see about that," pause for effect, "buddy!" That voice was disembodied. It wasn't mine. It was so sure of itself. Sure of its ability to achieve a desired effect by acting, by emoting. That person wasn't me. And yet it was my lips that were moving. Something big was happening.

I resented the Emperor. I started showing off. I'd run a whole range of emotions from moment to moment, stealing every scene with a fervor I could only connect to the greats I'd seen on my trips to the "library" from Jackson Heights.

I knew better than to be such an ego maniac on stage, but the guy deserved it. He had socks in his pants!

So I would go to the side of the stage and tell myself, "This is not what it's about. It's about being. Being in the moment, listening to that stupid narcissist, the television Emperor."

Then a thought occurred to me. "The Emperor is as stupid and narcissistic as the actor playing him. Just listen to his voice and you'll have all the contempt the beggar needs!"

On our opening night, right before the show started, Michael Dewell, the head of the Academy of Stage and Screen, came into my tiny dressing room and told me he had brought Florence Eldridge with him.

"How nice," I said, "thank you, and now I have to prepare."

Michael nodded that he understood and left.

"Florence Eldridge. Don't you know who that is?" the Emperor asked me snidely.

I shook my head no and shrugged.

"Florence Eldridge was the original Mary Tyrone in *Long Days Journey Into Night*. Fredric March's wife! She is a great actress!"

"That's nice," I said. My heart raced a mile a minute, but I kept my cool.

Then the play began. At twenty-three, I felt more alive than ever before. More than at Van Nuys High when I was in *The Road to Rome*, more than at Porter Junior High singing from *Mame*. That night I felt I had the entire world looking at me, being with me, breathing with me, and every emotion I hoped to portray came out of me, honestly and fluidly. No struggle, just being. Heaven on earth. No. Heaven on stage.

The play ended. I heard the applause. I bowed. Take it in, I thought, that's real love and it's all yours. You earned it and no one will be able to take it away from you.

I looked in the mirror in my dressing room and asked, "Who are you? Not Eduardo Machado from Cojimar. You are an actor."

When I went outside, Florence Eldridge was waiting with Michael Dewell. Hariette was standing next to them. I introduced her and she immediately knew who Florence Eldridge was.

"Your husband was such a great actor," said Hariette, her voice wavering for a split second.

"So is yours," Miss Eldridge said with absolute certainty. She repeated herself as if she could tell that Hariette didn't get it, or didn't want to. "Your husband is a great actor."

"I told you," Michael added.

Then she took my hand and whispered, "It's special, your gift. Guard it with your life." Her voice was full of pain.

"I will," I answered. And they walked away.

As we walked to our car, I could tell Hariette was on edge. Her jaw was clenched and her lips were pressed together. I looked at her every few moments, trying to get a read, but she didn't look back. I suspect she decided that enough people had looked at me that night. I wanted her to be supportive, but I knew that she, even as an ageless beauty, didn't like sharing attention. Of course she proved me right.

"She thinks you're a great actor?" Hariette said in disbelief.

"Don't you?" I asked, knowing the answer.

"No, not really," she snapped, and we got into the car.

The next night during *The Beggar, or the Dead Dog,* the same feelings overcame me. Emotions sat on the tips of my fingers just waiting to be called into being. Must be the zucchini soup, I thought. I will never eat Cuban food again.

As I walked out of the theater after the show, a tall blond man with blue eyes and freckles applauded me loudly. Something about his cockiness, the volume of his admiration—it was a little strange, but he could pull it off. I recognized him as the actor Darrell Larson.

"Bravo!" he shouted, "Ed Machado is a star!"

Without my knowing it, David Alexander, Michael Dewell, and Godeane Eagle had made Eduardo into Ed. Like La Habana to Havana, something had shifted, but it was too new for me to recognize it. Especially with this man shouting "Ed Machado" with such adoration.

Me in a publicity photo from
The Beggar, or the Dead Dog, *1976*

I told Darrell how much I had liked him in *Red Cross*, Sam Shepard's play about a colony infested with crab lice. He told me how much he liked Sam and that they were going to start a theater festival together in Padua Hills, just seventy-five miles outside of Los Angeles. He said he would make sure I was asked to act in the festival, the Padua Hills Writers Conference. His promise didn't hold, and I didn't get to participate in the festival's first year. Still, I went to see the plays, and everything changed because I did. It was that first summer at Padua that I met Maria Irene Fornes.

A famous New York avant-garde playwright, Fornes (whom I came to know as Irene) had just had a hit at the American Place Theatre with *Fefu and Her Friends*, a site specific, nonlinear play about a group of emancipated women in the 1930s. She was in her early fifties when I met her, and to say that she changed me would be a gross understatement. She, more than anyone, altered the course of my career, my life, my very way of being.

The day we met I was sitting in one of the gardens at Padua where a forgettable play was being performed. Hariette sat next to me with her daughter Natasha. Across the way was a small woman in a white man's tuxedo shirt, black linen pants, and a panama hat. Her curly black hair was cut into a tight bob that stuck out at angles from the sides of her hat. She looked in my direction and laughed a girly high-pitched laugh. Our gazes crossed and I was suddenly conscious of the fact that I was wearing a striped tuxedo shirt, white linen pants, and a panama hat of my own. My curly black hair was sticking out at the sides. I removed the hat to break the spell, but I was enchanted once again by the trill of laughter coming from this mirror image that was staring me down. She shouted above the action onstage, which was now playing second fiddle to us.

"You must be the Cuban Darrell told me about!" She could barely contain her mischievous glee.

"How do you know?" I asked.

"We all dress alike!" More laughter, peals like birdcalls at night.

"And you must be Maria Irene Fornes," I called back very seriously.

"What's your name?" she shouted.

"Ed Machado!" I yelled back.

"Ed?"

"Eduardo," I gave in.

The world receded as a curtain went up and our own play began to unfold.

The next year Irene asked me to stage manage *Fefu and Her Friends* at Padua Hills. When I had proved my competence, she asked me to sit in on one of the writing classes she taught during the conference. Afterward she told me I had talent as a writer. I ignored her and stayed focused on my acting.

Then one night I found myself in the middle of a deep depression. I was trying to reconcile my feelings toward my mother, revisiting the haunting images of family, guilt, and loss. I worked myself into a frenzy until I felt like I was drowning in a sea of forces that I needed to face but could not summon cohesively. Every thought would get lost in another, like snakes eating their tails, with nothing staying put long enough for me to figure it out and beat it into submission. I just tried to hang on as I spun around and around and around.

When I felt I couldn't take it any longer I sat down in front of a typewriter and wrote my first play, *Embroidering*. Two months later I had a reading of the play at The Ensemble Studio Theatre in Los Angeles where I was a member of the acting company. After the reading, the cast and audience encouraged me to apply for a grant from the National Endowment for the Arts as a playwright. I submitted the application and forgot about it soon after.

I was acting in a play called *The Adding Machine* at the time for which I got rave reviews. Other than that I was having a hard time getting work. No movies, very little television. Everyone who came to see *The Adding Machine* agreed that L.A. was wrong for me. They all thought I should move to New York, go for theater jobs and forget about the movies.

There was so much uncertainty that came with the thought of leaving L.A. My whole American life had been on the West Coast. My wife was there, my dreams were there ... but Greenwich Village had called me in my youth, and now it was time to answer.

And so I found myself in a black stretch limo in the middle of a blizzard, looking for Irene's apartment in Sheridan Square. I had been offered the executive ride by a friend of Darrell's who sat next to me on the plane to New York. Turns out he wanted to take me on more than one kind of ride. When I got into the limo there were two stewardesses waiting in the back. As we approached Manhattan, Darrell's friend tried to convince me to have an orgy with the three of them. I did my best to focus on the skyline and not make direct eye contact with the chesty gals in their uniforms. I was married, after all.

Sheridan Square couldn't have come fast enough. The moment the car slowed enough I jumped out with my bag and looked for Irene's number in the snow.

"Don't go and ruin the party!" called Darrell's friend.

"Maria Irene Fornes is waiting for me!" I yelled, crossing the street just to get away from him.

Irene had told me she would leave a key for me with the super. I was under the impression that I would stay at her place until she returned from a teaching stint at Smith College in Massachusetts, but when I rang the super, he let me in and told me that Irene was waiting for me.

Irene opened her door before I even knocked.

"In a limo. That's quite an entrance!"

"I thought you'd be away," I said.

"I decided to stay to welcome you!"

"That's so wonderful." I was relieved.

"I'm going tomorrow. I'll stay at my girlfriend's tonight so you don't have to sleep on the floor," she said with a giggle.

That night we went to see *Alice in Concert*, a musical at the Public Theater written and composed by Liz Swados. *Alice* was based on *Alice in Wonderland* and directed by Andrei Serban. Meryl Streep played both Alice and the Queen of Hearts. She wasn't famous yet, but her performance was unforgettable. I remember being wowed by the mercurial ease with which she moved between the roles.

That night, as we walked from Lafayette Street back to Greenwich Village, it felt like all my dreams were going to come true.

Still there was plenty of struggle. New York was not as welcoming to Ed Machado the actor as I had expected, but I managed to get an agent and a few fans when I did a play with Margaret Hamilton, who'd played the Wicked Witch in *The Wizard of Oz*.

I started flying between New York and Los Angeles on People Express, the greatest airline ever. You could buy your tickets on the plane and you paid separately for delicious meals. Five dollars for fried chicken and Mums champagne. Yummy. The plane was always filled with bicoastal actors, so the cabin usually felt like an in-flight pool party. JetBlue is great, but I miss People Express.

In the spring, to my great surprise, I received a letter from the National Endowment for the Arts telling me that I had received a grant for $12,500 for my one-act play *Embroidering*.

That summer I went back to the Padua Hills Writers Conference and acted in three different plays, including one by Irene called *A Visit*, about Victorian sex. We were dressed in authentic Victorian costumes, but the women wore exposed porcelain breasts with a little dark blue line around the nipples. The men wore matching erect porcelain penises with a dark blue line around the head sticking out of their pants.

"All very tasteful," Irene would say.

I noticed that the playwrights at the conference were not happy with my newfound talent, especially once news of the NEA grant was made public. At communal dinners they all stayed away from me, and if I forgot a word in a line while rehearsing, they would accuse me of trying to change the text. I decided to ignore their new hostility and just act. Irene let me sit in on more writing classes but was less kind in her criticism of my work. One night when I was in her apartment at Padua having a cup of wine she let her feelings be known.

"I don't think it's fair that you got all that money for one little play," she announced.

"Why not?" I was hurt.

"All these playwrights have been working for years writing many plays, and then you come along, write thirty pages, and you get a grant. They all applied for that grant. You got it and they didn't. They are very angry at you." She was giving a speech now.

"And you?" I asked.

"I didn't apply," she said. She took a long sip of wine, then cleared her throat.

"Listen, what I really want to talk to you about is that I am starting a training program for Hispanic playwrights at INTAR. They get paid a stipend of one hundred and fifty dollars a week to study with me. A lot of people have applied and . . ."

There was a pause in the conversation. INTAR (International Arts Relations) was the only theater in the country dedicated to producing new works by Latinos. I assumed she was going to ask me to join her class, which would have been an incredible honor. I should have known nothing was that simple with Irene. She took another sip of her wine and looked away from me.

". . . I don't think you are a talented enough writer to be a part of it. You're a wonderful actor. I'm going to do *A Visit* in New York, and of course I want you in it."

I thanked her, trying not to sound hurt.

"You'll be in it?" she asked.

"Of course I will. I love the play." I was relieved that I managed to get a compliment in.

"Good. It will be a whole new cast, so don't tell the actors here. The rest of the cast will be from New York. I am going to put songs into it, too, and you'll have a song."

"That's just great." I smiled and hugged her.

"Look, I just feel you got enough money from the NEA. You might have talent. Obviously someone thinks you do—they gave you the grant, didn't they?"

I felt another speech coming on, but I cut her off.

"You never read the play. So how would you know?" I couldn't believe I'd just said that. There goes the acting job.

"I've heard your exercises." She was defensive now.

"True," I conceded.

She looked at her cup. It was empty.

"I'll let you come to the classes. I just won't pay you. You can be my assistant. How's that?" She looked me straight in the eyes.

I wanted to say no. I was angry. I wanted to show her I didn't need her. I didn't need her consolation prize. But I did need her. I needed to be in her play and I knew she had so much more to teach me. And besides that, I worshipped her: her talent, the way she lived, her honesty.

I lit a cigarette, took a puff, and said, "Sure. I'll be your assistant." A tear rolled down my face, but she pretended not to notice.

"You are my little inspiration. I knew you'd understand! You are going to be wonderful in *A Visit*. I am going to write you a great song, a showstopper." Then she hugged me.

In that moment Maria Irene Fornes was pulling me in opposite directions: loving me, hating me, bringing me into her light, and keeping me in her shadow. All at once. Just like my father.

In the fall of 1981, Hariette moved to New York with me and we rented a studio in a renovated building on Barrow Street just across from Irene. I gave up my West Coast Bieler Diet soon after.

I worked tirelessly to help Irene organize for her classes. The meetings would be held at INTAR's second stage on 53rd Street and 10th Avenue. Their main stage was then at Theatre Row on 42nd and 9th, but we had been given a loft space above their smaller theater. It was a grim looking room at best, clean but spare. Irene saw a raw space ripe for molding minds. We set out to make it more than inhabitable. It had to be inspiring.

My first job was to paint the whole place off-white. Irene had small tables built for each of the students in the group with a couple of extras for guests (and me). The desks were made of pine and it was my job to coat their surfaces with several layers of linseed oil. We bought oak chairs and built coat racks with brass elephant heads bought from a gift shop in Chinatown. We found a very large Oriental rug to do Tai Chi on every morning before we wrote. We bought a coffeemaker and white porcelain cups with a line of blue at the bottom (just like the penis I wore in her play) as well as a set of light blue crystal glasses for water and a dish rack for me to place all the cups and glasses after I washed them at the end of each class. Finally, everything was perfect.

In early October it was time for our first class, which Irene set for nine A.M. A Tai Chi instructor was there to put us through an hour-long workout. Then we sat at the small tables, which I had arranged in a circle. Irene introduced me and her other assistant to the class. The other assistant was an attractive Swedish woman in her late forties, all blonde and body, but with enough brains for Irene to have a sometime affair with her.

The Swede was like a secretary who had to take notes on all the exercises Irene would give us. I would make coffee, serving it while the rest of the class wrote, running errands and cleaning up after the writers left for the day. If I had a spare moment, I sat down and wrote with them. Every time I did, Irene felt she had to call attention to the fact that she was not paying me.

There were six writers in the group, two Cubans—one male, one female—a Chicana, two Puerto Rican men, and a man who said he was from Spain. They were all older than me, and they seemed to agree that I should be treated with contempt. They were jealous because they suspected Irene and I were close in a way they could never hope to be.

And we were. We went to the loft on 53rd Street every day together, even when there were no classes. We'd get there in the morning, write for four hours, and then take a break for lunch. She showed me all her secrets in the Village, the perfect cookie shop on West 4th Street, Joe's Pizza on 6th Avenue, Faicco's and Murray's on Bleecker Street, where we'd buy sausages and cheese for supper. And while she was certainly in culinary command downtown, it was a place we frequented near INTAR that I was most fond of, a Dominican lunch counter called Melys, on 10th Avenue between 44th and 45th Streets.

Usually around two P.M., after the lunch rush, we'd go have a bite. Dominican food is a lot like Cuban food, but without any French pretensions. The beans at Melys were full of Cuban flavor, although they differed in color. *Habichuelas*, as they're called, are red, not black. The texture is similar, and I must admit the red beans can be a little creamier, and almost always easier on my stomach. They served the beans with fluffy white rice and fried plantains cooked whole. The plantains had a chewy, golden brown exterior while the inside stayed soft and sweet. And those were just the sides.

One of my favorite entrees was their sumptuous beef stew. The sauce, while thinner than the Cuban version, was quite flavorful, and its consistency allowed the soft chunks of beef to reign over the dish's minor players of fork-tender aromatics.

Another favorite of mine was their *bacalao*, or salt-cured cod. They prepared the dish in a thin tomato sauce similar to the beef stew, but it was thickened by the very Basque addition of diced potatoes. Clearly, though, it was the salt-cured fish that was the star. The flavor of the *Bacalao* was profoundly familiar, and yet I wasn't sure where or when I had eaten it before. My mother had made it into *croquetas* sometimes, boiling the fish in milk before adding it to the flour and butter and stirring, stirring, stirring, but this was different. This was a flavor I remembered but a preparation I did not. It was a confusing feeling.

Completely grounding, not confusing at all, were the diner's *tostones*. Twice-fried green plantains, not yet sweet and ripe, like thick, fluffy, ovular french fries. They served them with jarringly sour *mojo*, as an appetizer or on the side of a main course.

Green plantains are found all over Latin America in different forms, but I loved the truly Dominican variation of them, *mofongo*, a delicacy I discovered at that lunch counter. Hearty and forceful, *mofongo* is made from green plantains that are boiled and then mashed lightly. The mash is mixed with lots of raw garlic and pork cracklings, pressed into a mold, then fried so the edges get crispy. The whole conglomeration is then topped with spicy gravy, the same consistency as the sauce on the beef stew and *bacalao*. Wow.

Now, Cubans have a dish like *mofongo*, except that it's made from mashed ripe bananas and called *fufu*. Irene told me that was how she got the name for *Fefu*. We would always laugh about that whenever we had *mofongo*. We ate lunch at that counter at least three times a week. Even when we had writing class, we'd eat there alone, never inviting any of the other writers. *Mofongo* with Irene was reason enough to bear the contempt they were so eager to heap on me.

In December of 1981 I opened in *A Visit* at Theater for the New City, a three theater nonprofit institution on 10th Street and Second Avenue in the East Village.

We got mixed reviews, but the *Village Voice* ran a huge picture of me and the three other men in the play doing a soft-shoe with our four porcelain penises. My picture was in the *Village Voice*. I had arrived. Artistically, at least.

After we played a show on Christmas Eve, Hariette and I went to a Cuban restaurant on Fifth Avenue and 11th Street to eat roast pork with all the trimmings. She told me it was getting too cold in New York and that she was going back to L.A. until March when it warmed up again. I knew she hated the cold after long winters growing up in Detroit, but I also knew my East Coast life was getting to be too much for her. I said I'd visit her in February when we had a break from Irene's workshop.

Hariette left a couple of weeks later, and what followed was three months of writing and eating every day with Irene. At one point we had each gained ten pounds, so we decided to go on a diet of cream of broccoli soup made with only garlic, chicken broth, and broccoli, pureed. By the time spring came, I had finished writing my first full-length play, *Fabiola*, half of my second, *The Modern Ladies Of Guanabacoa*, half of another full-length play called *Broken Eggs*, and a one-act musical, *Rosario and the Gypsies*. I had written everything in the workshop and during our days of eating and writing. I was prolific if nothing else.

Then came a little recognition. The Ensemble Studio Theatre on 52nd Street between 10th and 11th Avenues agreed to produce *Rosario and the Gypsies*. The play was a rock-and-roll musical about an avantgarde Flamenco troupe that made a point of not trying to find an audience in San Diego, California. The characters resembled some of the people at Padua Hills. The essence of Rosario was based on Irene, which made her furious. She accused me of stealing her life, but I knew that what really bothered her was that the character was self-serving and obsessed with her art to a fault. All is fair in love and playwriting, I thought. I considered *Rosario* to be payback for the day Irene *didn't* ask me to join her workshop. No revenge like the written word.

Rosario and the Gypsies ran that summer; my friend Rick Vartorella wrote the music and Frank Rich gave us an amazingly positive review in *The New York Times*. He wrote that I was a playwright with real promise. I was terrified of what it would mean if he were right.

Ensemble Studio Theatre agreed to produce *The Modern Ladies of Guanabacoa* the following season. I hadn't even written the second act.

Ready or not, I was a playwright now.

‖ *Bacalao* ‖

Bacalao may be an acquired taste, but in the process of learning to love it, it helps to know what to look for: flavor and texture. The predominant flavors are salt and fish, two tastes that would be overpowering if you were to eat the stuff right out of the bag. The texture of the fish is quite chewy, too, as the salt cure has removed most of its moisture. Twelve hours is the minimum soaking time needed to remove most of the saltiness but twenty-four is ideal. The twenty-minute boil helps to tenderize the fish. It is possible to consider the *bacalao* as a supporting player, as the heft and heartiness of this dish comes from the potatoes. But when you taste the finished product, it's clear that the fresh, briny flavor of the cod is the star.

1 pound boneless *bacalao* (salt cod)
½ cup olive oil
1 pound russet potatoes, peeled and cut into ½-inch cubes
1 Spanish onion, peeled and cut into ¼-inch dice
½ red pepper, stem and seeds removed, cut into ¼-inch dice
1 teaspoon salt
½ teaspoon ground black pepper
4 garlic cloves, peeled and finely chopped
½ cup white wine
1 cup water
1 tablespoon distilled white vinegar
Two 8-ounce cans Goya tomato sauce
2 tablespoons finely chopped flat leaf parsley

1. Rinse the *bacalao* thoroughly and place it in a sealable plastic container. Cover with cold water and soak at least 12 hours, or up to 24. Change the water at least once halfway through.

2. After soaking, pour off the water, then transfer the *bacalao* to a large pot or Dutch oven. Cover again with cold water and bring to

a boil over medium-high heat. Cook at a rolling boil, uncovered, until the *bacalao* is softened, 20 minutes. Drain the fish in a colander and set aside until cool enough to handle. Slice or tear the *bacalao* into bite-size chunks. Discard any bones if you find them. Set aside until ready to use.

3. In the same large pot or Dutch oven, heat the olive oil over medium-high heat. Add the potatoes and cook, stirring often, until softened slightly, 4 minutes. Add the onion and bell pepper. Season with the salt and black pepper and cook, stirring, 3 minutes more. Add the garlic and cook, stirring, 1 minute more.

4. Add the wine, water, vinegar, and tomato sauce. Bring to a boil, stirring occasionally and scraping any caramelized bits off the bottom of the pot using a wooden spoon. Add the *bacalao* and stir gently, trying not to break up the fish too much. Reduce the heat to medium and simmer, covered, until the potatoes are cooked through, about 20 minutes, stirring every 5 minutes to make sure the potatoes don't stick to the bottom of the pot. Transfer to a serving dish, garnish with parsley, and serve with white rice.

Makes 6 servings

❙ *Tostones with Quick Mojo* ❙

Although I love *mofongo* and its exotic Dominican flavors, it is this preparation of unripe green plantains that I believe I could eat every day. To me they are like tropical french fries. Clearly they are bananas, with the familiar shape and subtle sweetness. But since the unripened green plantain still has lots of starch in it, this method of frying them twice gives you a satisfying crunch that is sure to become addictive. This is also a therapeutic recipe. My mother once gave me a kitchen gadget to smash the plantains in step 3, but these days I like to use parchment paper and a heavy skillet to take out all the frustrations of a long day in New York.

For the quick mojo:
½ cup lime juice
1 garlic clove, peeled and very finely chopped
1 teaspoon salt

For the plantains:
4 green plantains
2 cups vegetable oil

1. Prepare the quick *mojo*: Combine the lime juice, garlic, and salt in a small bowl. Mix with a fork and set aside.

2. Cut off both ends of each plantain and make a shallow incision along the length of the peel without cutting through the flesh. Peel the skin off by pulling outward from the center of the incision. Cut each plantain into 1-inch chunks.

3. Heat the vegetable oil in a 10- to 12-inch skillet with raised edges over medium-high heat until very hot (about 375°F). Fry the plantains, 8 at a time, turning once, 1 minute per side. The plantains should be cooked but not browned. Adjust the heat if necessary. As they're done, transfer the cooked plantains to a paper towel lined–plate using a slotted spoon. Set aside until cool enough to handle. Repeat with remaining plantains, then turn off the heat.

4. Place a piece of plantain between 2 pieces of parchment paper or 2 brown paper bags. Squash to ⅛-inch thickness using the bottom of a heavy skillet. Pull the plantain off the paper and set aside until ready to fry again. Repeat with the remaining plantains.

5. Bring the oil back to frying temperature (about 375°F) over medium-high heat. Fry the plantains 6 at a time until crispy and

golden around the edges, 1 minute per side. Using a slotted spoon, transfer the *tostones* to a paper towel–lined plate and sprinkle with a pinch of coarse salt. Repeat with the remaining plantains.

6. Serve immediately with the quick *mojo*, or reheat in a 350°F oven for 5 minutes after all the *tostones* are cooked. Do not keep the *tostones* warm for too long or they will get soggy.

Makes about 24 *tostones*

Ten

Sinking

After a summer surrounded by my plants in the searing heat of the California sun, I said good-bye to Hariette and returned to New York to begin work on the Ensemble Studio Theatre production of *The Modern Ladies Of Guanabacoa*. At the time the play was called *Maria Joséfa Circa 1929*, but Curt Dempster, the artistic director of EST, decided it would have to change.

"Maria Joséfa Circa, what?" Curt said when I walked into his office. "It's a play about bus drivers. What kind of title is that?"

Curt was not the kind of personality you saw in the theater all that often. He was a mixture of contradictions: tall and patrician with a rough-hewn edge. He was the consummate theater professional, and a mountain climber in his spare time.

"You are not García Lorca. You know what I mean?" I knew, but how to find the right title?

I had written a play about my family. I knew that much. But whose story was most important? My grandfather Oscar was a central character, with the main action of the play following his plan to convince Manuela's father, Eurgenio, to sell his butcher business to finance his dream of owning a bus company. I loved writing a young Oscar, a young Eurgenio, and imagining the machinations that made possible the life my family went on to lead.

Maybe then the story was about the family as a whole, unable to resist change, willing to give up their traditions to attain their dreams of fortune and power. Every title I came up with was worse than the next: *The Lie Underneath the Lie*, *The Buses*, *Every Nickel Counts*, or worst of all, *We Are in the Money!*

Maria Joséfa Circa 1929 did something right. It played up the importance of the matriarch of the family, which is probably why Curt accused me of trying to sound like Lorca. We began our search for a director while the title continued to elude me.

It was early September, and the show was set to start rehearsals in January, so I met with many directors, several famous old ones, even more not so famous young ones. I didn't connect with any of them. I wanted Shirley Kaplan, the woman who had directed *Rosario and the Gypsies* so beautifully, but Curt Dempster would not have it.

"This play is about Oscar Hernandez (yes, I used my grandfather's real name)," he said, "an orphan who seduces a family into giving him their business." He made it sound so cold. "It needs a man's touch. *Rosario and the Gypsies* was a whole other thing. It was avant-garde and about a woman." Curt had a habit of saying things like this at a dramatically amplified volume.

I had only been back in New York for about a month, but it was a trying time. Nothing seemed to be clicking and I was starting to run low on cash, as the money from my NEA grant had nearly run out. I started looking for a part-time job, but fortunately I was saved. The phone rang in the loft I was renting a room and a gruff voice grumbled over the line, "This is Al Pacino. Someone at the studio told me you were Cuban and that you were talented. I need help with a script. I am playing a Cuban in a movie and I don't know if the guy sounds Cuban."

I thought it was one of my friends playing a prank. All my friends knew I was a big fan of Mr. Pacino. I even tried to dress like him, in suits and trench coats, Armani if possible, a passable knockoff otherwise. So when the phantom voice asked for my address, I gave it to him and waited for one of my friends to call me and tell me it was all a joke. About half an hour later there was buzz at the door. I went downstairs to laugh off the prank, but when I opened the door I stood face to face with Al Pacino ... maybe not quite face to face, but he was there. I had to steady myself.

"Eduardo?"

"Yeah."

"Nice to meet you. Here is the script. Here is my number. Can you read it tonight? Call me after you read it. I need you to make me sound Cuban." He spun on his heels and was gone as fast as he appeared.

I hovered in the foyer, opened the screenplay, and read aloud, *Scarface*.

I read the script through in record time. I really just wanted to get it over with. It was so crass. I was appalled that anybody would think Cubans were like the characters in the script.

I made up my mind. I refused to be part of such an ugly story. My resolve lasted about twenty minutes, and then I remembered that Al Pacino was a hero of mine. Plus, I only had fifty dollars in the bank. Finally I buckled and called Al and told him I thought I could help him. He asked me to come to his house the next day and to bring a copy of my play, *Maria Joséfa* something.... I began to respond, but he had already hung up.

The next day I met with him and we read from *Maria Joséfa* something, Al Pacino and I, together in his living room. Out loud.

When we finished the play he paused. He closed the script, looked at me hard and said, "I like Oscar Hernandez. Good ear for dialogue. I know you can help me. Tomorrow I want you to see Marty Bregman so you can decide on a rate."

I had no writing agent, so I was forced to negotiate with Marty Bregman on my own behalf. He was an imposing man on looks alone, well dressed and solid, in his sixties but full of energy. His power made him even more intimidating, but I worked out a deal with him while he was having his shoes polished in his big Midtown office overlooking downtown Manhattan.

"Make him happy with his dialogue. That's your only job. Do not change the structure of the film. Or anyone else's lines. Only Al's. Make him sound Cuban."

We agreed on $1,500 a week. A fortune! As I was walking out of his office he asked, "Don't you want your shoes polished? I'll pay."

I showed him my feet. I was wearing tennis shoes. He scoffed silently but took the opportunity to reinforce his superiority.

"You're a smart boy. Do not fuck with the structure, you hear me?"

I nodded yes as I walked out the door.

I wanted to make Al Pacino sound more Cuban than Desi Arnaz, more Cuban than Fidel. I worked tirelessly, rewriting every little line, every little word, anything he had a problem with. In exchange, he taught me what a great actor expects from a part. Three months later I was fired. I was told it was because Mr. Pacino was heading to Los Angeles to prepare for the film. The real reason was that I had become a fan of the original Howard Hawks *Scarface*, the one starring Paul Muni.

After I watched the film about ten times, I met with Al to discuss it. I suggested integrating an incestuous subtext into the relationship between Al's character, Tony Montana, and his sister Gina. Al loved the idea, but I was fired anyway. I had definitely tried to fuck with the structure.

Unfortunately, in many moves from sublet to sublet, I lost the pages I had worked on for Mr. Pacino. I'm not sure which, if any, of my rewrites made it into the film. All I know is Al sounded Cuban enough to make the movie a classic, and my paystub said "dialogue coach."

Working on *Scarface* had made me some quick change, which left me free to meet every single director who was interested in *Maria Joséfa Circa 1929*. We went through the entire list of Curt's suggestions and I was made increasingly nervous as each candidate was rejected. In my pronounced state of anxiety I began to understand exactly what I was deciding on. *Maria Joséfa Circa 1929* was supposed to be fiction. And yet it was about Oscar Hernandez. What exactly was I sharing in my writing, and why was it making me so nervous? I knew there was a little distance between me and the material, but I also knew that I had mined some of the most powerful themes and secrets from my family's history to write the play. And this was only the beginning. Whomever we chose to direct would have to be someone who understood the depth of those themes, someone I could trust with those secrets. I spent most of my days convincing myself that I hadn't made some terrible mistake.

Then one brisk, sunny day in late October, I walked into the lobby of the Ensemble Studio Theatre to find a tall, thin man with gray hair and a beard removing bicycle clips from his pants. I knew who I was meeting, but I was surprised to see that he rode a bicycle. I introduced myself.

"Hi, I'm Eduardo," I said shyly.

"Jamie," he said, extending his hand. Jamie. As in James Hammerstein, the son of Oscar Hammerstein II, the man who wrote the musicals I had worshipped from Porter Junior High School up to that very day.

My friends in the theater had told me that Jamie was too conventional to direct my lyrical play. Maybe, I thought, but maybe lyricism is not at all what I'm looking for. Maybe what I need is naturalism.

I looked at him hard. His eyes moved quickly, and I could tell he was nervous. I thought, how strange for someone that tall to be that nervous. He began to chatter like he only had a moment to get it all out.

"So, your play. It really touched me. I thought it was very funny. You're ... original. Very original."

Funny, I thought? Original? I liked that much better than lyrical. He went on.

"But let me tell you, if I am going to direct this, we have a lot of work to do. I mean, there is also a lot of bullshit in it, too." I laughed, strangely relieved.

"Yes, there is a lot of bullshit." We both chuckled then.

"I know we are going to be able to work together," Jamie said, "so we meet at my house tomorrow."

"Yes!" I said, "tomorrow."

"It's 100 Prince Street, third floor. In SoHo. You know where that is?"

"Downtown," I said.

"I'll tell Curt it's all settled," he said. Suddenly he was taking charge; his nervousness was gone. He went into Curt's office and shut the door.

I almost tried to follow him in. I think I would have gone wherever he asked me to go. Not that he had power over me in a dominant sense. It was more like a gravitational pull, an unavoidable force that connected us, drawing us in the same direction. I didn't know where we were headed; I didn't even know if I had any say in the matter. Part of me wanted to leave EST then and there, just to avoid all that possibility. Then I noticed that Jamie's book bag was still there, bike clips and all. He had to return to pick it up. I wasn't sure what his return would bring, but something made me feel that I should wait for him. I took out my notebook and started to write. A few minutes later he walked in, tapped my back, and said, "It's all settled."

"Thank you," I said, feeling very little distance between the pages I was writing and the face in front of me. He picked up his book bag.

"Want to have lunch? They make the best turkey sandwiches across the street."

I nodded and put my notebook away, deciding that for now this was reality.

So we went to a diner on 52nd Street and Eleventh Avenue. The place was filled with truck drivers and the gals who love to serve them. We sidled up to a booth and Jamie went to the counter to order.

He returned with what were indeed the best turkey sandwiches I have ever had. They baked the turkeys every morning, then sliced them thin with a long serrated knife. They smeared mustard and mayo on spongy white bread piled high with both white and dark meat. Grilled onions to top it off, and a couple toothpicks to (barely) hold the whole thing together.

I bit into white meat that was just as tender and flavorful as the dark underneath and chewed a huge mouthful until I noticed Jamie looking at me. He reached across the table with a napkin and wiped a dab of mustard that had escaped from the confines of the sandwich. He was so gentle in his gesture, wiping from the side of my chin to the corner of my mouth. Finally, I thought, someone who wants to take care of me.

The next day I took the N train to SoHo and got off at Prince

Street. I looked up at the strange buildings, more like factories than houses. I had never been that far downtown before. I assumed New York ended on Houston Street. But there I was, south of Houston, staring skyward in the middle of an upmarket industrial block.

There was an art gallery on the bottom floor of Jamie's building at 100 Prince Street. The building was painted white and there were two other identical buildings on either side. Both also had art galleries on the main floor. I rang the bell for number three and I heard Jamie's voice.

"I'll come down and get you," he called through the intercom.

Down he came in an old-fashioned iron elevator that opened directly onto the street. He opened the sliding gate on the elevator, then the front door with a welcoming flourish.

"Good to see you. Come on in."

He pulled on a rubber rope, slid a hand crank, and up we went.

Then he opened the gate onto the loft, a big open space. The first thing I saw was a gold metallic waterbed. Low couches were clustered in welcoming arrangements, brightly colored pop paintings straddled the stretch to the ceiling. There was a kitchen in the middle of the space and a long wooden table for ten with gold metal legs and wooden cane chairs. A black grand piano was bathed in sunlight from the enormous windows. Doors that seemed miniscule in such space led to bedrooms and bathrooms around the perimeter. We sat down on one of the couches to read *Maria Joséfa Circa 1929*.

We worked every day in that cavernous space. It was cold at first, so big, so New York. If I needed to make a phone call or get a glass of water, I felt immediately uncomfortable. I asked politely no matter how many times I had to use the bathroom. But as I met with Jamie regularly, the details of his life started filling the place with a warmth that only comes with familiarity. I learned that he had a wife named Dena, his third, younger than he was, and that they had a young son named Simon. He had children from other marriages, too, a son, Andy, a daughter, Jenny, and another son, Will. He would talk about them all with great affection as we worked, referring to them or other personal experiences to help me dig deeper and deeper in rewrites of the script. It was inspiring, to say the very least, to hear tales of his mother, Dorothy, his father, Oscar, and his childhood friend Steven Sondheim. The play got better and better.

Auditions began in November and one day in the middle of the first scene an actress auditioning for Manuela read her line, "We will be the modern ladies of Guanabacoa."

Jamie hit me on the back and said, "There's the title."

And so *Maria Joséfa Circa 1929* became *The Modern Ladies of Guanabacoa.*

Jamie had come up with the title, and that was fine. What surprised me was how easily I gave in. I was learning that my writing was not something that was going to remain a secret. It was not going to be something that I did late at night or in Irene's class, something that only a few people would see. I was going to have to share it, and people might actually hear it, and, worse, have something to say about it. That was a scary thought. But a title decided on in a room full of people working on my play was a good reality check. I was going to have to get used to fighting my private demons in a very public sector.

Already I had paid a price in life for what I had written on the page. *Rosario and the Gypsies* had made dealing with Irene nearly impossible. She had been so personally affected by the play, and while I did want to rile her up a little, I ultimately saw *Rosario* as a farcical, musical love letter to the Padua Hills Writers Conference. If Irene couldn't separate herself from *Rosario*, what would my family feel about *The Modern Ladies?*

I found some understanding a few weeks into rehearsals. I had just seen the Stephen Frears movie *Sammy and Rosie Get Laid*, about the son of an anticolonial freedom fighter whose father visits him after a long absence. In the course of the movie the son, Sammy, learns that his father's political past contains an abundance of morally questionable behavior.

The night I saw the movie I found it impossible to sleep. I was deeply connected to the theme: internal conflict of trying to love a father figure whose behavior was reprehensible. Beyond that, Sammy had to make decisions about his life and his father with very little confirmed information. I wondered how I had arrived at the statements I made in my play, and I questioned their validity as they related to the creativity of my work and the reality of my family. I doubted the journey of my grandfather from fruit vendor to transportation executive. I dreamed up a dozen possible suspects who could have shot my great grandfather Eurgenio, several of whom were relatives of mine. I thought maybe it wasn't his mistress's husband who shot him, and maybe that was why the violence was never readily acknowledged in my family. The idea of secrecy surrounding so many events amplified their sinister potential until they loomed like bogeymen in my head.

Then, one day in rehearsal, the actor playing Oscar asked a simple question.

"Did I, Oscar, kill my father-in-law?"

I stood up in the audience and screamed at the stage, "No of course not!"

Jamie waited and then said, "I think, for the play, it's better if we think Oscar killed him."

I was stunned. What had I done? The words in my script had led Jamie and the actor to make that decision. And even though it did work for the play, I felt like I had destroyed the memory of my grandfather. Ultimately, that was the journey I had to take. I challenged myself to consider all the scary possibilities I could imagine, even if they made me uncomfortable, so that I could come back with the truth. What I really came back with was a dramatic situation that gave the appearance of truth. It wasn't Oscar who killed my great grandfather. Onstage that idea felt better, worked better, but the burden of that translation was on my shoulders, and I felt guilty. I tried to tell myself that Oscar forgave me. After all, he was alive onstage every night, and he would live forever on the page.

When *The Modern Ladies of Guanabacoa* opened, I felt somewhat vindicated when Frank Rich wrote that the play had epic dimensions, and that I was showing how Cuba came kicking and screaming into the twentieth century. I came to the ecstatic realization that my play, and every character in it, was speaking for my country, for Cuba. Their personal struggles and conflicts had taken on a broader context, and so the secrets of my family became secondary to their mythology.

Still, I had to deal with all my relatives, an exceptional challenge, especially in their reception of my play *Fabiola*, a darker play than *The Modern Ladies*, full of anguish and torment, and yes, family secrets. The play is about two Cuban brothers, one recently widowed, who have an affair with each other before and during Fidel's Revolution. I used memories of my uncles and cousins to inspire the play. In terms of incest, and real life, I'm not sure who was involved, or what really happened, but I don't think it matters. I wanted the play to capture the unspoken rules and desires of a big Cuban family in a dramatically charged era. Furthermore, I wanted to purge myself of some of my own deeply buried desires, in a way that I never would have been able to in real life.

All of this internal juggling feels very natural when you're writing a play. New rules of logic are formed with every scene, every line of dialogue. But working on *The Modern Ladies* with Jamie made me understand that the process of writing is very different from the finished piece. When the play is fully formed it makes a statement, and that is what people absorb and ultimately judge. I started wondering about the statements I was making in *Fabiola*.

Was I writing the truth about my family, about our secrets? More importantly, what would be the price if I was writing the truth? What would my father say? My mother? Cuca? And who was I to tell the truth in the first place?

Fabiola was, in fact, the name of my Uncle Pipo's wife, who died in childbirth. She and her baby had died just a few months before I was born. Her spirit had haunted my childhood, literally during my fainting spells, and figuratively in every whispered memory shared between relatives as if she'd walk into the room at any moment. So, even if I didn't have all the facts, Fabiola was just as much a part of my life as anyone else's. Did I not have the right to express it? I wasn't sure. All I knew was that the process of writing was saving me from the specters of my past and I had no choice but to keep going. On to *Broken Eggs*.

I had written ten pages of *Broken Eggs* in Irene's workshop, but after the success of *Modern Ladies*, I wrote the rest of the play in two weeks. This was due, in no small part, to the ease and immediacy with which the play was connected to real events.

When my sister Jeanette got married in 1979, the entire family came to L.A. from Miami for the wedding. The topic on everyone's tongue was whether or not my father would bring his new Argentinian wife. He did, which infuriated the rest of the family and made me want to kill him. And that's the plot of *Broken Eggs*.

I wrote the play two years after Jeannette's wedding, but I still felt an overwhelming anger toward my father. When I realized that I could channel this anger into the play, something broke wide open inside of me. The anger and its release fueled me, it filled me with rage and humor and passion, and I didn't care anymore whether it would make my family hate me. *Broken Eggs* begins with the following lines:

Mimi: I never thought that any of us would get married, after all—
Lizette: Pretend you come from a happy home.
Mimi: We were the audience to one of the worst in the history of the arrangement.
Lizette: Well, I'm going to pretend that Mom and Dad are together for today.
Mimi: That's going to be hard to do if that mustached bitch, whore, cunt, Argentinian Nazi shows up to your wedding.

My father never saw the play. But these lines got back to him and he stopped speaking to me. As word spread among the rest of the Miami contingent, everybody piled on the wagon of mass resentment. I was persona non grata in Miami for a long time after that.

The family at Jeanette's wedding, Woodland Hills, 1979

My mother, however, happily hung a framed copy of the play's *New York Times* review on the wall of her family room so my father would see it every time he came over to see my sisters.

Broken Eggs also marked the beginning of the end of my marriage. The character in the play that most resembled me was openly gay, not married to someone older than him. In fact, since Hariette had been spending less and less time in New York as my career gained momentum, I had started having occasional affairs with men. It never really felt like a big deal to me. I had always considered sexuality to be fluid, especially after my West Coast Reichian indoctrination where truly anything was allowed. Like I've said, the rules of living get blurry when you're buried in the theater, so it didn't actually occur to me that I was doing anything wrong until Hariette confronted me about *Broken Eggs*.

The cast of Broken Eggs *at Repertorio Español*

"Why does he do that?" she asked. "Why is he like that?"

I looked at her long and hard, and finally said, "It's my writing. And I cannot lie in my writing." I focused on the writing, but I was talking about so much more. She decided to ignore me, and the truth, for as long as she could.

After I finished *Broken Eggs*, writing became a conscious act of rebellion against those who tried to stop me from being myself. I was finally in control of my past and my future through the stage. I had been right,—the theater had saved me.

I had three plays that went together: *Modern Ladies, Fabiola*, and *Broken Eggs*. Jamie's wife, Dena, kept saying that they should be a trilogy, and that we had to find a title for all of them, but we could not come up with one. We found the title one day in a reading of *Fabiola* starring the incomparable Diane Venora as Sonia, the character I had based on my mother.

The idea for the title came in a scene between Sonia and her mother-in-law, when Sonia laments the loss of all the traditions she'd have to leave behind after the failure of the Bay of Pigs. At the prospect of moving to "a country where they don't even have bidets?!" Sonia tries to express her loss by sharing a recipe she'll never forget.

> I will always remember how to make Floating Islands. First you make an egg custard with milk, cornstarch, and three eggs. And a teaspoon of vanilla, of course. Then the syrup: a cup of sugar to two cups of water, and brandy to taste. While it's cooking you make the meringue: two tablespoons of sugar to each egg white and a little cream of tartar so they stay firm and fluffy. I know how to make them the right consistency so they stay firm. When the syrup starts to boil, you throw in the custard one spoonful at a time. Then you put a spoonful of meringue on top. If you're lucky they'll float, little islands like Key Biscayne. I can always get them to float.

As soon as the speech ended, I bolted out of the little theater in SoHo where we were holding the reading. I ran out into the street, overwhelmed by Diane, the speech, the way she stuttered just a little as the emotional potency of the words bloomed with all the heartache that I had felt since I was a child. The emotions were too intense. I was left wondering what connected Diane Venora and me? How was it that all the longing I had ever felt came out of her while she was basically repeating a recipe?

I wandered through the streets, and reality began to dissolve. I must have been on Mulberry Street—I know I was near Little Italy at least—but the details here get hazy. A crowd suddenly surrounded me, taking up the much-needed space my overflowing head was seeking. I couldn't move. Then a religious procession started coming down the street. There were candles, and music, and a statue of the Virgin Mary carried on a litter. I didn't know if I was in Manhattan or Guanabacoa. The revelers could have been Italians or Cubans. I could have been inside the world of one of my plays, projected into life, living on a stage larger than any theater. I felt like the only audience member who knew what was actually going on, but even I didn't have a clue. I stumbled, several hours later, into the loft at 100 Prince Street. Jamie was there with Dena. Hariette was waiting impatiently with a friend of hers. She wanted to leave immediately, but Dena stopped us.

"All the plays. Together. They should be called Floating Islands," she said.

I laughed, too exhausted to cry.

A floating island. That's me, I thought. If I was lucky, I would be able to float, past my own insecurities, through this hurricane of conflicting realities, into my new life as a writer. After everything that had happened, some part of me still felt like turning away and running. Possibility had become actuality.

That fall Jamie directed *Fabiola* at Theater for the New City. Frank Rich said it was in bad taste. But a week later it opened at the Ensemble Studio Theatre in Los Angeles, and all the critics there called it a major work. But, more importantly, my mother, sisters, and brother came to the play. My father refused to see it.

I was shaking during the first act of the play. I waited in the lobby until intermission, when my brother rushed up to me and said, "I never knew you loved me that much." He kissed me and hugged me tight.

My sisters were excited and proud, although no one mentioned the family secrets behind the play, or where the story had come from. "Good," I thought, "if they think it's fiction, then it must be fiction." I had been so scared of the truth that it never occurred to me that my family might rather believe in the drama. I felt slightly dizzy.

I had to leave before the show ended to catch a plane back to New York. So, after saying good-bye to my siblings, I went outside. My mother followed me.

She called out, "Tomorrow, call me."

"Yes," I answered. Shit. Maybe this wasn't going to be as easy as I thought.

On the red-eye to New York I agonized over what my mother might say. "You have demeaned all of us." Or "The only person in the family that's a pervert is you!" Or maybe (and it was a big maybe) she'd just say, "Thank you for telling the truth."

The next morning I waited until it was 8:30 in Los Angeles before calling. Mother answered after the first ring.

"I thought you'd be calling early," she said.

"So?" I said, wanting to cut to the chase.

She took a short breath, then said, "I knew who everyone was as soon as they walked in, even before they said a line."

"Everyone?"

"Yes," she said, "your grandmother, your aunt, your father." Big pause. "By the way, the girl that was supposed to be me, I didn't like her party dress. It looked cheap. I would never have worn a dress like that."

"Okay," I was bewildered.

"I hope your sisters weren't shocked by what you wrote."

"They are old enough to hear the truth," I mumbled.

"Not Michelle."

"She knows what's going on," I said.

"I hope not," Mother said. Another pause. "I just hope you never have that play done in Miami."

"Don't worry," I said. Was that it? I thought we were about to hang up, but then Mother spoke again.

"By the way, your father did not have an affair with his brother. He was kind to him after his wife died. That's all."

"Fine," I said, unable to argue with this woman who clearly had her own rules. I wondered if she'd ever understand mine.

"But anyway," she added, "it's still fiction." Maybe she understood more than I thought. With that we each hung up our phones.

One day while watching a performance of *Fabiola* in Los Angeles, I decided to make the Floating Islands trilogy into a quartet. I thought to myself, you've missed the most important moment, when the family lost everything. So that summer, at Hariette's house in Pasadena, I wrote *In the Eye of the Hurricane*, a play about how Oscar and Manuela lost their bus company to Fidel Castro. I felt the play was an act of forgiveness, after everything I had put them through in my world of plays. I needed to tell people what tragic characters they really were.

Jamie and I did several readings of *In the Eye of the Hurricane*, only to realize that while it was an exciting play, the ending didn't work. After the buses are taken away and Oscar is drunk from drowning his sorrows, Maria Joséfa, the character based on my great grandmother, dies. Oscar, Manuela, and her brother, Mario, toast to "the end of a noble life," and the play ends, without any drama. So one night I rewrote the scene. In it, Mario accuses Oscar and Manuela of stealing money from the bus company for their own use. When Oscar and Manuela exit, Mario looks through their account books and tells the family maid, Rosa, that they're just a bunch of mafiosos. He tells Rosa how awful it has been for him to have spent his life in a room next to his mother. Rosa merely replies, "You should have moved the bed," and the play ends. Mario had become a communist, and my grandparents gangsters. I had betrayed my grandparents again, but, of course, it worked dramatically.

That year, 1988, Repertorio Español, a theater company in Manhattan dedicated to producing plays in Spanish, decided to produce a translation of *Broken Eggs* called *Revoltillo*. They took the show to a festival in Miami and they wanted me to come, but I refused. I had not seen my extended family in a while, and they were all coming to the play. Dealing with them, all the aunts and uncles and cousins, after I had been away so long and written so unflinchingly about them, was not something I was prepared to do.

The night they performed the play, I heard from the director, René Busch, how shocked he was that the audience had booed from the first line. They had screamed obscenities like "faggots," "communists," and "whores." After the show a relative of mine had actually gone up to Rene and told him that if they ever brought *Fabiola* to Miami, they would bomb the theater. René said, "Eduardo, I thought you were paranoid, but you were right. These people don't get you. Stay away from Miami, and stay away from your family."

It was hard, but I accepted that the Miami contingent would never understand me or my work, be it fact, fiction, or somewhere in between. I couldn't help the matter, so I resolved to never let my family hurt me again. I was shocked at the freedom I felt to no longer live in fear of their judgments. I was even more shocked by how much I missed the fear, by how much it defined who I was.

I remembered meeting Hariette and being scared of salad. The idea that eating a few greens would somehow change me seemed ridiculous, but I felt it deeply. I was not a salad eater. If I became one, would I still be myself? Or did I need to hold on to that old persona to exist recognizably? Who would I be if I was not scared of my family and what they said about my writing?

Instead of worrying too much about my new identity, I dedicated myself to the work, and the freedom I found within it. I was fascinated by the world around me, supported and cared for by new friends and family. Practically overnight I knew that my life in Los Angeles was over. It wasn't that I had to get away. It wasn't that I was particularly unhappy, either, but there was room for a whole new me in New York, and I felt most comfortable in that skin. The facts of the transition were not so simple, but the truth of where and who I was wouldn't allow for any other way. It was inevitable that a few people would end up getting hurt in the process.

While I had always been a little bisexual, once I hit my thirties I could feel my sexual pendulum swing toward men exclusively. There had always been homosexual themes in my plays. I had known about sex in all its permutations, instinctively, primally, since my childhood when I would watch my cousin Hugo showing off as he rode his dark brown stallion. My shift to dating men began secretly at first, but I soon brought all my internal contradictions into the light.

Hariette and I began an ugly separation that lasted for years. While it didn't always make sense to me, I had a new life, and I was ready to start living it.

In the spring of 1990 I found a new friend to go with my new life. I was in California rehearsing a play at the Los Angeles Theater Center called *Stevie Wants to Play the Blues.* I felt the play was the most intimate I had written to date even though it was not about Cuba or my family. I was suddenly a writer without a past. What a relief.

The story was inspired by the life of Billy Tipton, a female jazz musician who pretended to be a man to get into the business. Amy Madigan was the star, having just finished the film *Field of Dreams.* She was funny and feisty and beautifully androgynous, like nobody I had ever met. And though she was nervous about having to play the piano onstage, she held her head high with the drive and confidence of a film star.

All this would have been enough to endear her to me, but I really fell for Amy as I watched her act. She knew she couldn't get away with a half-assed job, and so she threw herself into the play with obsessive fervor. I watched, fascinated, as she created the role of Stevie. I marveled at how she managed to materialize the darkest, most hidden, gender-bending side of myself right before my frightened eyes. I knew Amy's husband, Ed Harris, from the summers in Padua. He too uneasily registered Amy's transformation as it happened. He saw how complete it was, and he must have sensed how much closer it made her to me. None of this was spoken about at the time. We all just worked and worked under the helpful eye of the English actor, writer, and director Simon Callow.

Stevie helped me rediscover my respect for the theater. It was such a pure experience, perfectly exemplified by the way Amy went into the show as one person and came out entirely different. Billy Tipton had to transform to realize her dreams, and Amy Madigan did it eight shows a week. My own transformation took longer but was just as intense. Everything seemed to reflect everything else, and though it might have been chaotic, there was a through line. We were all subject to the power of art and its ability to change everything.

My God, I thought, I have come so far from my roots. I have become my own creation.

The play got a mixed review in the *Los Angeles Times* but raves everywhere else, and people were coming in droves that filled the four hundred seat theater nightly. It was a hit! The excitement (and the audiences) quickly overwhelmed me, so I went to New York and hid, but I was immediately in planning mode.

The attention I had received in L.A. made me want more. I plotted for the one thing I had wanted since seeing Angela Lansbury and Bea Arthur in *Mame* when I was just thirteen. I was going to get a play produced at the Mark Taper Forum, the biggest regional theater in Los Angeles.

I saw my chance when I was asked by Oskar Eustis, then employed as the theater's director of new projects, to teach a writing class in late 1990. While I was there, I persuaded Oskar to hold a reading of *The Floating Island Plays*. He eagerly agreed, and we read all four plays over a weekend at the Taper. I became playwright-in-residence soon after, receiving a large grant from the Pew Charitable Trusts that enabled me to work out of the theater.

Over the next few years we had workshops of *The Floating Island Plays*. Gordon Davidson, the artistic director of the Taper, hired Oskar to direct the workshops and ultimately the productions of all four plays, which were slated to open in the fall of 1994.

I became bicoastal, traveling between New York and L.A. when work called me in either direction. On one trip back east in early 1993 I went to New Haven for a production of *Once Removed*, my play about a wealthy Cuban family that loses everything after the Revolution and moves to Dallas, Texas, then Los Angeles. The play was produced at the Long Wharf Theatre by Betty Ann Solinger, a very sophisticated Upper East Sider who had taken an interest in my plays. Betty Ann was chic, smart, tall, blonde, and classy, and she wanted to help mold my future. Frank Rich came to review the show. He was about to retire as the head theater critic for *The New York Times*, but not before giving me a lovely front page review. It was a parting gift that I appreciated tremendously.

In 1994 I was in the middle of rehearsing *The Floating Island Plays* at the Taper. I was on my own once again, but I felt like there were people watching every move I made. There were stories about me and my family everywhere, in *The New York Times Magazine*, on the cover of the *L.A. Times Calendar*, and countless others. It was a big deal for the Taper to devote two slots out of their season to one playwright.

The production itself was a disaster. The entire idea was ill conceived. The four plays ran a total of eight hours. Audiences would have the choice of seeing *Modern Ladies* and *In the Eye of the Hurricane* one night, or *Fabiola* and *Broken Eggs* the next. There would also be a marathon showing of all four plays on weekends. When the producers realized how much they would end up paying people in overtime, they decided that I should cut two full hours from the plays. My rewrites, in an attempt to make the story more cohesive after the big cuts, just seemed to sink the plays further.

Most of the major critics enjoyed slashing me to pieces after my fifteen minutes of pre-Taper fame. *The Hollywood Reporter* and *The New Yorker* ran blessedly good reviews. John Lahr came to my defense, calling me a modern day Molière, but to me and the theater world it was a total failure, something I had somehow managed to avoid in more than a decade of life as a playwright.

If I was my own creation, how had this happened? The life I dreamed of had given me what I wanted, then taken it away, and I had to figure out who I was all over again. I was a mess, for sure, but I came away from the experience with an emptiness inside me again, so I felt strangely myself.

I went back to New York and did little but lay in bed. In the mornings I would lift my head, but I had forgotten how to get up. Everyone stopped calling. In the early dawn, after a stint of sleepless tossing and turning, I'd start shaking as the sun rose. After about three hours of shaking I'd need a taste of something and so, fuelled by the promise of caffeine, I'd wander down to the Lower East Side to drink a barrio version of *café con leche* as slowly as possible. I wanted to delay my return to the purgatory of my bedroom, where I would end up in the early afternoon, shaking for the rest of the day.

Me, in a publicity photo from The Floating Island Plays, *1994*

I had started teaching writing in 1990. I put the word out and got a succession of adjunct positions at Sarah Lawrence, Columbia, and NYU. I mixed Irene's techniques with Stanislavski's method via David Alexander and adapted the whole amalgamation to teach writing. The results must have had a lasting effect because a month after the Floating Islands fiasco a group of students I had taught at NYU four years before reappeared to support me. They were the only people calling, and I was grateful.

The students, Colette Burson, Kate Robin, and Dmitry Lipkin, had started a theater company called the Playwrights Collective. They had just rented a production office in a building on the corner of Varick and Canal Street. I asked them if I could do a play in the office, and they agreed. I needed to discover, once again, why I kept returning to the sadomasochistic lure of the theater. So I went home and wrote.

Three Ways to Go Blind was about people who were waiting to have eye operations after having been blinded by unrequited love, denial, and art. I rehearsed the play for four weeks with several actors, including my friends Lázaro Pérez, Victor Argo, and Ellen McLaughlin. I directed the show, designed it, and ran the lighting board.

Regardless of what happened to the show once we started performing, my students had been so helpful getting it up, it would have felt wrong to not unite with them somehow. They had all worked selflessly to help me heal from my West Coast battery, and in the process they became my best friends. Just before we opened, they were gracious enough to let me join the Playwrights Collective officially.

None of us could have predicted how *Three Ways to Go Blind* would be received. The faces in the audience were a steady rotation of movie stars and downtown youngsters, a few critics, and countless actors, actresses, and theater professionals. Old friends I knew from L.A. and many new people were moved by the play and the event as a whole. Sometimes there was wild applause. Sometimes people in the audience would sit in the space and cry for quite a while after the play was over.

After the Taper it was important for me to do something that stood on its own legs. And so I didn't let the play get reviewed. Instead I wrote personal letters to all the critics who wanted to see the show, asking them to write me letters about their thoughts in lieu of printed reviews. It was my way of making theater for theater's sake, for the audience, for the actors, and for me. The experience made me feel like a writer again. After so much exposure before *The Floating Island Plays*, followed by such rejection, I was deeply and personally wounded. And while *Three Ways to Go Blind* set the writer in me free, the person whose life was on display was still suffering from shaking spells and panic attacks.

I was back, in some way, but still fragile. I'd get up in the morning to teach at Columbia, then go to a meeting at the Collective. Then it was back home to shake for the rest of the evening. This went on for about a year. I started wondering if I would ever get better. There was no way for me to know that Betty Ann Solinger was planning my recovery. She wanted me to become a film director.

Floating Islands

What's not to love about a sea of sweet, milky egg yolk custard? I also appreciate the thrifty aspect of this recipe, as it uses all the egg whites to make the fluffy, sugary floating islands. This is a different recipe from the one I include in my play *Fabiola*—if you tried to follow that version, I'm not really sure what you'd end up with. But when Sonia recites the recipe for this fine French dessert, she is on the verge of coming undone, so we can't exactly fault her for confusing a few things here or there. I suppose this is a fine lesson in culinary and dramatic license.

1 quart whole milk
½ teaspoon salt
6 large egg whites
1 cup granulated sugar
6 large egg yolks
1 tablespoon cornstarch
2 teaspoons vanilla extract
Powdered sugar or ground cinnamon for sprinkling

1. Combine the milk and salt in a 2 quart saucepan. Bring to a barely noticeable simmer over medium heat. The milk should always be barely simmering. If it starts to boil, turn the heat down a little.

2. Meanwhile, in a large mixing bowl, beat the egg whites with an electric mixer until frothy. Continue mixing and add ½ cup of the sugar, a little at a time, until the meringue is shiny and holds stiff peaks. Do not overbeat.

3. In a separate bowl, whisk together the egg yolks, cornstarch, and remaining ½ cup of the sugar until smooth, shiny, and pale yellow, about 1 minute. Set aside.

4. When the milk is fragrant and just starting to simmer, drop heaping tablespoons of the meringue into the pot, 2 or 3 at a time. Be sure to keep the meringues separate or they will stick together. Cook for 30 seconds, then flip with a slotted spoon to cook the other side, an additional 30 seconds. Transfer the cooked meringues to a serving dish with raised edges. A 9 × 13-inch baking dish works just fine, but you may use a more decorative dessert dish if you like. Repeat with the remaining meringue.

5. When you've finished cooking the meringues, add the remaining milk to the egg yolk mixture, a little at a time, whisking thoroughly after each addition. Return to the saucepan and reduce the heat to low. Cook, stirring constantly with a wooden spoon, until the mixture is thick enough to coat the back of the spoon, about 7 minutes. Turn off the heat and stir in the vanilla.

6. Pour the custard through a fine mesh strainer into a mixing bowl to remove any unwanted bits. Carefully pour the thickened custard around the edges of the meringues in the serving dish, not on top of them. The meringues should appear to be floating on a sea of golden custard. Cool to room temperature, then cover with plastic wrap and refrigerate until chilled completely. When ready to serve, sprinkle each floating island with powdered sugar or ground cinnamon. Serve the meringues in small bowls or dishes, with a little custard spooned around them, and additional powdered sugar or ground cinnamon sprinkled on top.

Makes 18 floating islands, about 6 servings

Eleven

Swimming

In 1994, with money Betty Ann had raised, we shot footage of the Halloween parade in Greenwich Village from inside the parade route. We planned to use the parade footage as the backbone connecting three different stories that would make up the narrative of my debut feature film, *Exiles in New York*.

Two years later we still hadn't raised the funds needed to shoot the rest of the movie. Then the company producing the film with Betty Ann went belly-up. Like a true auteur, I wanted to finance the film myself, but I was flat broke. Betty Ann decided to produce just one of the stories with her own money so we could show it to other backers in an attempt to convince them that I could direct a successful feature.

And so we shot the first third of the film, the story of a young Englishman living in New York who unknowingly falls in love with his mother, who has been in absentia for twenty years. We shot all the scenes in a week using actors I knew and

Phillip Courtney and Josie DeGuzman on the set of Exiles in New York, *New York City, 1996*

had worked with before. I edited the footage on a home computer with the help of my student Rogelio Martinez.

Betty Ann showed the rough cut around, but there were still no buyers. Betty Ann was driven, though, and managed to raise enough money to shoot the second story, about an Ecuadorian busboy who falls in love with an Irish maid. We never had enough money to shoot the more expensive third story that Amy Madigan had agreed to do with her husband, Ed. Even without the third scene, we still had enough footage to make a film. We found a young editor named David Frankel and took six months to edit the final cut.

It was slow, strenuous, and stressful work. I was still nervous, anxious, and prone to panic attacks, but at least I had something to show for it. It didn't occur to me until 1999, when I was sitting at the American Film Institute (AFI) Film Festival, that I had made it through Betty Ann's Five-Year Film Rehab. *Exiles in New York* was being screened. I had become a film director.

I was sitting next to Betty Ann and her niece Annie, surrounded by the actors from the film. I felt both supported and grateful to look around and see my good friends Ed Vassallo, Joe Quintero, Tatyana Yassukovich, and Josie DeGuzman, waiting for the lights with the same excitement I had bubbling in me. They knew what it took to get here. They had seen me at rock bottom. They had worked with me on the way back up. If we hadn't gone anywhere but AFI, it would have been enough for all of us. Fortunately, the film was accepted to a number of other festivals, so the party carried on for a little while.

The icing on the cake came just moments before the film screened that day. Betty Ann leaned over to me as the film started and whispered, never one to disturb the audience around her.

"They want to show the movie at the Latin American Film Festival."

"That's great," I said.

"The festival is in Cuba." Gulp. "You're coming, right?"

"Yes, I am," I said. And I meant it.

Or did I? Aside from the emotional issues, as a purely practical endeavor the thought of getting to Cuba was enough to give me a migraine.

As a Cuban citizen with an American green card, I was subject to every imaginable restriction. First, I needed to get a visa from the Cuban government that would allow me to return to the country, the same visa that would then allow me to leave. This mandatory clearance was a way to protect the country from returning exile terrorists. They had reason to be worried after a bomb set by exiles was detonated at the Hotel Nacional in the summer of 1997, but as it goes with so many things in Cuba, the message sent is more important than what actually happens. So while there was no screening process for explosive devices, the extra hassle carried a clear meaning: You left before, as a traitor to the Revolution, so we're not going to make it easy for you to just walk back in.

The American end of things was even more complicated. At the time, if you wanted to go to Cuba from the United States legally, you had to get permission from the United States Treasury Department, filling in multiple forms detailing the purpose of the trip and how it would be spent. But in 1999 Clinton was still president, and there were concessions granted to cultural exchanges, educational initiatives, and artistic projects. This made it both easier to get approval if you filled out the paperwork and less likely that you would be stopped and hassled upon returning to the United States if you didn't. If you had a project in the festival, you were pretty likely to get permission. Most of the filmmakers and actors who went were allowed to bring back rum and cigars, two of the perks of getting U.S. clearance.

Then there was the emotional side of it. I manage better now, but then the idea of traveling to Cuba caused immediate terror in the very depths of my being. Forget my mother. Forget my grandparents. Forget that going would be such a flagrant act of betrayal that I wouldn't know how to forgive myself, much less ask forgiveness. At that point, after years of mounting anxiety, getting on planes was bad enough. Even if I was staring at the destination on the ticket, some part of me always doubted where I was going, how long I'd be there, and if I would ever return. My body responded with sheer mind-numbing panic.

Now make the destination Cuba and multiply the panic by a thousand. Add to it my feeling that all the red tape on both sides had been put in place to make me, specifically, miserable. That's what it's always felt like. I know it's a bit much to take government regulations personally, but when such a basic need for home is at the center of your life for so long, anything standing in your way feels pretty damned personal.

Betty Ann's offer was the third I had to go back to Cuba. The first was during the production of *The Floating Island Plays* at the Taper when I was so overwhelmed by Rome burning that I said no immediately.

The second chance was in 1997 when Repertorio Español decided to take their production of *Revoltillo* on a tour of Cuba. It was to be the first theatrical exchange between the United States and Cuba since the embargo started, a trip that came on the tail end of Ry Cooder's project with the Buena Vista Social Club, which brought Cuba onto the U.S. cultural radar like nothing had for decades.

The exchange was helmed by Repertorio Español's executive director, Gilberto Zaldivar, a Cuban who had left in the early sixties but had returned several times. Gilberto had decided to try to fight the embargo with theater, and his controversial plans got him a feature on the front page of the Sunday *New York Times*. He had managed to bring a Cuban company to perform at his theater and he wanted *Revoltillo* to complete the exchange. The show would open in Havana and then tour the entire country. I was going to be the first Cuban-American playwright to have his work performed in Cuba after the embargo.

When the Cubans in Miami found out, all hell broke loose. We were the subject of many a Cuban talk radio show, where they made sure to use every nasty name in the book to put down anyone involved with the project. One of the actresses in the play, a well-known Cuban-American named Ana Margarita Martinez-Casado, was told that if she went to Cuba with *Revoltillo*, all of the commercials she had running on Spanish television would be pulled. Sure enough, when she didn't back down, her commercials were taken off the air.

When we began performing the play in New York, Repertorio got bomb threats and protesters on the streets. Every night they would yell obscenities at me when I walked in the theater. I would turn around and look at the mob for at least five minutes every night, taking them all in from the barely protected foyer of Repertorio. They were young and old and filled with venom and vengeance.

When the play went to Cuba, even though I had agreed to go, I could not do it. I could not betray Oscar Hernandez by going back to the place were he lost everything. I would let the play make the trip for me. Reporters from *The New York Times* went along with the company, and every few days I would read the paper and cry as I heard about all their experiences. The electricity went off on opening night. Ana Margarita was reunited with her brothers after more than forty years. In Havana an audience member was reported to have said, "It was thrilling. Incredibly, culture brought us together."

Culture. My plays had become a part of the culture, part of several cultures: Cuban, American, and the conflict between them. But still I could not find the courage to go home.

Part of me thinks I turned the trip down because it was all a little too perfect. At the time I chose to believe that the Cuban government was lying to me. The Cuban liaison to Repertorio promised me that my visa would be waiting at the airport in Mexico, but I imagined myself stranded at the Cancún airport waiting for a piece of paper that would never come.

To add to it all, I had lost my Cuban passport. Since I never claimed American citizenship, I had only my green card until the United States granted me a stateless passport. It was a lovely white rectangle with no commitment attached, a fact I enjoyed immensely. It was like working on *Stevie* when I was a writer without a past. Now I was a person without a state. I had always felt like I was stuck in limbo anyway; now I had proof. I didn't have to betray anyone by deciding who I was. I was neutral. A little white rectangle.

I wish I could say my decision to return came with some soul-wrenching revelation, but that didn't happen until later. I took Betty Ann's offer, the third time charmer, because my desire to go home then was stronger than the fear holding me back. The first offer was inconceivable, but it planted a seed. The second chance was tempting, but I backed down at the last minute. By 1999 I knew I needed to go home, and I was ready to fight in order to do so.

First things first, I had to get a passport. The Cuban embassy told me that if I had my passport, it would be easy to get into Cuba, but since I didn't it was going to be hard.

I called my only friend in Cuba, a talk show host and TV personality named Lizette Vila. I had been hooked up with Lizette during the planning phases of Repertorio's tour of *Revoltillo*. She had the combination of status, visibility, and behind-the-scenes know-how that actually got things done in Cuba. Of course I couldn't reach Lizette by phone, so I sent her an e-mail. A day later I received a call from the wife of the Cuban ambassador in New York, a perfectly poised woman named Olguita.

I had met Olguita during the protests in front of Repertorio Español. She was impressed with how I handled the protesters, how I never lost my cool and even relished their discontent, absorbing their jeers to fuel my creative fire.

"Lizette wrote me," Olguita said when she called. "We are so happy you are finally going to Cuba, Eduardo. It's time to go home. We will get your passport and all your papers in order so you can go to the festival."

I don't think I wanted to trust her, but I really didn't have a choice. She assured me that everything would be taken care of.

It hit me like a bus. I was going home. Panic. Tempered by resolve, but still panic. Deep. Quiet. Crippling.

By then I was teaching full time at Columbia and living alone. I would often wake up in the middle of the night screaming from nightmares about going back home or being sent back to the United States once I landed there. I liked choosing to be stateless, but the thought that neither the United States nor Cuba would want me was far less enjoyable.

Beyond that, I started doubting myself. I was terrified that I would arrive in Cuba, take everything in, and then realize that it was completely different from what I imagined. Once again I started to doubt my feelings, my memories, and my plays. What if my plays were as illegitimate as I was? What if they portrayed a Cuba that did not exist, and my whole trip was spent facing the sheer inadequacy of my life's work? I knew I had to deal with some serious stuff, but I didn't want to face the possibility of my life, my work, being lies when I saw home again.

Home, again.

Could I go back? Could I return? During the month that I waited for word from Olguita and the embassy, all I wanted to eat was Cuban food. I went back to Melys, the diner on Tenth Avenue. Irene's diner. Our diner. I went to Cuban stores in Spanish Harlem and Jackson Heights. I even took the bus to Union City to be around Cubans. Did they all know? All these refugees? Did they know that I was about to betray them? That by going home I was going to disregard their bitterness and resentment to serve my own agenda? How would I tell my mother? God. I decided that I would wait to do that until the night before I left.

My friend Ed Vassallo decided that he would come to Cuba with me. The trip was for the film festival and he was in the film, so it made sense, but the real reason he came was that he saw that I was cracking. Ed was just the right person to accompany me. He is a man with that rare combination of strength and sensitivity. He was aware enough to know I was terrified, and gentleman enough to not remind me. I hoped he would know how to pick up the pieces if everything fell apart.

Then one day I got the call from Olguita at the Cuban embassy. She told me that the passport had been arranged and that all I had to do was go to the Cuban Intersection in the Swiss embassy in Washington, D.C. They would give me the passport. Simple?

"What's the Cuban Intersection?" I asked.

"Cuba does not have relations with the United States. So Cuba cannot have an embassy."

"What about your embassy? Your husband is ambassador."

"To the UN," she said. "It's different."

"Can't they just send it to you in New York?" I asked.

"No, you have to go there. When do you want me to get you an appointment?" she asked.

"Next Tuesday," I said. I taught at Columbia on Mondays and Thursdays, so Tuesday gave me time enough if something went wrong. Ed offered to drive me. What a friend.

So at six o'clock Tuesday morning, Ed was waiting for me outside my apartment to accompany me on the journey to retrieve my Cuban identity. I got in the car and panicked.

"Wait," I said. "I think I forgot my green card."

I looked through my papers, birth certificate, passport pictures, money order, and green card! I settled into the passenger's seat. Ed got on the West Side Highway.

"Are you sure you know where we are going?" I asked.

"I Mapquested the address," he said with alpha-male confidence. I had no idea what he was talking about.

"What?"

"I looked up how to get there on the computer. Here, you read the directions. We'll get there."

So I read the directions, over and over, and we both chain-smoked our way there. Ed tried to distract me by talking about how great it was going to be to bring the film to a new festival. We followed the directions to the letter but three hours later found ourselves in front of a suburban house somewhere in Virginia. Ed had entered the address correctly but had forgotten to put in Washington, D.C. Was he conspiring against me, too? Paranoia. Fear. More driving.

It took us another hour to reach D.C. I made it to the Cuban Intersection with just enough time. I stood on a line with about a dozen Cubans who looked equally conflicted about where they were and what they were doing. A hand touched my shoulder and startled me.

"Mr. Machado?"

I turned around and saw a good-looking Cuban man in his forties standing in front of me. I nodded yes, not finding words fast enough.

"You don't have to stand in line. Please come into my office."

All the Cubans in line were staring at me. I could hear their taunts. You communist asshole, traitor, that's why you're getting special treatment. They didn't actually say anything, of course, but I could tell they wanted to.

The man escorted me to his office and asked his secretary to get me a cup of café. He asked me for my paperwork, which I handed to him. He told me it would take a few minutes.

The secretary handed me a cup of café, strong and sweet. It was delicious. She smiled at me. These are very Cuban Cubans, I thought to myself, always relaxed and comfortable in their bodies. You can tell they know where they're from. Would I be like that after I went home?

For a moment I saw something scary in the eyes of the secretary. Maybe they're all like panthers, I thought, waiting for a moment of weakness before they strike? No. They are being nice. Kind. They are comfortable and kind. They don't want to hurt me. They want to help me.

The man came back in and we talked about teaching at Columbia and how Cuba was doing and how sad it was that I had left the country so young. The secretary knocked at his door and handed him my passport, which he handed me. I put it in my pocket, thanked him, and left. I hurried to Ed, who was waiting in the car.

"Did you get it?" he asked anxiously.

"It's in my pocket." I got into the car.

"What does it look like?" He wanted to see if it was all true.

"I haven't looked at it," I whispered.

"Don't you think you should?" he said sweetly.

I took out the passport. It looked just like the one I had when I got here. I opened the blue jacket slowly and flipped through the pages. It was like a U.S. passport but with ink that seemed more exotic. I found the front, the photo page. The picture was different, not the young boy I expected to see. It was a man in his late forties, full of hope and doubt. A citizen of Cuba. I wanted to cry but did not let myself.

Ed instinctively put his arms around me. He drove us to a diner for breakfast and we planned our trip. Ed didn't care about permission from the Treasury Department, so we would travel without Betty Ann, through Cancún instead of Jamaica. We'd buy the tickets to Mexico and I would arrange the flight to Cuba through a travel agent who would meet us at the gate in Cancún. I booked the tickets and contacted the travel agent, whose number I got from the producer of *Revoltillo* at Repertorio Español. The details were in place and he would meet us in Cancún. We were going to Havana!

Then a week passed and my visa from the Cuban government was nowhere to be found.

I knew it! They were playing a dirty trick on me. In the end they would never let me back in. Now I really couldn't sleep. I started coming undone. I found myself ranting and raving to my students at Columbia about the great injustice forced upon me by the Cuban government. Then the Mexican travel agent called me asking me to send him a copy of my visa. I was in trouble and I knew it. I e-mailed Lizette, who told me not to worry. I called Olguita, who said to be patient.

And then it was two days before I was supposed to leave. Betty Ann was already packed and had figured out a way to take the film on the plane with her, all four heavy cans. I suggested that I take two on the plane with me. She refused.

I took the refusal as a sign that she knew I was never going to get the visa. Ed assured me that if we had to stay in Mexico we'd have a nice vacation. They're all conspiring against me, I thought. They all know the visa is never going to come!

That night I went to Repertorio Español to ask for help from some of the actors who were there from Cuba as part of a government-sanctioned cultural exchange. Everyone called somebody: friends, family, even the head of ICAIC, the Cuban film ministry that ran the festival. Finally the actress Adria Santana said, "Let's call Lizette right now. She is the only person in Cuba with enough influence to get this to happen tomorrow."

Adria called Lizette herself, and amazingly enough, she got through. We caught her just as she was on her way to the opening of the film festival. Lizette assured us that I would get a fax of the visa the next morning. She took my Columbia fax number and told me to call her at eleven if it hadn't gotten there.

I started teaching my class at ten, and by eleven I told the students I needed to call Cuba. I went to my office phone and could not get through on my line. So I went into someone else's office and called Lizette. Thankfully she answered.

"Its not here yet," I said, my voice shaking.

Lizette was surprised. "I faxed it an hour ago," she said.

"But it's not here!"

"I have it in my hand. It will be waiting for you at the airport. Don't worry."

"Try again," I pleaded.

I heard her tell her secretary to fax it.

"Is it there?" I called out into the main office. One of my students rushed in and said no. I told her to go down to the film department and ask them for their fax number. She ran.

I whispered to Lizette, "Someone is keeping it from getting here."

"Either God or the CIA," she said, only half joking.

My student was now there with the number. The rest of her class had joined her.

"All right," I told them, "half of you go to the film department and run up as soon as you get it. The other half, keep your eyes on the fax machine up here."

I got back on the telephone and gave Lizette the other fax number. While we waited, Lizette gave me all her office numbers and the names of her assistants just in case the authorities gave me a hard time in Mexico. She assured me that everyone knew what flight I was coming on and that they had already sent a fax and e-mail to the airline telling them my visa would be waiting for me in Cuba. I thanked her sincerely but still couldn't believe her. At that moment a student ran in with my faxed visa.

"It's here!" I yelled. The students cheered.

"I'll see you tomorrow in your country," Lizette said sweetly.

"Tomorrow in my country," I answered back.

And then three copies of the visa came through the theater department fax machine.

"A miracle," said one of my flightier students.

"A miracle or the CIA," I said.

I called Ed and Betty Ann to tell them the good news. On the way home I had a drink at a bar, something that I rarely do. I had one more call to make: to my mother.

I trembled as I dialed the phone. She answered, and I spoke without stopping for breath.

"My movie got into the Cuban film festival. I got my Cuban passport back and a visa to go back to the country. And you know, Mom, all my life I have wanted to go home, and this is my chance. I hope you don't see it as an act of hostility toward you. But the way I left when I was young was very hard on me, Mama. I need to find the person I left there. I left someone else there, Mama, and the older I get the more I need him. I'm going home. I'm going to see the house. I'm going to face it all. Our past, my youth, my plays. Everything. I have to. I'm going tomorrow morning."

There was a long silence. I didn't know if she was crying or angry.

Then she said, "I wish it didn't have to be this way. I wish you didn't feel like you had to go there. I hope they let you come back."

She was scared.

"They'll let me come back. It's a big film festival with newspaper people. My producer is going, and nothing will happen to me." I tried to sound calm.

"I hope so, son. Call me when you get back. Yes?" She was trying to be sweet.

"Yes. It's going to be a great thing." I was surprised at just how calm I sounded.

"I'm not going to tell your grandmother," she said, "and do not tell your sisters. Or your brother. Not till you get back."

"Fine," I said, keeping it all together.

Then with a quick clipped good night, she hung up.

All the terror came rushing back in. What am I doing? What if they put me in jail? What if they don't let me come back!? A friend had given me thirty Valiums for my trip. I took the first one and went home to pack. Believe it or not, I slept that night. Who knew the unwanted medication of my youth would prove so beneficial in my adulthood? And I wasn't even in Cuba yet.

❧

I was awoken by Ed's voice on my answering machine telling me that he was waiting outside in a limo. I rushed to get dressed and hurried down with my bags. Ed had his handheld video camera on when I got into the car.

"So what does it feel like?" he asked, pointing the camera at me.

"Like I'm lost. Is this Elysian fields?" I drawled with the syrupy accent of Blanche DuBois in *Streetcar Named Desire*. He laughed.

I added, "If anyone asks where we are going, just tell them Cancún." That would be the story just in case we were questioned. You had to have a story if you were going without permission. I ran over the fabricated resort stay in my mind.

Before Cancún, we landed in Mexico City. I handed Ed his first Valium. We went to a bar and Ed noticed a bottle with a label that read, "Havana Club siéte años." Cuban rum, aged for seven years. We each had a shot.

I know of no other rum better than Havana Club. Sorry, Mr. Bacardi, but some things truly are lost in translation, among them the taste of authentic Cuban rum. My first sip of Havana club siete años— coated my mouth with the clean taste of distilled sugar cane and made my throat swell with heat. I found myself craving a tumbler of *guarapo* for a cocktail of which Oscar would surely have approved. Between the booze and the Valium, we got on the plane to Cancún more than a little wobbly.

Upon arriving in Cancún we rushed to the Air Caribe counter to meet our travel agent, who was, thankfully, waiting for us. Ed turned on his camera just in time to capture the ticket agent informing me that my faxed visa was not good enough. I told him that people in Cuba had told me everything was taken care of, that I was a film director going to the film festival, and that everything had been explained to the airline!

I caught myself sounding very grand. He flatly told me to call Cuba.

"How?" I asked, challenging him with the impossibility of being able to find a reliable connection to the island.

He pointed to a pay phone. My God, you could call Cuba from a pay phone. I rushed to it, hearing Ed talk into the camera as he filmed me dialing Lizette frantically.

"The first snag."

I got Lizette on the phone and she told me she would fax all the information back to the Air Caribe people.

"Tell them to look at their fax machine. People are waiting for you at the airport. I faxed everything to the airlines again this morning, just to be sure."

I told Ed what was going on. He suggested we bribe the ticket counter guy. When I went back I discreetly handed him a fifty and he magically found my name on a list. He presented us with two tickets and two tourist cards that would be stamped in lieu of our passports. Then he said the plane was already boarding, to just go through the gate.

"What gate?" I asked.

"The gate that says LA HABANA," and he pointed to a sign.

I looked up. La Habana. I had forgotten. I had been calling it Havana. Was it happening to me? Had I forgotten the real name? Had I lost its source inside me? What else had I lost? I felt sick as I boarded the final plane home.

When we got inside the plane Ed noticed that the glass covering the window in the cockpit was missing. They had a piece of cardboard covering part of it, and this was more than he could take. For the first time he started to panic. I handed him another Valium to calm him down.

The plane was a small jet, very old and dangerous looking, but I was sure that I was not going to die on my way back home. Ed was not as certain. His seat was directly behind mine and I was sitting next to a businessman from Spain who dealt in imports from Mexico to Cuba. He told me he took this plane once a week, that it was a short flight over the ocean and that they didn't go very high. I told this to Ed, but it did not make him feel any better.

The plane was full of people, the tourists easily distinguishable from the Cubans. The tourists were clearly on holiday, clad in brightly colored shirts and hats, smiling and laughing. The faces of the Cubans were either stone cold or on the verge of tears. I fluctuated between both.

We sat on the runway for what seemed like forever. It was about halfway through forever that I started shaking, an honest-to-goodness panic attack. Ed was worried about the plane; I was more concerned with the trip.

What the hell was I doing? Was I ready? No turning back now. What about the visa? Could I actually trust the government? Was I going to be able to control myself? My emotions? Who was waiting for me there? The same frightened child that left forty years earlier? I did not know if I wanted to feel him again. And then all at once I missed Othin. Where was my brother? Should I have made him come back with me? My brother, my dear little brother. We had become strangers over the years, but at that moment I needed him so much. I was about to start crying but instead I wrote in my notebook a poem to my brother and myself for having survived that flight forty years ago.

But had we? Had we survived? Was I about to risk it all? My body started to shake. I took another Valium and the plane took of. I wrote, "Took off to / Never / Never / Land."

As soon as the plane took off, Ed fell asleep. It had been a long day made even more stressful by the specter of the U.S. government. Even if you can distract yourself, some part of you knows that you're breaking the law. But that's where the personal comes in again. Of course I would break a ruthless, useless, forty-year embargo against my country. I was breaking the law so I could find myself. Ed was breaking it so he could be my friend. But no matter how you justified it, the tension was exhausting.

I started talking to the Spaniard next to me. I told him there was a visa waiting for me on the other side and that I was afraid they would send me back. He handed me a pack of Cuban cigarettes and told me not to worry, that they would be waiting for me. I believed him for a second and then I convinced myself that he was a conspirator, too. There would be no visa and I would be sent back.

I spent the rest of the flight writing in my notebook, lost in my head until the wheels screeched on the tarmac. Ed woke up and squeezed my shoulder. The door opened soon after. I ran out of the plane into the airport.

I was the first person out, and I didn't see anyone. It was around eight-thirty at night, and my body was betraying me. "Don't start shaking, Eduardo, please," I said to myself.

Ed was behind me and I heard him say, "Look, Eduardo, there's a guy waving the visa at you."

I looked up, and sure enough there was a very white young man in his late twenties. He had dark black hair, was strikingly handsome, and he was waving a sign that said MACHADO. The visa fluttered slowly in his hand like a butterfly just before it takes off. I ran toward him.

He introduced himself as Eugenio as he handed me the visa. He said he'd wait for us on the other side of customs, and then before he left he said, "Lizette is sorry she could not be here, but there was a big party for the film festival at the Hotel Nacional. You might be able to go to the end of it. Señor Machado, I cannot wait to see your movie."

Film Festival? Movie? I suddenly remembered that was why we were there. I thanked him about three times as Ed and I walked toward customs. We noticed that everyone was smoking. Ed was thrilled.

"A place where people smoke at customs. Wow."

I pulled out the Cuban cigarettes the Spaniard had given me and handed him the pack. He lit two cigarettes for us.

I inhaled and the taste of Cuba filled my mouth with smoke. Aah, cuban cigarettes are made with what's left over from the tobacco leaves used to make cigars. Wrapped in sugar-laced paper that leaves a taste of sweetness on your lips, they may be the most soothing things on God's earth. The Spaniard saw me smoking. He waved from his place in line as if to say see, I told you everything would be all right.

I started to breathe, calmed by the smoke and the ground beneath my feet. I took in my surroundings. It was definitely a new airport, not the one I remembered. There were *milicianos* and *milicianas* with machine guns pacing up and down the lines at customs and hovering around the doorways. I passed through customs, choosing to keep silent and present my paperwork. Thankfully, blessedly, all I got was a raised eyebrow and a quizzical glance from the agent who stamped my tourist card.

I reached the other side before Ed, gesturing back to him that I was going to look for cigars. Instead I went outside, lit another cigarette and breathed in the smoke now tinged with the mineral taste of salty air. The air. The air I had been waiting all my life to breathe again. I saw the landscape that I had seen as a child. My vision clouded with thick dense foliage rippling on the ground, waxy leaves ribbed with yellow framing the edges, and dots of bright red hibiscus blossoms accenting the air. The world of people and airport receded, and I was at the center of a swirling tropical kaleidoscope. It felt like I had gotten to heaven on earth, and I recognized the feeling.

When Ed found me, Eugenio was close behind with two people who worked for Sundance, nebbishy Los Angelinos with the pasty complexions of film freaks. They immediately got into showbiz talk, about the movies they were interested in, and then they pummeled me with questions. Ed did his best to intercept their barrage of business talk, and they switched gears, asking Eugenio if Rory and Ethel Kennedy had arrived yet. Apparently they had. The Kennedys are here? I thought to myself. What's the world coming to?

I got into the back seat of the van and put Ed between me and the Sundance people. He told them that this was my first time back since I was a child, and they pretended to care. Ed asked if we could smoke, and Eugenio said of course. The Sundancers rolled down their windows immediately but did not say a word; they were too hip to complain. Instead they started babbling about how great Rory Kennedy's documentary was. Then they, too, started to recede from my field of attention until they were nothing but a little buzz in the background.

I looked out the window as we drove. I felt like I was snuggled in a warm blanket, cozied up to some long-extinguished fire that had suddenly burst into flames. The landscape billowed around the van like smoke. I had seen all this greenery right before I left, but now it looked more rural than I remembered. Had I fabricated a sophisticated city named Havana? Or was this what La Habana looked like? All trees and greens and flowers and billboards? The billboards! Huge murals on the side of the highway or on cinder block walls at intersections with brightly painted slogans of the Revolution. They would probably be car ads if they were along the Long Island Expressway, but here, in the land of socialism, they were richly colored portraits of Fidel and Che, with mantras printed alongside to stir the soul of any Cuban with a nationalist bone in his body.

But wait, I didn't remember any of this. What if I had gotten it all wrong? I exhaled when we drove into La Habana. The town. The city. With its fountains and colonial buildings and majestic tree-lined boulevards and the blue Caribbean Sea guarded by an undulating stone wall. The cars. Buzzing past my eyes, pulling me back in time. All of a sudden it was 1958. This is my mother's world, I thought. This is a place of history, of beauty, a city with a soul. It's a sophisticated playground for your deepest desires, made safe for those who appreciate the finer things. I flashed back to the present. I felt my heart swell with everything my mother missed. Everything she refused to let go of. No wonder she was never able to give it up. I don't think I will be able to give it up, either.

Then we turned into the grand driveway of the Hotel Nacional, a 1930s architectural masterpiece. The cream-colored walls and arching doorway, terra-cotta-colored roof caps and row upon row of windows all gave off an air of genteel exclusivity. The hotel had been renovated recently and so it hurled me headlong into another flashback. For a moment, just a moment, I was my father, my grandfathers, pulling up to the classiest spot in town to gamble, drink, and cause a little trouble. This is who they were. This building, this monument to an ended era of elegance. No wonder they are so angry.

Eugenio walked us into the grand marble lobby and conferred with his friend Mario, who also worked for the festival. It was about nine-thirty.

"The party is over," he said. "It was just cocktails. Everyone has gone to dinner now."

The Sundance people decided to get settled into their rooms. They waved good-bye and went to check in. Ed was polite, but I just breezed past them and through the open double doors that led to the hotel gardens overlooking the Caribbean. I ordered mojitos for Ed, Eugenio, Mario, and me. The craggy face of El Moro Castle was visible in the distance. I looked up the flagpole at the center of the courtyard and saw the Cuban flag flapping in the breeze from the ocean. All the patriotism I felt as a child when I recited José Martí's poetry or sang the national anthem came flooding back and I thought, this is who I am, Cuban.

I took my first sip of a real mojito made with Havana Club. The bartender had used the clear white rum, not the darker aged variety, combining it with fresh lime, sugar, and several stems of mint muddled in the bottom of a glass with a wooden pestle. I would later learn why Cuban mojitos are so much better than any I've had in the United States. They use spearmint—*yerba buena*—which has a sweeter, smoother, almost creamier taste than the peppermint that's usually available in American supermarkets.

That first sip was satisfying in the way that only a perfectly made cocktail can be. When the ingredients are well blended in exactly the right proportions, the result is both tranquilizing and clarifying. I was calmed, cooled, and collected, the chatter of all my nerves and anxieties quieted, if only for a moment. I felt good. I was ready to party!

Ed went to see if Betty Ann had registered, but her flight had not yet arrived from Jamaica. We decided to go to the house we were staying at a few minutes away from the hotel, in the neighborhood of El Vedado. Eugenio and Mario offered to drive us there. We told them we would leave our suitcases and then take them out to dinner. Ed had found a cigar store and bought us some Montecristo No. 5 cigars, my favorite kind next to the smaller cigarillos that I smoke as a habit. They are like a miniature version of the big cigars that businessmen like to smoke. They're compact—about five inches long with a one inch diameter. They give you the satisfaction of a bigger cigar, but they don't require the same kind of commitment. Perfect for a ride through downtown Havana.

We smoked as we drove along the streets of El Vedado. The neighborhood was built in the twenties and thirties for the most part and looks a lot like parts of Beverly Hills. Some of the fancier houses were noticeably run down, their Art Deco splendor more than a little rough around the edges. It was quite a sight to see such aristocratic elegance tarnished by years of struggle nestled in the swells of tropical flora. The effect was amplified, made more ethereal and dramatic by the cool white light of the moon beaming through a cloudless sky.

Eugenio found the place we were staying, the home of a lighting designer named Carlos who was a friend of the actress Adria Santana. It was a three-story house with a courtyard and several trees, in front of it. A family of four lived on the ground floor, and Carlos occupied the top two floors. He had his residence on the third floor, but he had permission from the government to rent the three rooms on the second floor. This kind of setup is common in Cuba, known as a *casa particular*, a Cuban bed and breakfast.

Ed rang the doorbell, and a few moments later we were greeted by a black man with a shaved head and the straight-backed posture of a dancer. He looked about thirty, though we later learned he was in his forties and had, in fact, been a member of the National Ballet of Cuba. He greeted us with hugs and kisses and introduced himself as Fidel.

He told me that Carlos and his partner Nelson would take care of the paperwork in the morning because everyone was at a rehearsal for a show they were working on. It was exciting to hear that we were staying with artists. Maybe we'd have more in common than I expected.

Fidel took our bags up a dimly lit marble staircase. He led us down the corridor into a slate-tiled hallway that would have been exposed were it not covered by a hard green plastic roof. Wrought-iron windows along one side opened to the moist night air. The hall had a wooden bench with floral print cushions and hanging plants overhead. We passed a glass fish tank overflowing with plants that dipped their roots into the bottom of the tank. There were two gigantic goldfish and a strange little swimming thing that seemed to be sucking the life out of the glass on the edge of the tank. Fidel caught me staring. "They

keep the tank clean," he said with a smile. "No filters. This way."

Me and the fish tank without a filter,
Carlos and Julio's hallway, El Vedado, La Habana, 1999

Down the hall we went, into a dining room with more ornately tiled floors and a mahogany armoire full of little mementos and objets. I saw the kitchen to the rear, a wooden table with six chairs, and a spiral staircase in the corner that led to the upstairs bedroom and roof. Fidel opened a door off the dining room that led to a tiny bedroom. He set our bags down on a neatly made double bed. Ed glanced at the bed and swallowed audibly. He was scared, but I reassured him, "Tomorrow we will get you your own room."

"I don't care," he said, trying put on a brave face.

That night Eugenio took us to our first *paladar*, a restaurant run out of a private home. He claimed, with typical bravado, that it was the best place in El Vedado. I can't remember where it was exactly, but it doesn't matter. The experience was what counted.

Going to a *paladar* is a great way to eat in Cuba. They're almost always small, with room for a large party (usually at a family's dining room table) and maybe a few tables for two. Some of them are approved by the government, but often it's the illegal places that are the best. Depending on how big or well known the place is, you may or may not get a choice from an actual menu. You are almost always guaranteed fresh seafood, but beyond that anything goes. We didn't get seafood or a choice that first night, but I was fine when I heard what we'd be eating: breaded pork cutlets with *Moros* and *yuca*. Yummy.

There was only one other couple at the *paladar*, an American man in his fifties and a very beautiful Cuban woman in her early twenties. She treated him like he was a god from Mount Olympus, which he definitely wasn't. Ed told Eugenio and Mario that he would like to get his hands on a girl like that. They looked at him, a little confused, as they had assumed he was my lover. That would be everyone's assumption for the next two weeks.

The food came, and the *Moros* weren't overseasoned but they were a little dry. The thin breaded pork steaks were lemony and crisp but a little bland. The *yuca* was undercooked and very unpleasant. Was this what I had been waiting for? My first meal back in Cuba? I had hoped it would be a revelation. Then I remembered the mojito. That did it. That was like a gift from heaven. I decided to postpone judgment until I had eaten at a few other places.

After a dessert of little cubes of guava paste, Eugenio and Mario drove us home. They said they would pick us up in the morning so we could register for the film festival. Oh, God, the film festival! I kept forgetting about it!

Ed went to buzz the doorbell as I got out of the car. Eugenio stopped me before I said good-bye.

"Anything I can do for you, just let me know," he said, and then he leaned in and hugged me just a little too intimately. Just before we separated, he held on to my hand—a few seconds more than necessary—staring intently at me with his deep brown eyes. He was letting me know that he was for sale. This made me feel both guilty and excited. My first come-on in La Habana!

"Thanks for picking us up today," I said, "and thank you for bringing me my visa." I moved toward the house.

Ed held the door for me and I walked by him without making eye contact. We went upstairs to our little double bed and stripped down to our underwear, falling asleep when our heads hit the pillows. It had been a long day.

I was awoken by the sun shining on my face. We had been too tired the night before to remember to close the curtains. Ed's legs and arms were tangled in a pile on top of me. I gently moved them away, stood up to close the blinds, and put on a pair of shorts. I walked into the dining room and put on my tennis shoes at a smaller table in front of the kitchen. Fidel was making café at the stove, and he whispered that he wanted to give me some. I told him I was going for a walk but I wouldn't be long.

Outside the house, La Habana was waking up. Dogs were barking, women were cleaning their sidewalks. People were

Me on the street in La Habana, 1999

waiting in clusters for buses that were brimming with bodies when they pulled up. Sometimes one of the many old cars ratcheting along would pull over and pick up a small group that had been waiting for a long time. I wondered if they charged them taxi fare but liked the idea of the ride being free: all in a day's work for a good socialist.

I walked about a dozen blocks to El Malecón, the stone sea wall that runs along the length of the ocean from El Vedado to La Habana Vieja, Old Havana. At night Cubans gather in droves along El Malecón to gossip, kiss, or just hang out. But that early in the morning there was only an occasional fishermen or passing pedestrian for a good distance in either direction. I sat on a stretch of wall across from a beautifully run down building. I became hypnotized watching the waves collide with El Malecón, and in that trance I was happy.

When I got back to the house, Ed was still asleep, but Nelson was awake. He was a short man in his fifties with longish gray and black hair. He was fit if a little soft in the middle, but his demeanor was what made him unique. He was flamingly queer. Not feminine, really, but very grand and flowery. He embraced me like a long lost brother and asked for our papers. I went into the room. Ed was snoring, so I quietly got both our passports and my money belt. I paid Nelson for a week, in case we wanted to leave after the festival. Fidel served me breakfast, which was included in the price of the room.

I sat down to my first cup of Cuban *café con leche* with lightly buttered toast. Delicious Cuban bread with butter. *Café con leche* with freshly boiled milk and maybe even a pinch of salt. This more than made up for last night's so-so dinner. The simple beauty of the butter gathering into shiny bubbles on the surface of the coffee was made even more enjoyable by my memories. This little meal was mine, in my past, in my mind, and in this moment. They were all the same, and they were all pretty damned good. I munched and sipped, content, then I saw Fidel bringing out the rest of the breakfast.

He set down a platter of fresh fruit salad made with papaya, mangoes, and pineapple. Then he brought a smaller dish with a few slices of homemade cheese. It was fairly firm and a little crumbly, resembling a block of tofu, but tangy and slightly bitter. I appreciated the delicacy of the cheese and the care that went into making it, but it was a little off-putting.

The eggs, however, were perfect. Fidel didn't prepare them sunny-side up or over easy. He fried them. Just fried them. In lard. Yeah. They were still soft on top, with the yolks running at the center, firm on the bottom. The wisps of white that had turned golden in the pork fat had a pleasant crunch in my mouth. So many textures in two little eggs. I wasted no time in using as much Cuban toast as possible to dab up every little drop of egg yolk.

While I ate Nelson chewed my ear off, and I loved it.

"Carlos and I were lovers," he said matter of factly, "but now he has a younger lover named Julio. I had a younger lover, too, but he ran away with all my savings and married a girl. He comes by sometimes, but I won't give him any, not anymore. I just pick up a different young one when I need one, right?"

I nodded my head yes.

"It would be wonderful if you could get us tickets for your movie. Could you?"

"Sure," I said through mouthfuls of eggy bread.

"My sister can get her own tickets; she works for ICAIC. But I am a theater actor, you know?"

I nodded, "Now I do."

"Yes, I am an actor. And at this house I play the role of waiter."

We both laughed.

"I belong to the same company Adria belongs to." We agreed that she was a lovely woman. Then he asked me what I had planned for the day. I told him we had to register at the film festival.

"Well," he said, "my brother-in-law just bought a 1955 Chevy and he wants to start driving tourists like you around for twenty-five dollars a day. Would you like that?"

I knew we'd need to get around, so I agreed. "I think I'd like that very much," I said.

"What time do you want him?"

"We'll have to meet up with some people after we register for the festival, so how about three?"

"Where do you want to go?" he asked.

"Home," I said, "I want to see my house."

"Where is that?" he asked.

"Cojimar."

"Nice. I will call him and he will be here at three."

He went toward the phone.

"Wait." I stopped him.

"Something else?"

"Is there another room?"

He smirked. "Are you having problems with your boyfriend?"

"He's not my boyfriend."

"Sure. Whatever you say." He gave me a sarcastic look.

"We are just too big for that little bed," I protested. He smiled a knowing smile. Then he sighed.

"Well, we are booked. There is a Spanish couple and their two women friends. Girlfriends. They are coming tomorrow, and I gave them the bigger rooms. But I guess the couple can have your room. And you can have the one in the back. Fidel!" he called, "show him the room in the back."

Fidel smiled. He lit me a cigarette and we walked toward the back of the house.

The room in the back had two single beds, its own private shower, and a sitting room that faced the street. As soon as Ed woke up we moved our luggage, unpacked, and made the space our own. We tipped Fidel generously, which made him our best friend and protector for the rest of the trip.

That morning we went to the Nacional and ran into David Frankel, a big charismatic guy in his late fifties. David had a documentary about Fidel Castro showing at the festival. He had made the film with an American director who was living in Havana. As it happens, his son Davey was the editor of my film, but he wasn't able to join us in Cuba. David was accompanied by his wife, Linda, a Southern beauty in her fifties, and their other son Greg, in his early twenties, slim, blond, and sure of himself, a perfect combination of his parents.

We made a little small talk, but David immediately took us upstairs to meet the director of his film. As soon as she found out I was a

Peter Pan kid she wanted to set up an on-camera interview. She literally dragged me to a television set up on the sixth floor, in the business center where much of the publicity for the festival was being handled. She cued up a tape and showed me a clip of Peter Pan kids leaving in the fifties, then turned to me with a series of questions to find out how I felt and what I thought. It was more than I could take my first day back. I excused myself sheepishly and said I had to find Betty Ann.

Thankfully I found her downstairs in the courtyard, sipping juice with her niece Annie. Betty Ann had already planned our day, how many movies we were going to see, and who we had to meet. As we were checking in at the festival's registration desk I told her I would have to sit the day out.

"I need to go home," I said, "I need to see my house." She paused for a moment, pursing her lips, deciding whether or not she would make an issue out of it. I told her she was more than welcome to come along for the ride.

"No. Thank you. You go. But before you leave we have to talk to the festival people to see what time the film is showing."

They told us that we had been given a prime slot, that the film would be screened on Tuesday afternoon, and that it was going to show at a seven hundred seat theater. The color drained from Betty Ann's face.

"How will we get such an audience?" she asked.

"People will come," said the festival official. "He is a Peter Pan kid who has come back. People will want to meet him." I didn't even want to think about what that would be like.

Ed and I took a cab back to our house while Betty Ann and Annie went off to a seminar about pornography.

❧

Around one P.M. our driver, José, was waiting for us in the dining room with Nelson. He was early and eager. He told us that he had made all the lamps and stained glass windows in the house. Apparently he'd had a show in Paris and had used the money to buy himself his "new" car. I was ready to go, so I handed him the twenty-five dollars and told him we had to leave right away.

We drove to Cojimar in José's boat of a car: a spruced up '55 Chevy with a reupholstered burgundy interior. Ed got in the back with his camcorder, and I sat in the front with José. Ed started filming as soon as we got in the car. I asked José if we could smoke, and he said yes. When I took out the Montecristos he quickly told me he could get some for less money. He had a friend who worked in the factory. I bristled for a moment.

"Maybe," I said. "We have enough to last us the week. We can talk after that." I knew that anything you bought outside the official cigar stores were usually fakes.

"Okay. But whenever you need anything, you know where to come."

Was that another come on? I hoped not.

As we made a slow turn on the road I realized we were approaching the tunnel that would lead us from Havana City to the eastern part of the province. El Tunel de Amor. The Tunnel of Love. All of a sudden the car sputtered then stalled in the middle of the road. José was furious. He steered to the side of the road, shifted into a gear-grinding park, and popped the hood to get a look at the engine. Ed pointed the camera at me and asked a simple question.

"What does it feel like?" I was staring at the sea. "Eddie?"

"What does what feel like?" I asked, turning to face the camera.

"Coming home."

"Like I've been born again," I said, and I held back a tear.

José walked to the car window and told us that he needed to clean the spark plugs. Ed pointed the camera toward him and asked, "Where do you get the spark plugs from?"

"Russia," José answered, and went back to the front of the car.

"Russian spark plugs in a 1950s Chevy! Did you hear that, folks?! I have to get a close-up!" And he got out of the car.

Had I been born again? Maybe. Born again in the eyes of Fidel. I began to remember my childhood. The buses, the stores, my grandmother's exercise bicycle, the smell of my mother's perfume. The rose bushes in front of the house in Cojimar had so many different colors, especially when the butterflies would float around them. I remembered catching them with a net, putting them in a jar, turning the lid, and watching them suffocate slowly. I watched them die so I could place them in a book and see them when I pleased. If I kept them for myself, I'd always know where they were.

Then the car started. We drove on and we were in the Tunel de Amor, built by Batista to look like the Lincoln Tunnel in New York City but much smaller. After the tunnel we drove along a bigger highway, flanked by more revolutionary billboards and a big concrete soccer field in the distance. The landscape started to change. The highway got smaller and for another ten minutes we drove on roads lined by craggy trees and snaggly brush. I started to smell the sea, but it was a different smell, of a cleaner breeze, unfiltered by the buildings of La Habana. We took a long bend in the road and went over a looping ramp, emerging on a crest of road that made visible the Playas del Este, the beaches of East Havana. Beautiful and tropical. Trees and bushes giving way to beach brambles and grass-covered dunes.

Then I saw a sign with an arrow that said COJIMAR. We exited the highway and passed a cluster of trees that I recognized. They were taller, of course, but I was not prepared for the shocking bursts of red flowers that seemed to stretch to the sun and cascade to the earth. We went up a hill, and from the movement of the earth beneath me I knew instantly: this was the hill I had driven up every day on my way back from school in Guanabacoa. Guanabacoa. We must go there after Cojimar, I thought. But for what? To see the school, well, maybe some other time. My priority, after the house, of course, was to have lunch at La Terasa. But after. After the house.

My house. My houses. Manuela and Oscar's modern design wonder, on the same block as Fernando and Cuca's stone fortress. I would go there first, because in spite of the memories of Manuela's backyard, it was Cuca and Fernando's house that I slept in most nights. That was the house I dreamt in, the house I dreamt of. It was the house I first wrote about in my plays, the most dangerous building full of the most unrequited longing.

"So how does he get there?" Ed's voice broke into my daydreaming.

"You know the address?" José asked.

"330 Maceo," I quickly answered.

"You remember your address?" Ed said into the camera.

I gave him a dirty look. How could I have forgotten? Besides, it was what was printed on my birth certificate.

We hit the top of the hill that dipped into Cojimar and all at once the past and the present melted in my head like one big collage of images. I saw the fifties and the nineties bleeding into each other. Memory after memory stood alone in my mind and then mixed in with the rushing reality of the present.

We passed the house of one of Manuela's friends, Beatrice, an interior designer in the fifties. I saw the shell of the building bathed in a blast of technicolor, and suddenly there was a cocktail party of well-dressed drunken sophisticates chattering in the early afternoon sun. The edges of my imagination started to drip grays, and I found myself staring at a chunk of plaster missing from the side of the house.

To the right of Beatrice's house was a tiny park with a José Martí statue that I used to pray to. I could see myself as a child making the sign of the cross in front of the statue, kissed by yellow sun under a blue sky, my collar rising on the caress of a sea breeze. I blinked to see vines on the base of the statue, dappled shadows from the shade of trees grown more than twice the size I remembered them. I took in the rest of Cojimar, tired and proud all at once. Some of the houses were in ruins, picked apart by the vultures of Revolution and time. But for every house that lay in shambles, five houses had been restored to their glory.

I was confused by the contrasts around me, but soon instinct took over. I heard myself directing José, "Make a left; now when we see

Maceo, make a right." I could feel myself riding my bike, following behind my cousin Hugo's horse as Uncle Miguel drove by on the bus, honking the horn at us. I was almost home. But then I spaced out again, lost in memory.

When I came back we were lost, going in circles around the town. Then I saw the church I went to every May to bring flowers to the Virgin Mary, and I snapped, "Turn around, next street corner make a left, in two blocks make a right."

And there we were at Maceo. I could see the neighbors' house across the street to the right of me, the one that had its entire contents thrown into the street. Their beautiful mansion was crumbling. I asked José to park the car, and I turned to Ed as we sidled to a stop.

"It's a block away," I said, "across the street."

Ed turned on his camera and got out of the car with José. They went ahead to get the lay of the land. I paused for a moment, lit a cigarillo, and deeply inhaled all that Cuban earth to give me strength.

I heard José say to Ed, "It sure is a big house," and I began to walk toward my past. I found myself silently describing the house in my head, just in case I didn't recognize it.

It is a big house. A very big house. A colonial house built in the 1800s with a white wall surrounding it. There is a red tile porch in the front with an awning overhead. And on the roof there is a huge room with a large terrace surrounding it. You get to the room by going up a spiral staircase. That's where my parents lived when they first got married.

And then I saw it. My home. I proceeded cautiously, step by careful step. Images of the houses in all my plays collided with memories of this building from my past, the force of their meeting keeping me at bay until I felt safe enough to get closer. Each time I looked at the building I felt threatened by the possibility that it would just dissolve into nothing. Spectres of actors who had lived there in my plays seemed to appear in the courtyard, playing out scenes of secrets and intrigue. I felt like one of my worlds could easily swallow the other, and I had no idea which one was real.

I stopped. I breathed in smoke. I told myself this was really happening, and I tried to look at the house as if it were an old friend. She was still there. Solid but withered with age. I peeked over the stone wall and gasped. The rose garden was gone. But the round cement

Cuca and Fernando's house, 1999

stage where I made up plays was still there. I saw me. Standing there. Speaking the speeches I lovingly crafted at six and seven and eight years old. There was a whole world contained in that stage that hadn't been visited for more than forty years. And yet it was playing out before me as if I had never left.

If a dream—no, if a memory of a dream could have that much power thirty years later, maybe there was hope. Maybe I could get through the day in one piece.

I walked through the front gate and down the path that led to the front door. There was a sign that informed me that my house had become a school.

A woman and her baby were sitting on the porch. The woman was in her twenties, with caramel-colored skin and curlers in her hair. The baby was wearing just a thin pair of underwear. I walked toward her, sitting there like a guard dog keeping me from my past, and I became possessed by a fit of demonic rage. All the anger of losing the life that stood before me came out from inside.

"Who are you?" I demanded.

"The janitor," she replied matter of factly.

"This is my house. I want to go inside and see it."

"This is a school now," she said. "I am not allowed to let people in on the weekend."

"It's my house!" I argued.

"It was your house," she corrected me. It was like getting punched in the gut. I turned to walk away.

José took me by the arm. He told me he would convince her. I gave him five dollars and went to sit on the round cement stage, which now had a bust of José Martí rising out of its center. I did the sign of the cross and lit the Montecristo No. 5 I had in my pocket. Ed was busy doing a close-up of my face with his zoom lens. I wanted to swat the camera away like a fly, but it was too far and I was too drained to move.

I smoked. I was eight years old. It was Christmas and the pigs were being slaughtered. I had a new coat that I didn't want. I was leaving soon. The characters in my play were dancing in the ballroom, partying in the last throes of a lifestyle that would soon be obsolete. They were my kindred spirits. They shared something with me. We faced different futures, but they were equally uncertain. I sat, sharing the blurred space between fantasy and reality with the characters in my mind. Smoking, there, they became more real to me than the people in my past, more real than I myself felt in that moment, and the whole effect was strangely comforting. Was I really home?

José could not convince the janitor to let us in. I lifted my chin and walked around the side of the house, peering through the shutters. This made the janitor stand up with a hand on one hip, her baby resting on the other. She stared me down until I left the courtyard, exasperated.

I crossed the street and walked toward Oscar and Manuela's house. It had been kept up and looked exactly the same. I told the man standing in the yard that my grandparents had once lived in that house and asked him if I could come in.

"No," he answered evenly, but his eyes betrayed him. He didn't claim the property outright, but the flash of animal in his eyes made it clear that this was his territory now. He sensed that I wanted to take the place back, and he was right. I wanted to stake my claim, mark the perimeter with branches or fences or something that said it belonged to the grandson of Oscar Hernandez; that it had been built by him and his wife with nickels from all those bus rides!

I wanted to tell him to fuck himself. Instead I thanked him for keeping the house in such good shape. He turned and went inside, making sure to let a snarling dog back out into the yard. He barked several times until I got the point.

When I got back to the car I uttered two words: "La Terasa." Everyone was hungry. I hoped I would be able to hold it together long enough to eat some food. I half-thought that I would be haunted by the ghost of Ernest Hemingway, drinking at the same bar as my grandfather Oscar, grumbling jokes to the fishermen who hadn't even tried to get rid of the smell under their nails. We found the bar right away. The old man parking the cars out front remembered my grandfather Oscar. He welcomed me home. I needed a drink.

La Terasa had become a tourist destination, so it looked strangely the same as the last time I saw it, its big, long mahogany bar stretching toward the dining room with the black and white tile floors. All the way in the back I noticed the picture windows that opened out onto the bay, nestled in a crook of sandy beach.

The menu was basically the same: *escabeche* and *paella*, featured alongside a smattering of traditional appetizers and working-class seafood fare. The only thing different was that the once-bare walls were now covered in pictures of Papa Hemingway and Fidel together for a rare photo op. They were on the old dock in front of the bar. The same place the boat was docked when I met Fidel as a child.

We all ordered *escabeche* and *paella* with Cuban beers to wash it down. The swordfish *escabeche* was perfect, firm fish with pickly onions and peppers. The *paella* was nothing like it used to be. No lobster, shrimp, or spoonfuls of briny liquor, just well-made yellow rice with some fish. I'm sure they didn't use *bijol* for color, as I definitely could taste saffron. I suspect they substituted powder for the costly whole filaments. If I had known how hard it must have been to pull the meal together, I may have been a bit more forgiving, but all I wanted was for the present moment to stand up to my memory. Sadly, the *paella* just couldn't cut it. Mind you, I still cleaned my plate.

After I finished eating I ambled to the rear of the restaurant and opened one of the windows overlooking the bay. A breeze hit my face, the breeze that I had described so many times in my plays, a breeze that symbolized safety and security for my characters. As I looked at the bay, the memory of lunch disappeared and all that was left was Cojimar. The water became a looking glass, reflecting all the power of my home. My town. For better or worse, I had been able to return to Never Land. I had made it to La Terasa, to a place I thought I would never see again in my life. I treasured the brief moment of peace, hanging on to it just in case it was the last one.

When we got back to La Habana in the late afternoon, the main highway that ran along El Malecón had been closed. The word on the street was that there was a rally being held for a boy whose mother had taken him on a boat from Cuba to Miami. Everyone on the boat had drowned except for the little boy, who had been rescued by some fisherman off the coast of Florida. The Cuban government and the boy's father wanted him back in Cuba. The Cubans in Miami and his cousins wanted

to keep him in the United States. Apparently it was a big news story in both places, but I had not watched the news since I arrived in Cuba. José knew all about it, though, and gave us a detailed account. He left us a couple of blocks away from the Hotel Nacional where we were supposed to meet Betty Ann and Annie for drinks. Instead Ed and I walked toward the march at El Malecón. History was happening—new history—and I was not going to miss it.

El Malecón

We ran into Annie and Betty Ann as we got closer to the hotel. They had heard the march from their room and had come down to check out the scene. Ed got his camera out and we rounded the final corner between the hotel and the people. I nearly fainted from the sight.

A wave of people seemed to ripple along the sea wall. They stretched from a stage set up in front of the United States intersection (because Cuba would never give the United States an embassy) all the way to Old Havana, at the extreme opposite end of the Malecón. We all excitedly walked toward the stage, where a very pregnant revolutionary stood giving a speech next to a girl in a Cuban school uniform.

She intoned passionately, "We will not give our children away like we did during the Peter Pan airlifts."

My heart sunk to my knees.

The crowd yelled, "We will not!"

The pregnant girl continued with a fervor clearly learned from watching Castro speak.

"This child that I have in my womb will be born in Cuba, and I would never hand him over to the imperialists."

Tears began to roll down my cheeks.

"He is going to be born in Cuba and he is going to be Cuban! Like Elian! His unstable mother took him away from this country without his father knowing. But now the father knows, and the father wants Elian, his son, back. At home in Cuba! Imperialists will not get to keep him. The Miami mafia does not get to keep him! Return Elian!"

"Return Elian!" the crowd shouted back, pumping their fists in the air.

I found myself joining in. I heard myself screaming at the top of my lungs.

"Return Elian! Return Elian! Motherfuckers. No more Peter Pan imperialists! Return Elian! Return Elian!" I had found a way to put to good use all the rage I had held back in Cojimar.

The speech ended and the crowds began to disperse. We milled around the people—the Cubans—for a while after but eventually decided to stumble back to our room in El Vedado. So much excitement in less than a day.

We returned to find that the two Spanish couples had arrived and were looking to have fun. The two "girlfriends" were not lesbians at all and even seemed to have their eyes on Ed, though something about the way their lashes flitted toward him and then away just as quickly said to me that they were just sizing him up. I could tell what they really wanted was someone darker, someone Cuban. It became clear that they, as well as the straight couple, had come to Cuba to have sex, and not with each other. They went out in the early evening for dinner and a night of hunting for pleasure.

It's no secret that people come to Cuba to fulfill their fantasies. While the social and economic implications of a country with prostitution as a tourist draw might be depressingly stark, the attitude toward sex in Cuba is so different that it's easy to overlook the grittier aspects of the sex trade. I know this sounds naive, but we get such a wealth of information about people being oppressed in Cuba that we never hear about the ways in which they're actually more liberated. We have just as much prostitution in America, but somehow it's more acceptable because we don't talk about it. Sex is a force in Cuba that shows itself on many levels of daily life. It is accepted as such and utilized, if possible, to eke out a living when other means are impossible. I'm not condoning it, but I will not judge or deny it, either.

That night we got very drunk. Fidel made Cuba Libres with Coca-Cola imported from Mexico and slices of fresh lime.

As we drank, Nelson told off-color jokes. At around eleven we finally met our host, Carlos, and his new love, Julio. Carlos was a short, plump man in his sixties with a shock of white hair streaked with charcoal gray. He looked more like a butcher than a lighting designer. Julio was in his mid-thirties, tall and muscular, a lightly tanned white with brownish short hair. He wore a pair of very short shorts and a T-shirt. They welcomed us to their home and quickly went upstairs. Nelson made a snarky remark about Julio as soon as the latch closed on the upstairs gate, but the party continued immediately after. By the time we got into our room, both Ed and I were dizzy. We barely noticed that someone had pushed the two beds together. Too drunk and tired to move them, we each took our place on opposite sides of this haphazardly constructed "Cuban king."

When I woke up the next morning, I was holding on to Ed for dear life. Both my legs were wrapped around him. Such open vulnerability embarrassed me, even if I was asleep. I had to keep it together, so I put on a robe and went to the dining room for breakfast.

When Ed woke up, he and I separated the beds without a word. We each smoked a cigar, planning what we were going to do for the day. I had a lot of interviews about the film that morning, so I started feeling the grip of nerves. We each took a Valium to soothe the tension. Valiums had become my little friends again, although this time I was taking them voluntarily. I was glad I had Ed to accompany me this time on the slow, sedated ride.

When we got to the Nacional, Betty Ann was waiting for us in the lobby. Annie had gone to a screening, but Betty Ann was in business mode. She led me through the double doors to the courtyard in the rear of the hotel. I sat down in a high-backed wicker chair at one of the wicker and glass tables on the patio overlooking the sea. Peacocks roamed the grounds freely. Songbirds twittered wildly in their cages, which were placed at strategic intervals. Canons for firing mortars at approaching ships were visible at the edge of the Nacional's property, before the land sloped down to the highway and the Malecón beneath. El Moro Castle was outlined in the distance. What a funny place for a press junket, I thought. I lit a cigarillo to prepare for the onslaught of reporters. Betty Ann brought the first one over.

What followed was a blur of the same questions coming out of different mouths. They all wanted to know what it was like being home again, and the moment they knew I was a Peter Pan kid they wanted to know what I thought about Elian. I kept trying to bring all the interviews back to the movie that was showing the next day. Each time I did, Betty Ann nodded approvingly. My personal transformation was all fine and well, but she had paid good money for the film and the trip down, so I was expected to work it.

Ed sat behind the reporters and filmed them interviewing me, his camera often wandering toward the beautiful young women that were walking in and out of the hotel. After five hours of relentless questioning, Betty Ann and Ed went to meet Annie at a screening. I had a date with Lizette Vila.

We were to meet close to the edge of the hotel, near the cannons in the ground at a smaller bar for strolling couples who wanted to share a *guarapo* with rum while they gazed at the sea. *Guarapo!!!* I ordered a glass.

The machine looked at least as old as I was. As the bartender fed precut stalks of sugar cane into the machine, I expected some kind of automated innovation to make the process more efficient but had to contain my glee when I saw him turn a four-pronged crank, pressing every drop of juice out of the tough cane. I took a sip of grown-up *guarapo* with a jigger of Havana Club for heat. I felt like my grandfather, looking to my side for the child I used to be. The breeze stroked my cheek, and my belly went warm.

I turned to see a small woman approaching me. She wore a clean-cut gold dress and an embroidered silk shawl. Her curly reddish-brown hair was cut in a bob. She was both warm and severe, stark and rosy. I knew immediately that it was Lizette Villa. I ordered her a drink.

Underneath us at El Malecón another rally had begun for Elian. Lizette embraced me warmly, kissing both my cheeks. She held me at arm's length, a familial gesture that said "Let me get a good look at you." Then she squeezed my hands, sat me down on a whitewashed wrought-iron bench, and began chattering as if we were long-lost friends with our whole lives to catch up on. She spoke in cooing, soothing tones as she said how good it was to meet me and how much she was looking forward to seeing my film. Then when she heard rumbles of applause from the rally below, she became rigid, her voice staccato, and she punctuated her statements of socialist dogma with typically Latin hand gestures. She drew talk of the Revolution in and out of her commentary, talking about why the collective we had to get

Elian back. She began to talk about her projects, her favorite being a documentary about Cuban transvestites. An oration on the new sexual politics of the Cuban people flowed into her love of *guarapo*, but not when she's dieting. She was like a perfect storm of the personal and collective. Like your favorite gossipy neighbor crossbred with a progressive activist who only speaks Russian.

I was distracted by flashbulbs flaring on either side of us. Two couples sat at little white wrought-iron cocktail tables, sipping mojitos and chatting quietly. I squinted to get a better look and almost spit out my *guarapo* when I saw Mariel Hemingway to my right, Ethel and Rory Kennedy to my left. I heard the crowd underneath me chanting, "Return Elian! Return Elian!"

I looked at Lizette and sighed, "Here you and I are at the Nacional having drinks. To my right is a Hemingway, to my left are Kennedys, and the masses are protesting in the streets below. What's changed?"

Lizette looked wounded, angry, but she paused to collect herself before she spoke.

"The people down on the street believe in the Revolution. They are not homeless and they eat. That is what's changed."

Nothing could have convinced her otherwise, and in that moment I began to understand, if only a little, what was going on around me. Cuba had become more than just the place I lost. It was still that, and there were plenty of personal trials I would have to go through yet. But I understood the bigger picture, if only a little, and I was grateful. I looked at Lizette and held her hand.

"I love you," I said.

"Because I'm a good communist?"

"Yes," I answered with a smile.

We took a long sip of our *guarapos*. I could smell the freshness of the sea.

Then I whispered, "Maybe you should keep Ethel hostage in return for Elian," and we both cracked up.

That night David and Linda Frankel invited us to go with a bunch of film people to a popular restaurant, El Aljibe. Betty Ann and Annie decided to eat at the hotel, but the rest of us took black Mercedes cabs to Miramar.

Miramar is a few miles outside the center of La Habana through a tunnel in the opposite direction of El Tunel de Amor and the Playas del Este. It was built in the forties and fifties and looks like Coral Gables or Beverly Hills, all Spanish hacienda-style houses and neatly manicured boulevards. Most of the Cuban elite and all the foreign businessmen and ambassadors live in the area. There are blocks and blocks of mansions and one of my favorite parks, with a central gazebo surrounded by ropy-looking mangrove trees offering shade from the sweltering heat.

El Aljibe is a government-run restaurant comprised of three open-air dining halls with thatched roofs and varnished wood floors. Wooden tables and chairs are clustered under numerous ceiling fans that disperse the smoke from cigars bought at a well-stocked shop just a few steps from the restaurant. It is clearly a place for rich tourists, clean and smoothly run, with a huge selection of expensive wine. They have a menu of à la carte items if you ask for it, but their main attraction is the house special: chicken. Again, in my naiveté chicken still felt like an everyday item. I had no idea how hard they were to come by in a country with strictly regulated meat rations. Most likely it was because the restaurant was a government-run operation that they had such ready access to chicken.

We all ordered the special, and soon after the first course appeared: a platter of chicken *croquetas* and chicken *empanadas* served with *galletas* and thinly sliced plantain chips called *mariquitas*. The *croquetas* had been sitting under a heat lamp, but they were appealingly crunchy and creamy. The *empanada* filling was delicious, strands of moist chicken in a light Cuban tomato sauce, but the pastry had clearly suffered in its layover between kitchen and table. I snacked on the *mariquitas* and smoked one of Ed's cigarettes while I waited for the main course.

It appeared in a cloud of citrusy steam—a huge pile of chicken parts lacquered in a deep golden brown sauce. This was not your mama's roast chicken. The waiter set the platter down in the center of the table, and we all eagerly dug in. A moment later two more waiters appeared. One carried a tray of *yuca* in *mojo* and a dish of fried sweet plantains; the other brought a big bowl of white rice and a crock of black beans. I waited for them to set the platters down, but they began to serve us like we were dining in some kind of European court. The formality was jarring, to say the least. I wanted to take the bowl and serve myself, but I went along for the ride. Before the waiter left he informed us that if we wanted more of anything, all we had to do was ask.

"Anything?" I asked in wonder, and then I understood. This place was all you can eat! They had to serve the sides that way so we didn't eat up all their profits. It was a regulation to prevent waste, knowing full well that hungry tourists, American or otherwise, weren't likely to care if they ordered a second platter of food and only ate one bite. We devoured the chicken and ordered another tray, which we consumed just as quickly.

The sauce was an addictive blend of caramelized chicken juices, sweet roasted garlic, and mellowed-out sour oranges. It was *mojo* in its ideal form, reduced to a concentrated sludge that I wanted to pour over everything on my plate. It tasted the way I wanted it to—better even—and then I realized something: This was what those restaurants in Miami never quite managed to capture. The flavors and dishes of Cuba, amplified, but still teetering on the edge of restraint. At El Aljibe, they knew what to do, and they did it well: clean, simple Cuban food, well seasoned and served with pride.

We ate into the night and then went to hear jazz at a club. It was thrilling to be immersed in Havana's nightlife; it felt like anything could happen. Ed and I agreed that if one of us scored, the other would go home alone. Maybe such potential was too much for us. At around two A.M. we decided to take a cab home together. When we got to our room, we found the beds were pushed back together.

Ed joked, "Come here, Romeo!" and we fell into bed laughing.

Ed and I woke up early the next morning. We wanted to be fresh and ready, as the movie was going to play at three that afternoon. At breakfast I handed movie tickets to everyone in the house.

Carlos made an announcement to the Spanish guests who were all eating breakfast, "Eduardo was on *Primer Impacto* last night." Clearly they were impressed.

Primer Impacto is a high-rated show like *Entertainment Tonight* that plays all over Latin America and on Spanish-speaking stations in the United States. I had done an interview for the show when my movie was at the AFI festival in Los Angeles but had long since forgotten about it.

Julio continued the housewide address: "It was a five minute segment," he said, tilting his head and raising his eyebrows. "Everyone in La Habana watches it."

Carlos interrupted, "So you two better be ready for the crowds, and the rest of us should get there early."

"We have VIP tickets," Nelson snarled.

"Still we should get there early," said Carlos. The Spaniards agreed.

I hoped they were right, but I chose not to believe them. I had bigger worries on my mind. I knew I had to introduce the movie, and so I spent the whole morning trying to figure out what to say. We met Betty Ann for lunch and then someone from the film festival drove us to the movie theater.

We drove along 23rd Street, a two-way avenue known to Cubans as La Rampa. We passed a long line of people, and I got excited when I thought they were lining up to see my movie. I asked our driver if this was where we were headed, and he chuckled.

"That's Coppelia," he said, "for ice cream. The tourists can eat outside at the carts. But if you're Cuban you wait on line to go inside." Great. I was being shown up by an ice cream shop. We drove another moment, and then the driver gestured and said, "That is the movie theater."

Cine La Rampa. I don't know if that was always its name, but I recognized the building immediately. It was the same theater where I went with my father to see cartoons. The same one where he saw *Some Like It Hot*. At that moment something clicked, like when I was at La Terasa, and I felt stronger knowing that I was about to walk into a building I never thought I'd see again.

Then I saw the line. It was at least ten times as long as the one in front of Coppelia, and people had already started filing into the theater. *Milicianos* strutted back and forth, showing off their guns to keep the crowd in order.

Ed looked at Betty Ann with a sarcastic smile. "I guess we have an audience," he said.

"We sure do!" Betty Ann replied. She looked unbearably happy.

We met a film festival representative at the door who ushered us in past the crowd. We waited in an anteroom until the audience had taken their seats. A man came to bring me out to the stage.

The theater was filled. Seven hundred seats. Not a single place left. I waited as a representative from the film festival introduced me as a great playwright making his first film and a Peter Pan kid who had come home. I walked up to a microphone and faced the crowd. They went wild, applauding for no less than three minutes. Generous, welcoming, grateful applause. I felt so accepted and loved.

I began to speak, but the mike was not working. I refused to get flustered. I turned to the people from the film festival, dizzy with gratitude and excitement.

"Don't worry," I said, "I didn't study voice with Godeane Eagle for nothing." They looked at me funny, but I just turned back to the crowd. When they quieted down, I used every voice class I'd ever taken, every speech I'd ever spoken, every memory of every stage I'd ever stepped on, and I projected.

I told the audience how we had shot the film in two weeks. I introduced Betty Ann and I thanked her for coming. I thanked the audience for coming, and then I paused. I took a deep breath.

"It is not easy to come back," I said. "Years of separation make you

scared and paranoid. But I have missed you, my people, all of my life, and I am so proud to stand in front of you. To quote an old Cuban song . . ." I began to speak the lines, but my voice gave way into a resonant vibrato and before I knew it I was singing.

"Cuando se quiere, de veras / Como te quiero yo a ti / Es imposible mi cielo / Tan separados vivir / Tan separados vivir."

«When you love truly / As I love you / It's impossible my loved ones / So impossible to live apart / So separated from you.»

The crowd sang with me and then burst into more applause, this time even louder and longer. The movie began and I waited for the first few jokes to make sure the crowd laughed. When they did I knew they'd understand the movie, and so I decided to step outside for some air.

But air in Cuba is not complete unless there's smoke to go along with it. I lit a cigarillo and took a long, slow drag. I felt more whole. If not complete, then at least a part of something that I had been missing for a very long time.

❙ *Mojito* ❙

Like Cuba, this drink is full of contrasts. It is both sweet and sour, strong and bright, warming and cooling. All of the notes get a nice accent from the grassy, herby, creamy flavor of spearmint, or *yerba buena*. Even if you're making mojitos for just a few people, buy plenty of mint. Because no matter where you are, in La Habana, Miami, or New York, after one sip of a good mojito, you and your friends are sure to want more.

2 teaspoons turbinado sugar*
3 sprigs fresh spearmint (stems and leaves), rinsed well and dried
½ lime
2 to 3 ounces white rum
Seltzer water or club soda

Crushed ice
Extra mint and lime wedges for garnish

*You may substitute granulated sugar, but I like turbinado because it reminds me of *guarapo*.

1. In a metal cocktail shaker, combine the turbinado sugar and spearmint. Add the juice of the lime along with the flesh and skin. Mash with a wooden pestle or the base of a wooden spoon until the mixture is slushy and the mint and lime skin have released their fragrant oils.

2. Add the rum and a splash of seltzer. Stir until the sugar dissolves. Strain into a rocks glass filled with crushed ice. Top with additional seltzer and stir. Serve with a cocktail straw, garnished with a wedge of lime and a small sprig of mint.

Makes 1 cocktail

▌ *Cuba Libre* ▐

Free Cuba. The words remind me of the feeling I get when I smoke a Montecristo and sip an *añejo*, or aged rum. As such, I like to drink my Cuba Libres with aged rum. Obviously, I think Havana Club is the best, but there are many high-quality imported *añejos* available in liquor stores today. Be sure to distinguish between aged rum and spiced rum, which is full of overpowering flavors. A good *añejo* is a deep golden color and subtly accented by sweet and spicy aromas.

Crushed ice
2 to 3 ounces *añejo* (aged) rum
¼ lime
Cola
Lime wedges for garnish

Fill a highball glass with crushed ice. Pour the rum over the ice and add the juice of the lime quarter. Top with cola and stir. Serve with a cocktail straw, garnished with a wedge of lime.

Makes 1 cocktail

Twelve

Gladys

Soon after I got back from Cuba it became a new century and I became a new person. I had confronted the world in my head, my past and all its ghosts. I had taken in my country and my home, not as it was when I was a child but in that present adult moment with all its harsh realities. I was not prepared for the clash of those worlds, the old Cuba and the new. There were parts of me that I understood more than ever, and there was even more that I didn't understand, but that was okay. It would have been typical but hypocritical to try to force some clear-cut conclusion out of the obvious chaos. So I decided to embrace the complexity of my own Cubanness. What surprised me was that as soon as I got back to the United States I was equally willing to embrace the parts of me that were American.

This presented even greater complexity. What did it mean for me, after discovering that I would always belong in Havana, to also feel American? What kind of American was I? An immigrant? An exile? Was I a Los Angelino? A West Coast kid who had spent twenty years in New York? Or had those twenty years earned me the moniker of a real New Yorker?

Whatever the identification, when I got back from Cuba I loved New York City the way I did as a teenager. For a while I wrote a series of poems about the Hudson River. I would sit in Riverside Park just staring at the water and all its majestic beauty. I wrote about how every day was different in its swirling waters. Thankfully my endless fascination was not the result of too many Valiums.

Still, I was constantly reminded of Cuba because the Elian battle was on full force. Every morning I would turn on CNN and wait to see the reports from Cuba so I could glimpse the sweeping shots of El Malecón or a building that I had seen only weeks before. When I watched those reports I felt I belonged equally in both countries. I was a citizen of two cities, La Habana and Nueva York.

I began to work on a play about going back. At first it had many characters, but then I focused in on three: Federico (Me), Fred (Ed), and Ernesto (José).

What resulted was a play about belonging and finding your identity, both nationally and sexually. The story followed Federico, a writer and professor returning to Cuba for the first time with his best friend, Fred. They meet a cab driver, Ernesto, who takes them around the country, to Federico's family home and eventually to a huge rally for Elian. All of this gets filmed by Fred on his camcorder. I included Valiums, fears of flying, and even some Blanche DuBois role playing.

One of my favorite parts of the play is a letter given to Federico by Ernesto for him to deliver to his sister, who lives in the United States. Federico can't bring himself to deliver the letter without knowing what's inside, so he and Fred open it and read it before returning to the states.

The beginning of the letter is about their ideological differences and how

Bruce MacVittie and Ed Vassallo in Havana Is Waiting *at the Cherry Lane Theatre in New York City*

the politics of their lives have kept them apart for more than twenty years. It moves into a passage where Ernesto reaches out to his sister and encloses a picture of his daughters and himself. Then Federico becomes a part of the story.

"If this man gets this letter to you it means he forgave us. All of us that wanted a Revolution. If he forgave me why can't you? I'm still here. In our house. The same telephone number. Nothing's changed in twenty years. Time is still here. . . .We are here . . . It is here . . . changed. But still recognizable. . . .Waiting. Waiting for you. Everything . . . including my love. . . .Your brother, Ernesto."

I wanted to express that even though an embargo is an act of governance, one that doesn't care about people or relationships, it is those very people and the relationships in their lives that are most affected by the indifference of bureaucracy.

I called the play *When the Sea Drowns in Sand*, to emphasize the inevitable collision of one world with the other.

As I wrote each scene I was sure the play would get produced. I finished the whole thing in a couple of months and immediately sent it to my friend Michael Dixon, the dramaturg at the Actors Theatre of Louisville. My play *In the Eye of the Hurricane* had been a hit at the theater's Humana Festival of New American Plays in the early nineties, so I hoped they would be interested. Michael loved the play and said they would produce it in the same festival in March of 2001.

In December of 2000 I took a group of friends back to the film festival in Havana. I was not going to wait forty years to see home again, no fucking way. Landing in Cuba again was less threatening but equally emotional. So I bolstered myself behind a no-nonsense business approach to the trip. I ushered my friends about town, proving to them that I knew my way, that Cuba was indeed my home. It's scary enough for people to go through the hassle of getting to the island, so they're usually relieved when somebody is willing to take the reins, especially if they know where to find real cigars.

On the opening night of the festival I sat two rows behind Fidel Castro. It was the closest I'd been to him since I was seven, floating on the bay next to the dock in front of La Terasa. The *Los Angeles Times* published a picture of Fidel at the opening , and you could clearly see my face staring at him from behind. The Actors Theatre of Louisville jumped at the chance to use the picture as part of their advertising.

When I got back from the trip we began casting the play. I had insisted that Louisville hire a young Cuban-American director named Michael John Garcés. We agreed that Ed should play himself, or his fictional self, Fred. As Federico we cast Joe Urla, a short, muscular actor, who was appropriately nervous and Basque. Félix Solís was chosen to play Ernesto, the scrappy cab driver, always ready to hustle a tourist. We set off for horse country, ready to be received by the hat-wearing, julep-sipping denizens of Southern hospitality.

But Louisville was not as welcoming as I remembered. The city had a hard time with four Latino guys walking around it and we were often heckled. Nothing special, just the usual "faggots" and "spics." One day we all went to a restaurant together and were told we'd have to wait two hours for a table when there was a whole row of empty banquettes right in front of us.

The barely veiled hostility of the city unfortunately carried over to our experience at Actors Theatre. The new artistic director of the theater was doing his best to let me know that he wasn't happy to have my play as a part of "his" festival, and so I got the silent treatment from him through the entire rehearsal process. I think he felt stymied by Michael Dixon and the previous artistic director, Jon Jory, who had chosen half the plays in that year's festival before resigning. The whole business obviously upset the new guy, but I seemed to bear the brunt of his scorn. Fortunately I had Michael Garcés, Michael Dixon, and a wonderful stage manager, Chuck Turner, to take care of me during the draining rehearsal process.

To add to the pressure, I was scared to be sharing such a personal story. I had written about myself in plays before, but this was an emotional retelling of something that had happened in the recent past, and what's more it was barely fictionalized. I felt totally exposed.

But as Irene always told me, "If you don't feel like you're showing your tits to the audience, then why do it?"

I felt I was showing more than my tits. It was my soul that was naked on stage, all of my longing, despair, and joy up there to be judged. After the plays run a few weeks at the Humana Festival, people from all over the country are invited to see the audience favorites, packed into two weekend programs. The first weekend is for college professors and students, the second for producers of theaters around the country and most, if not all, of the nation's major critics. So by signing up to be part of Humana, you are inviting the buzzards to pick you apart. My vulnerability was amplified by the pressure of criticism. I understood that the show could be a comeback or the end of my career.

During the first performance of *When the Sea Drowns in Sand* I was tense and raw like an open wound. The new artistic director was kind enough to pour salt all over me when he introduced me before the show, in all seriousness, as Eduardo Muchacho.

Muchacho. I felt that twinge of otherness that sent me into a panic. I suddenly worried that my two cents would not be accepted by these people who obviously had no idea how to relate to me. What would all these Americans think when they saw this play, which tells them they are hurting people by their ruthless embargo? The excerpt from the letter wasn't even the most incendiary moment in the play. I saved that for a direct address from Ernesto to the audience that comes immediately before the play's ending—but I'll get to that in a little bit.

Suffice to say I was so terrified I couldn't even watch the play. Instead I watched the audience. One man was trying to get his wife to leave because he was angry and insulted. She refused to go. Good. Another man wiped away a tear while Federico read from the letter. Yes! It was working!

When the performance was over, the audience stood up and applauded for a very long time. Michael Dixon ran up to me and said, "In the fifteen years I have been here, this is the first time I have seen a standing ovation on a first preview."

One of the audience members came up to me, held my hand, and said, "I always thought the embargo was about trade and money. I never knew it tore families apart." They had gotten the message. I was triumphant. So I returned to New York while the play ran.

I got a phone call from the theater's press person a few weeks later, at the end of the students' and teachers' weekend. She could barely contain herself.

"Your show was the big hit of the first weekend," she said. "Please be ready to do a lot of interviews when you get back here. Oh, and the big party on Saturday night when the critics are here is going to have a Cuban theme. Please tell us what kind of food we should make."

I thought about what I'd like to eat and what would please the masses. So I told them Cuban fried shrimp, *tamales*, roast pork, *yuca*, *Moros*, and, of course, Cuba Libres and mojitos.

The play's success carried over to the second weekend, when the show received a rousing standing ovation, even from the critics.

After the Saturday night performance, we went to the party. The theater had hired a Cuban band, a ragtag bunch of musicians who had only gotten to the United States a year earlier. They rocked the place with mambos, sons, and rumbas until the wee hours of the morning. For catering, the Cuban food was pretty darn good, especially the fried shrimp—crisp, tender, and, of course, completely overseasoned.

The reviews were mostly raves, except for critics who were either politically or sexually insulted by the play. But theater's not supposed to be comfortable. It should stir things up a bit. I never said people would like seeing my tits.

That summer I decided to go back to Cuba again. I needed a vacation before returning to New York to remount the play in September of 2001. Angelina Fiordellisi wanted to produce the play at her beautiful venue in the West Village, the Cherry Lane Theatre. I agreed to do the production, but I decided to change the title of the play. I wanted to do away with poetics and dramatic imagery in an attempt to emphasize the work's political aspects. I also wanted something a little catchier, and so I decided to call it *Havana Is Waiting*.

Once again I stayed at Carlos and Julio's house. It was different, as poor Nelson had been excommunicated. Still, I felt at home. But it was

Fidel that I really grew closer to on that trip. He took good care of me and treated me like a friend. On my last trip I had brought a boom box with a CD player that I had lent to Fidel in my absence. Without my even mentioning it he had set it up so that it was waiting for me in my room when I arrived. I played Ella Fitzgerald and drank his addictive coffee and got down to the real business of my trip. I wanted to write a play in Cuba.

Who was I kidding? I didn't need a vacation. I had taken three weeks off so that I would have enough time to write a play in my country, a place that positively oozes inspiration. At first I wanted to write a play about male and female prostitutes, but that quickly became boring and sensationalistic. I didn't want to write about my family, so I looked for other inspirations: industry, agriculture, history.

I couldn't make up my mind. I knew that I wanted to have something truly Cuban at the center of the play, but what? It had to be something people might not understand initially but that they would come to know deeply, in a way that connected them to Cuba and its people.

As I thought and searched, it was inevitable that I would also eat. My favorite place to go that trip was a *paladar* in El Vedado, just two blocks away from Carlos and Julio's house. It was called Gladys's House.

Gladys ran her business out of a grand Art Deco villa that had been meticulously kept up over the years. Her dining room had high ceilings and a long wooden table, with two smaller tables to the side. You could hear the echoes of her cooking in the kitchen as the sounds bounced off the shiny marble floors. The house specialty: Garlic Chicken, cut into pieces and roasted in the perfect *mojo* of lime, *naranja ágria*, and oregano. It was like the stuff at El Aljibe, but so much better. The sauce was stronger but not vulgar as it was in Miami. It was potent because it was native, truly Cuban, almost dangerous. The sauce was sticky, the meat was juicy, and I was hooked.

I was also partial to Gladys's homemade ice cream. Julio insisted that Coppelia, the store we had passed on the way to the film festival, made the best ice cream in Cuba. He loved their tropical flavors, *guayaba*, coconut, and mango best of all. While I appreciated their exotic tastes and smooth, light consistency, it was Gladys's old-fashioned strawberry ice cream that I craved. With its dense, creamy, hand churned richness, it reminded me of Paris, or at least Paris as it was experienced by the women in my family: through couture bought at El Encanto or continental cuisine eaten at a fancy restaurant in downtown Havana.

The truth is, Gladys made food that reminded me of my childhood more than anything I had ever eaten. Gladys herself reminded me of my grandmother Manuela, beautiful, direct, and poised. Her black skin was smooth and flawless, her energy like that of a twenty-year-old even though she was well into her seventies when I first met her.

Me at a paladar *in El Vedado, La Habana, 2000*

I went to her house later than usual one night, after a siesta that went on a little too long. Fortunately for me that was the night that all the customers left before I finished my dinner. I sat and ate, and when I was done Gladys made café and sat down with me. I talked to her that night about her business and the insignificant details of both our lives. And then something caught my eye. I noticed a picture on the dining room wall of a striking blonde dressed in fifties couture.

"Gladys," I asked, "who is that?"

"The lady who owned this house," she answered.

And then she looked at me. Her eyes said, "That's it. Stop there," and I knew that I was not permitted to ask anything else.

That night I sat down and began to write *The Cook*, about a woman named Gladys who works in a beautiful mansion for a wealthy white woman who leaves Cuba right before the Revolution. It was miraculous for me to be writing a play in my own country. I was so taken by the atmosphere and language around me that I started writing the play in Spanish, but I soon switched to English out of practicality.

I wasn't sure how the story would progress, but the things I needed for the play seemed to fall into my lap. I knew I needed 1950s recipes, but I didn't want to wait till I got home to ask my mother. One day I was walking through the Plaza de Armas in Old Havana with Chuck, the stage manager from Louisville who had come to Cuba for a week before we started work on *Havana Is Waiting* in New York. As we strolled the cobblestone streets we admired the shady park and statue at the center of the square. I loved browsing the tables of book vendors that were set up around the park. There was plenty of revolutionary propaganda, posters and books and cards with pictures of Fidel and Che, but there were also pulp novels, romance stories, and even some carefully selected classics. I happened upon one table where I found a cookbook from the fifties, *To Cook in a Minute* by Nitza Villapol. The book had the same title as the cooking show Nitza hosted in the fifties. It was full of Cuban and European recipes, as well as bizarre brand name advertisements and the most hilarious illustrations. The chapter on cooking meat has a picture of a terrified little piglet being chased by a housewife with pert, bullet-shaped breasts and an impossibly tiny waistline. She's also wielding an ax to hack the little piggy into pieces. I had struck inspirational gold, and I poured myself into the writing.

One morning I got a call from Gladys. Fidel rushed into my room and whispered, "Gladys wants to talk to you."

Oh no, I thought, she found out I was writing a play about her and wants to yell at me! I took the phone and heard her gentle voice.

"I made you a plate of *tamales* and I am sending it over," she said. "You know *tamales* are the only food we have left from the indigenous people that once lived here. Their souls comfort us when we eat *tamales*. I made you the *tamales* because I know you love this country."

The plate she sent had more than a dozen *tamales* on it. They were unbearably delicious, the perfect consistency: uniform and creamy, surprisingly chewy and savory when you got a bit of pork. Without knowing it, Gladys closed a circuit inside of me. She gave me the foundation that I would build my entire play on: the power of food. I ate her *tamales* like I had eaten other *tamales*, but the experience was different. The little bundles of corn told a story, my story, the story of those that came before me, and the story I was trying to tell through my play.

From that moment on it was clear that Gladys and I shared a deep connection. With only a few words exchanged between us, she had given me the greatest of gifts. The play came out of me without struggle, so easily, in fact, that I wrote it longhand in notebooks, something I had never done.

One afternoon when I was almost finished with *The Cook*, I decided I deserved a break. I took a cab by myself to La Terasa in Cojimar and sat there as the sun set over the bay, casting rosy shadows on the long bar. I ordered a Havana Club siéte años on the rocks and sipped it slowly. I felt like I was celebrating a victory. I had won. I had beat the sons of bitches on both sides of the embargo. I was writing a play and having a drink in my hometown bar.

In September I was back in New York City ready to get down to business. The first day of rehearsal for *Havana Is Waiting* was supposed to be September 11, 2001. Obviously, after the attacks on the World Trade Center, none of us made it below 14th Street.

There was some talk about canceling the play, but when I met with the producers I told them what my friend the Polish actress Elzbieta Cysewski had once told me: "The time to do theater is when the city is in trouble." So now was the time.

On September 12, the cast and crew met at Ed's apartment to sign their contracts. The producers had decided that the show was going on. We sat down and read the first act of the play.

We took a break between acts, and just before we sat back down the room filled with a horrific stench. We walked out onto Ed's terrace to find that the wind had changed. We felt so helpless; all we could do was go inside and read act two.

It was almost a week before we could all get down to the West Village to rehearse at the Cherry Lane Theatre. But we were determined, blindly determined. I can honestly say that in the haze of the Towers it didn't occur to me that a play that openly criticized America was not going to get the standing ovations it had the year before.

In an interview for an article in the Sunday *The New York Times*, I had told the reporter that some of the producers had asked me to change the ending of the play. They wanted me to cut Ernesto's speech just before the final blackout, his direct address to the audience. He says:

> Miami Mafia. Yankee politicians. Exxon and United Fruit Company. Meyer Lansky and all his disciples. Motherfuckers. You've kept us apart long enough. Return us. Motherfuckers! You've kept us apart long enough. Return us. Us. Elian. Peter Pan. Give them back. Give them back to us. Motherfuckers! Let us come together. End the embargo. Please. Fuck you. Motherfuckers! Give them back!"

The Sunday before we opened, the article in *The New York Times* ended with this:

> When someone asked him whether he would alter his play to remove any material that could be deemed unpatriotic, like his anti-embargo stance, he also said no. "The United States has been an imperialist power and I have the right to say that," he said. "We can't, at this point, make ourselves victims and blind ourselves. It's important to see how other people feel about you and try to understand why they feel that way about you." Risky words these days, but spoken like a true American."

After the article came out I got scads of hate mail sent to the Cherry Lane. Even some of the people working on the play refused to talk to me. For my part, I loved the contradiction in that it took my returning to Cuba, the reclaiming of my true, "foreign," Cuban identity to earn me the title of a true American in the press. And yet there

I was, characterized by a quiet majority as unpatriotic. Maybe Marx had it wrong, I thought, maybe patriotism is the real opium of the masses. The play closed after a month.

I tried to gain perspective, but with all the gloom and doom in the air it was almost impossible. Still, for me, September 2001 was a magical time. My friend Nicole LaLiberté, a nymphlike creature, all legs and big eyes and real red hair, had spent the summer trying to convince me to meet a friend of hers named Michael Domitrovich. Every time she told me his age, nineteen, I told her to forget it. I later found out that he did the same. We were many years apart, and so I put off meeting him indefinitely. But when the towers went down, I said to myself, you might be dead next week, so why don't you meet this guy that the magical Nicole thinks is so right for you? So I called him. We sat for hours in Washington Square Park on September 15, watching people light candles and sing songs, looking up at the smoke from the still-burning towers. I looked at him: tall, dark, and handsome, sweet and insecure. I decided to hold his hand, and when he did not pull away I knew that something really good had just happened to me.

As the weeks passed, in the middle of all the chaos in Lower Manhattan, Michael and I spent more and more time together. We did our best to distract ourselves, overloading our senses with as much good food as we could get our hands on.

At the time I was living in Hanover Square, near the South Street Seaport, only a few blocks away from Ground Zero. Every morning I'd go downstairs to a little chocolate shop that served coffee from an espresso bar in the rear of the store. I'd order two large fresh-squeezed orange juices, two *pain au chocolat*, and two cappuccinos (which came with two little dark chocolate truffles). I'd bring them upstairs and Michael and I would share our Parisian breakfast while gazing at a thin strip of the East River, visible between two tall office buildings.

The neighborhood around Hanover Square, Manhattan's Financial District, has a high concentration of commercial and office buildings. Even though people thought I was crazy, I loved living down there because the streets would empty out as soon as the work day ended.

The weekends, too, saw very little action, even less just after 9/11, when the whole area felt like a ghost town. Michael and I took to roaming the streets, looking for obscure restaurants that needed patrons. At first we only went to holes in the wall. We found random places that served Indian, Japanese, Mexican, Italian, and French food. There was a great place near the river that served a wide selection of soups for lunch. As we branched out in the neighborhood we found our naughtiest pleasures. We'd have homemade sausages and duck confit at Les Halles, oysters on the half-shell at Delmonico's, steaks and creamed spinach at Harry's, or piles of fried shrimp and spaghetti marinara at Carmine's. Eventually all the eating out put a dent in our pockets, so I suggested to Michael that we check out a gourmet grocery store on John Street called Zeytuna. It was then that I learned the nineteen-year-old could cook.

I knew Michael came from a family of restaurateurs. His mother and father had owned restaurants in New York and Detroit, and when I met him they had a successful Cajun place called Lola's on Martha's Vineyard. I thought buying groceries and cooking out of the tiny kitchen at Hanover Square would save us money, but we ended up spending, and eating, even more.

Every trip to Zeytuna was the same. We'd get a selection of cured meats, a few nice cheeses, and a loaf of crusty bread for starters. We'd pick up some pastries or cookies to make sure we had something sweet, and then we'd buy dinner.

Over the next year I tasted all of Michael's Cajun specialties: jambalaya, étoufée, and gumbo, fried oysters, fried catfish, and fried soft-shell crabs. Everything had a sauce or a gravy to go with it. Sometimes Michael would prepare five-course meals just for the two of us. He didn't like it when I helped in the kitchen, but if he asked, I was there. I preferred setting the table and lighting the candles and picking the music.

As the terror alerts went from high to low to elevated, my belly stayed at a steady full. We were fat, happy, and together. I couldn't think of a better way to spend what seemed like the end of the world.

Eduardo Machado & Michael Domitrovich

All the eating proved to be very inspiring, too. I finished writing *The Cook* in 2002 and started preparing to hustle for a production. My efforts were cut short, though, when I heard that Lucie Arnaz was thinking of doing my play *Once Removed* in Miami. Maybe it was time to conquer the Cuban refugees.

In April of 2003 I was back in Miami rehearsing *Once Removed* at the Coconut Grove Playhouse. I was nervous about showing the work in Miami. I didn't want to deal with the trouble I knew would arise when

Michael and me, 2002

my plays went up before the notoriously confrontational exile community. I also remembered René Busch's warning. If my family in Miami didn't get me, how could I expect anyone else to?

Two things made me agree to do the play. The first was that *Once Removed* is one of my least political plays. It's about a Cuban family that comes to the United States and realizes the American Dream, if tenuously at first. I figured the Cubans couldn't hate the play that much.

The second and most important deciding factor was that Lucie Arnaz had, in fact, decided to star in the play. Lucie Arnaz. The daughter of Desi Arnaz and Lucille Ball. I had met Lucie ten years before when she did a benefit reading of *Broken Eggs* with Olympia Dukakis, Sigourney Weaver, and John Leguizamo. They were all wonderful in the reading but Lucie seemed to have channeled Desi and all of her Cuban ancestors for the performance. The audience went wild. I got a call from her assistant the next day saying, "Lucie thanks you for yesterday. It made her feel very close to her father."

I did that? She didn't even know what watching her father had done for me. How he had made me feel closer . . . to what? To being? To existing? While living in a scary new country, a strange new home where so much was uncertain, her father had made me feel like I at least had a chance.

And then there was Lucie herself. The connection was not as direct as the one I had felt watching her father, but I had followed Lucie and her career for as long as I was American. When we got to Los Angeles, the first house we drove to was Lucy's and Lucie's. I had watched her on *The Lucy Show* and seen her in *The Black Dahlia*. I had even seen her sing to her mom and grandmother from *Mame* on *The Mike Douglas Show*. I had envied the fact that she was friends with Patty Duke. I sometimes think that I only learned English so I could understand *The Patty Duke Show*.

Naturally I thought that my interest would be matched by hers and that Lucie and I would become fast friends. After *Broken Eggs*, I asked her to do a reading of *Once Removed*, in which she was equally good. She even came to rehearsals with a Cuban cookbook of her own. I had a drink with her at Sardis and never saw her again.

Then in the winter of 2002 I was contacted by the artistic director of the Coconut Grove Playhouse. He told me Lucie wanted to do the play at his theater but that she wanted me to do some rewrites first. I imagined tragedies of Floating Island proportions unfolding before me, but I decided to go with my gut instead. Something told me that Lucie and I would work really well together.

We met to read the play for the first time with Lucie's husband, Larry Luckinbill, and the director, Michael John Garcés. When we finished, Lucie gave me notes. She told me every line that didn't feel right, all the kinks and quirks that she knew wouldn't work well onstage. I took the majority of her advice, simply because I was so impressed by her professionalism. There is very little that Lucie takes lightly when it comes to work. She is so incisive, so thorough and specific, that it is impossible to not hear her out. I hadn't met a pro like that since Jamie Hammerstein.

After several months of work we all agreed, in a manner that would have made Jamie proud: We had gotten rid of the bullshit in the play.

Heading down to Miami, arm in figurative arm with Lucie, I felt like none of the Cubans would be able to stop us—not the exiles, not the critics, not even my family. Because I felt connected to the Arnaz family, and my family positively worshipped at their altar. I think it's safe to say that Lucie and her father are about as close to Cuban-American royalty as you can get, and no good Cuban would ever disrespect their queen.

As we rehearsed and promoted the play, I watched Lucie fall in love with Miami and Miami fall in love with Lucie. At our first big fundraiser cocktail party Lucie spoke lovingly about her dad. She explained how her grandmother never learned English and that as she lay on her deathbed when Lucie was a teenager, she heard her yell, "Mi casa! Mi casa!" "My home! My home!" She was referring to the house she had lost in Cuba forty years before when President Machado's dictatorship ended, after her dad's family lost everything and escaped to Miami. She told the audience that was her reason for doing the play—for her grandmother who she never quite understood until now. I felt proud.

The cast and crew were all staying near the theater in the quaint little town of Coconut Grove. We occupied our off-time by strolling the sun-baked streets, avoiding the boutiques and chain stores, instead frequenting a few of the town's outdoor cafés. There was a Mexican place, an Italian joint, and a little French café called the Green Street Café that served strong drinks and snacks well after most of the other places had closed.

Michael and I preferred to dine at a little Cuban café across from Green Street called Mambo. I started going there early in the morning because it was the only place within walking distance that served a strong cup of Cuban coffee. They had the right machine: all copper tubes and polished chrome, the requisite sandwich press, and a glass-front case with a heat lamp on top to keep their selection of *croquetas* and *empanadas* warm through the day.

I liked to start each day with a meat *pastelito* and a *cortado*, a big shot of coffee with a splash of steamed milk. Michael would meet me on the corner for coffee when he woke up, and then I'd head off to rehearsal.

When we ate dinner at Mambo we would always start by sharing a plate of *tostones*—the crispy fried green plantains—served with a little dish of garlicky *mojo*. We'd then split an avocado salad, all tomatoes and onions and creamy green slices of the fatty fruit. We'd always say we would try something new, but every time our main course was the same: we'd both order *Vaca Frita*, shredded and fried flank steak served with even more *mojo*.

Now, I should say that it occurred to me that nothing had changed in Miami. The flavors were still too strong, too salty, and too garlicky. Both Michael and I usually ended up with big tummy aches after scarfing down the fried plantain discs and fried beef. Garlic burps, swollen tongues, and headaches. I knew I was back in South Florida. But something had changed. I no longer cared that Miami didn't quite live up to the Cuba in my mind. How could it? It was Miami. Not Cuba. It was on that trip that I learned to take the goodness where I could find it. We ate *Vaca Frita* and *tostones* with reckless abandon. The swollen tongues and aching bellies were just part of the experience.

And so Miami began to feel more and more like home, despite the fact that I had not called any of my relatives who lived there. They were not happy about that. They knew I was in town—they were reading about it in all the promotions that were running in the papers. I had wanted to call them the minute I landed, but I just couldn't do it. It was partly because I wanted some privacy while I was working on my play. My nerves about the rest of the Cubans in town were starting to get the best of me. Otherwise I think I just felt bad that I hadn't visited in so long, and I didn't know where to begin. I had not been to Miami since I was nineteen years old, except for a secret three-day trip to do research for a screenplay. What was I supposed to say—"I'm back and I'm going to do a play that's going to piss off all your friends!"?

I decided to remain silent and guilt ridden until my sister Didi called me and said, "Call them before I get there. I do not want to deal with the drama."

I was really excited that Didi was coming for the opening, so I listened to her. A day later I called my aunt Maria, my father's sister, and I invited her and her children to the opening. Then I called my aunt Chichi, on my mother's side, and invited her and her children to the opening. Then I did the hardest thing. I went and saw my grandmother Cuca.

I found her sitting in the same room at my aunt Maria's house where I had last seen her thirty years before. She was listening to the same radio back then, tuned to the Cuban station, waiting for Fidel to be overthrown. And there she was, still listening, still waiting, still twiggy-thin, but with long black and gray hair. I walked in and sat on the bed. She looked at me.

"Grandma, it's Eduardo."

"I know who you are," she said curtly. "The rest is gone, but my mind is still intact." She punctuated her sentence by rapping on the arm of her chair with her knuckles. Then silence. She was ninety-eight at the time. The radio played a quiet ballad. Then she snapped.

"You are too fat."

"I know. I got old," I replied.

"I saw your picture in the newspaper."

She showed me a stack of newspapers with my picture, and we both smiled. That was the last time I ever saw my grandmother. She died at ninety-nine.

The opening of *Once Removed* was very glamorous. My aunts, my cousins, my sister Didi, and Michael were all there. Several of my friends from New York, as well as a former student, Sandi Goff, and her husband, Andrew Farkas, had flown in to give me support on my Miami debut. It felt like a Broadway opening. The thousand seat theater was packed—there is nothing like a theater filled with a thousand people listening to your words. Michael Garcés, the director, was too nervous to watch even a moment of the performance. I walked outside with him for a few minutes, but then I had to go back in. Miami was doing strange things to me, so I did something I rarely do. I watched the play until the end.

It wasn't that I liked the play any more than others. It wasn't that I felt particularly welcome, either. Like the comfort that comes with a familiar feeling of emptiness, or the greasy burps that go along with Cuban food in Miami, I wanted to enjoy the whole joyous spectacle of a play I knew would piss at least a few people off.

Later that night there was a huge party at a Cuban furniture store in downtown Miami, on Calle Ocho, the main Cuban thoroughfare in town. The store was surreal—its facade was shaped like a huge castle, and the theme continued on the inside. The walls were painted like a stacked stone fortress with little windows and arched doorways that led to neatly arranged furniture sets. The owners, Cubans of course, had opened all the rooms so people could wander freely. They set up bars at opposite ends of the store and little tables with lots of Cuban hors d'oeuvres—*croquetas*, *empanadas*, and little meat pies. They were tasty, but they didn't have heat lamps so they got cold and rubbery pretty fast.

But I was too excited to eat. The audience had loved Lucie's performance. And sure enough, a group of Cubans in the balcony were so offended that they left the theater screaming at one another. Does it get any better than that? To top it all off, the mayor of Miami was at the party!

I watched my family as the mayor spoke about how important it was to have Lucie as a member of the Miami community. He presented her with the key to the city, and her acceptance speech moved the entire crowd. She was sincerely grateful, to the theater, the play, and the city of Miami for welcoming her with open arms. I felt the same. I loved the place. Even if I found it slightly repulsive.

When I looked at the faces of my aunts and cousins I could tell that they were happy to be related to me, happy to be a part of that night. Later, when I introduced them all to the mayor, I felt like I had conquered Miami. This was the place where I felt so lonely and desperate as a child. The place I had dreaded returning to. But I was there. I had gotten over the fear of my childhood, and I had gotten my family back in the process.

That Sunday we went to my godmother Yolanda's house for a barbecue. As we ate grilled flank steak with *Moros*, and flan for dessert, I could feel the warmth of my family surrounding me.

My family. I didn't think I needed them. I even ran away from them. Finally, I just gave in and admitted it: No matter how much I wanted to get away from them, I had loved them all more than I had ever let on. The first and second and third cousins, all the parents and children, but especially my aunts.

And as I sat there and ate the food that fed my soul, I knew that time had not separated us. We were still cousins, aunts, uncles, nieces, and nephews. We still had shared history. We knew how to make each other laugh and just which buttons to push. We still loved each other. We still needed each other. I had found home again, one of many, in the place I least expected.

❚ *Gladys's Garlic Chicken* ❚

I know I'm going to get hassled for not including Gladys's recipe for *tamales*. I do not pretend to be able to reinvent such perfection, and honestly I'd rather make the trip to El Vedado. Her Garlic Chicken is another story. There are, of course, subtle differences between Gladys's version and mine, but this is a quick and easy way to make a Cuban classic, inspired by a Cuban classic.

Two 3- to 4-pound chickens, cut into parts
1 cup sour orange juice (or ½ cup orange juice and ½ cup lime juice)
1 tablespoon distilled white vinegar
12 garlic cloves, peeled and coarsely chopped
2 tablespoons salt
1 teaspoon ground black pepper
1 teaspoon dried oregano
1 teaspoon ground cumin

1. Place the chicken parts in a container large enough to hold them all. In a small mixing bowl, combine the sour orange juice, vinegar, garlic, salt, pepper, oregano, and cumin. Stir gently, then pour the marinade evenly over the chicken. Cover with plastic wrap and refrigerate at least 1 hour, preferably overnight, mixing halfway through so the chicken is evenly marinated.

2. Preheat the oven to 450°F. Transfer the chicken to a roasting pan so that it sits in one layer. Pour the marinade evenly over the top. Roast in the lower third of the oven until the chicken is cooked and the sauce begins to caramelize, about 45 minutes. Be sure to stir the chicken and shake the pan in the last 10 minutes of cooking to coat the chicken in sauce and prevent it from scorching. When it's done, transfer the chicken to a warm platter and spoon the garlic sauce left in the pan evenly over the top. Serve with rice and beans.

Makes 6 servings

Vaca Frita

Every time I eat this dish I feel like I am being personally welcomed back to Miami. The big, bold flavors of beef, onion, and salt stand out. And I love the play of textures, the soft boiled beef that is crisped up in hot oil, topped with sweet, slippery onions, and sauced with garlicky sour *mojo*. It makes me want to do the mambo just thinking about it.

To start:
1 piece flank steak, about 2 pounds
6 garlic cloves, peeled and smashed
1 jumbo Spanish onion, peeled and quartered
2 bay leaves

2 tablespoons salt
15 black peppercorns

To finish:
½ cup vegetable oil
1 jumbo Spanish onion, peeled and sliced into ¼-inch-thick rounds
1 teaspoon salt

1. Cut the flank steak against the grain into 3 smaller pieces of uniform size. Place the meat in a large pot or Dutch oven. Cover with cold water. Add the garlic, quartered onion, bay leaves, salt, and peppercorns. Bring to a boil over high heat. Reduce the heat to medium and simmer, covered, 2 hours, or until the meat is fork tender. Transfer the meat to a plate and set aside until cool enough to handle. Discard the cooking liquid. Slice each steak into 1-inch-thick strips, cutting with the grain this time. Set aside until ready to fry.

2. Heat ¼ cup of the vegetable oil in a large skillet over high heat. Separate the onion rounds into rings by pushing out their centers. Add the onion rings to the pan and season with the salt. Cook, stirring occasionally, until softened, 5 minutes. Transfer to a paper towel–lined plate. Blot any excess oil with more paper towel. Set aside.

3. Add the remaining ¼ cup vegetable oil to the pan. When the oil is hot, fry the strips of flank steak until browned and crispy, turning once, 1 minute per side. Transfer to a paper towel–lined plate when cooked. Blot any excess oil with more paper towel. If you like, sprinkle with a pinch of coarse salt.

4. To serve, take a few chunks of steak and top them with a little fried onion. Serve with *Tostones* and Quick *Mojo* (see pg 224) on the side.

Makes 6 servings

Thirteen

Their Souls Comfort Us

We began rehearsing *The Cook* in the fall of 2003 for a production at INTAR that winter. In the two years since I had started writing the play in Cuba it had become a story of truly epic proportions. The action spanned nearly forty years, following the changes in Cuba between 1959 and 1997, the one constant being the central character, the fiercely passionate and loyal Gladys. In the first act, the mistress of the house she works in is fleeing Cuba on New Year's Eve, just before Fidel and his *compañeros* take Havana. Before she goes she gives Gladys five hundred dollars to keep the house as it is until the day she returns. The rest of the play shows what Gladys is prepared to do to keep her promise. Then when her mistress's daughter returns to see the house her mother lived in, Gladys must confront her inevitable disappointment at just how much has changed between her and her former employer. Ultimately she adapts, as she has to all the other challenges she's met throughout the Revolution, and she decides to turn the house into a *paladar* called Gladys's Place.

As I was doing rewrites of the play, I had in mind my friend Wanda de Jesus for the role of Gladys. But when it became clear that Wanda would not be able to do it, we had a reading with an actress named Zabryna Guevara. It turned out she had played one of the sisters in the production of *Revoltillo* that had toured Cuba. She had been charming and graceful and a delight to watch then. Six years later she had really come into her own as an actress. She had a laid back confidence, a fierce but subtle sexuality, and, most of all, the technical chops that would be required to originate such a demanding role. She worked her ass off and she became, completely, Gladys, "the Cook."

Zabryna, only in her thirties, went from the age of thirty to seventy without much make-up. She used her technique and inhabited the soul of the woman from the pages I had written. Her acting alone brought out the warmth and good-heartedness of the character.

We had to turn people away at the first preview, and from that first show on the audience fell in love with her night after night.

For me the play was a return of sorts. We presented the piece at INTAR's small theater, on 53rd Street, right downstairs from the room I had set up with Irene years before. I chose to work with Michael Garcés again, and he had the brilliant idea of turning the lobby of the theater into the living room of an old Cuban mansion in El Vedado.

Garcés took this conceit a step further and started each night's performance by having two of the characters who played servants in the play pass hors d'oeuvres as the audience waited for the house to open. All the food had been generously donated by a new Cuban restaurant called Havana Central. Their ham *croquetas*, meat *pastelitos*, and miniature Cuban sandwiches were a smash hit before the show even started. The restaurant now has three locations in Manhattan; I love the branch on 46th Street if I'm nearby and need a little Cuban fix. What I love the most about their restaurants is that they're built to resemble *paladares* in Cuba, and they look a lot like our set for *The Cook* did.

When the show was about to begin the audience was led into the theater. The set from the lobby continued along the walls until it opened up onto the stage, which housed a fully functioning 1950s kitchen that aged along with Gladys and the Revolution.

At intermission we gave the audience little sips of rum poured out of a Havana Club bottle I had saved from one of my trips to Cuba. Without much of a publicity budget the play was extended three times, thanks to word of mouth and *The New Yorker*, which praised it all through the run.

For my own part, I felt a surprisingly thorough satisfaction after the show closed. All the surface pleasures were there—I was grateful for the good notices, relieved that audiences kept filling the house, and delighted at Zabryna's brilliance onstage. Beyond that, I knew that I had accomplished what I set out to do with the play: I had presented a truly Cuban character in a uniquely Cuban story, in which a more general understanding of Cuba and its people was reached through a personal narrative.

Most importantly, I had honored Gladys, and not just because I wrote about her. The play was full of her food: strawberry ice cream, Baked Alaska, cream cheese and pimiento sandwiches, Steak with Fried Onions, Garlic Chicken, and of course, *tamales*. Everything was prepared onstage, and other foods and recipes were mentioned in the action of the play. So when I say I honored her, it was because I felt I had communicated her story in the way she would have wanted it told: through food.

That summer I returned to El Vedado with all the good reviews in hand. The first thing I did after unpacking was to send Fidel over to Gladys's house with the stack of articles. I wanted to see the look on her face, but I remembered the day I asked her about the blond lady in the photos. If she didn't want to talk about it then, I didn't want to make her talk about it now, but I needed her to know just how much she had done for me. It was she who inspired my play, but it was her food that inspired so much more. Those *tamales*—the meaning in their taste and the way they were so generously offered—for me they opened up a whole new understanding of food and its power to communicate. I'd had an inkling of this power the year before, on Michael's first trip to Cuba, and it was all thanks to fruit salad.

Michael always slept later than I did, but I would wait until he woke up to have breakfast. After coffee in the plant-lined hallway, we'd sit together in Carlos and Julio's dining room and have those perfect fried eggs with bacon or a link of hot-dog-like sausage. Toast was served with butter and jam or a long block of cellophane-wrapped guava paste. There was homemade cheese, sometimes yogurt, and always a big bowl of fruit salad.

The fruit itself was supremely sweet—mangoes that burst with floral notes, firm little baby bananas, and chunks of pineapple so tart and juicy that eating them was a revelation of its own. But the boys quickly learned that we liked the fruit best when they served it in the form of a frothy blended fruit smoothie. The pureed stuff was like a magic potion. The smoothies had no milk in them, no yogurt, no ice cream or sorbet. If they hadn't been made and chilled the night before, they weren't even particularly cold, but they didn't need to be. The carafe of brightly colored liquid set before us each morning was all about the fruit. It was so thick from all the different pulps and natural sugars that one glass had the rejuvenating power of two cups of café, with the added bonus of sending you running to the restroom mere moments later.

Carlos, Julio, and Fidel at one of the tables in their dining room. El Vedado, La Habana, 2004

The turning point in my culinary relationship with Carlos and Julio was on the day Michael asked them why the fruit was so delicious. Julio was flattered that we liked it, as he took pride in picking the produce they served for breakfast. So he offered to take us straight to the source: the outdoor market on 19th Street.

He drove us to this greenest of green markets in his new car. The tourists and guests that frequented the house had made it possible for Carlos and him to buy a miniature red Citroën. It wasn't a particularly long walk to the market, but he insisted on driving to give us the full experience.

The market was overwhelmingly beautiful. All the vendors' tables were situated under a wooden roof in four long rows with space to cross over in between. The perimeter along the right side when you first walked in was where the meat was sold. I don't doubt the meat's quality, but its refrigeration left something to be desired . . . since there was no refrigeration. Meat and flies don't really go together in my mind, but I was not there to judge, so I turned my attention to the vegetables.

The minute Michael saw the piles of brightly colored produce, he took off to get a better look, returning every few moments to pull us toward another stall. There were vibrant red and green peppers, spicy green chiles, and bright orange *habaneros.* Fresh tomatoes and three different kinds of eggplant. A whole table full of roots: *yuca, malanga, boniato, ñame* (African white yams), and potatoes. And one section was nothing but citrus fruits—limes, lemons, oranges, and my favorite, sour oranges. Julio showed us the best pineapples, papayas, *guayabas,* and mangoes as large as my head with pits no bigger than my thumb.

"See this?" he said, holding up an ovular fruit with a papery brown skin, "mamey. This is what I use when I make the juice red."

I hadn't seen a mamey since I was a boy. I had forgotten they even existed. I had just assumed the color was from extra papaya, but when I saw the papery shell of the mamey, I remembered the ruby tone of the flesh inside and matched it to the smoothies. After that I asked Julio to put chunks of mamey in his fruit salad, even though he only liked it pureed.

Next at the market were collard greens that looked like ancient Egyptian fans. Big rippling stalks of broccoli. Michael almost had a heart attack when he saw the spinach—the leaves were so big, their color so green, and sprouting out of their tops were clusters of tiny purple flowers.

"I've never seen anything like this," he said. Julio smiled.

"It's because they're organic."

"No," I said.

"Of course," he scoffed, "why should we waste all that money on pesticides?"

Amazing, I thought. The organic food we pay an extra arm and a leg for in the States is sold here out of necessity. Perhaps it was risky—you could lose your crops if a blight of something or other came along, but the cost of expensive chemicals didn't make sense in Cuba. I could see the pride in Julio's eyes as we ogled all the goodies. He knew about quality when it came to produce.

"*Soy un guajiro,*" he'd always say. A *guajiro* is a farm boy, a bumpkin, someone who's spent his whole life in the country. Julio loved to identify himself as such, in a self-effacing manner that was totally endearing.

Since the market only accepted Cuban pesos, no dollars, there were mostly Cubans there, maybe one or two tourists besides ourselves. Everybody I know that's been to Cuba complains that the food is sorely lacking in fresh vegetables and green salads. I always tell them to go to the market on 19th Street.

Later that day Julio and Carlos invited Michael and me up to their roof for the first time. It became clear that Julio was more than just a *guajiro*. He was a master of plants.

I loved the fish tank and the hallway and the pots overflowing with greenery in every corner, but nothing could have prepared me for the garden on the roof. After going up the stairwell and crossing the threshold, you emerged onto a deck covered in terra-cotta tiles, shaded by a wooden grape arbor with vines and leaves and bursting green fruit running wild. Julio led us around, pointing out the highlights of his garden. He had potted palms, rubber plants, tropical shrubs, and two different orchids—one with tiny butter yellow blossoms, another with burgundy-flecked pink petals that smelled like chocolate, "But only in the morning," said Julio.

The show-stoppers were Julio's bonsai trees. He had taken five or six different species of trees native to Cuba, snipping and trimming them over time until they were perfect miniature versions of their larger relatives.

Sitting on that roof, I could sense that things were shifting in my relationship with Carlos and Julio. They had always been perfectly polite, but they had never invited me upstairs to see their garden of treasures. When they went off to run some errands, as Michael and I lazed about, smoking and sunbathing, we decided to make them dinner. It just seemed like the right thing to do. But what to make? We knew it would have to involve vegetables from our favorite new market, but we weren't sure what other ingredients would be available to us. Michael looked up at the arbor and said, "Grape leaves!"

We told Carlos and Julio about our plan, and they agreed to let us cook them dinner that weekend. We bought all the vegetables at the market, some rice and ground lamb at one of the dollar stores in Miramar, and then went home to prepare dinner.

Michael and I spent hours in the small kitchen, blanching the grape leaves and stuffing them with a mixture of rice and lamb. It was July, and so between the sweltering air and the heat from all four burners on the gas stove, it had to be at least one hundred degrees in there. But we worked and worked, and sweated and sweated.

Galletas, *plantain, and lizard in Carlos and Julio's kitchen, El Vedado, La Habana, 2002*

In addition to the grape leaves, we made a big leafy spinach salad with a warm bacon dressing. There was no way we were going to miss eating those little purple flowers. Michael made another Greek dish, a sweet and sour eggplant salad called *Melitzano Salata*, similar to Italian *caponata*. Julio wanted the recipe—he could not believe that eggplant could be turned into something that good.

Even though he declined to sit at the table with us, I made Fidel a plate, but all those vegetables were a little too foreign for him. Even if vegetables are available, some Cubans still want rice, beans, and meat with nothing else to accompany them.

It didn't hit me just how much this shared meal affected our relationship until the following year, when I returned to Cuba after *The Cook*. As soon as we got to their house, Julio and Carlos started asking Michael what he was going to cook for them this trip. The boys insisted that we eat at home the two Saturdays we were there. The first one Michael would cook, the second Carlos and Julio would. What a sweet surprise.

After a lot of thought, Michael decided he would make Chicken Française and his grandfather's recipe for pasta with burnt butter. There would have to be some kind of vegetable side dish, but we put off that decision until we reached the market on 19th Street. We knew the meal would have to be simple yet splashy. Even in a utopian cultural cooking exchange, Michael was not one to be shown up in the kitchen. The priority for both of us was that whatever we made had to be easy to cook on the boys' small stove in sweltering heat.

So on Saturday morning we set out with Julio to the dollar stores in his red mini. We took El Malecón toward Miramar and began our hunt. I say hunt literally, not figuratively, because if we had learned anything cooking the year before it's that what you set out to find is not always what you come home with. The dollar stores in Miramar were stocked with European imports to feed the diplomats and celebrities that live in the neighborhood, but even their stock was unreliable. Some days the shelves were full of Serrano ham, chorizo, imported cheese, and chocolate, as well as delicate wafer cookies, sweet drink mixes, and, of all things, quail eggs. Other days there would be cheese but no chocolate, ham but no chorizo, cookies but no quail eggs. It occurred to me that the products were there on the shelves out of their own kind of necessity, like the organic vegetables in the market. The groceries represented their countries of origin and carried a deeper political meaning: They were from the only countries willing to trade with Cuba.

The previous year we had noticed a predominance of Italian imports in the dollar stores, so Michael figured a meal based on those flavors would be easy to pull together. If only it were that simple. We found dry pasta and butter but no Parmesan cheese. After much sniffing, Michael picked a piece of firm, waxy-looking white cheese with a pungent aroma. "It should be fine," he said, but I could tell he was uncertain. He couldn't hide the panic, though, when we went to find chicken breasts. He looked at me with fear in his eyes.

"They have frozen turkey legs, lamb shanks, and rabbits."

"Rabbits?" I asked.

"Whole rabbits," he said.

We made a few more purchases, some white wine, Spanish olive oil, ground black pepper, and flour for breading the nonexistent chicken. Then we told Julio the bad news.

"They don't have chicken," I said.

"None?" he asked.

"No breasts, thighs, legs, or wings," said Michael, utterly dejected.

"Don't worry. We'll go to another store."

We drove a few minutes to another, larger dollar store but were equally unlucky there.

"Do Cubans even eat rabbits?" Michael asked incredulously.

"Today they do," said Julio with a shrug of his shoulders.

"What are we going to do?" I asked.

"We'll go to the market on 19th Street," said Julio. "See what they have there."

Michael took one glance at the meat counter and gave me a look that was clear. Absolutely no way was he going to cook or eat anything on that table. He went off and bought a big bag of lemons and several bundles of long beans.

"I love these things," he said, bouncing the rubber-banded green tentacles up and down like a big brush at a car wash. "They'll make a great side."

We bought several heads of garlic and two bunches of Italian parsley. We were postponing having to commit to the meat on the open air table.

All of a sudden Julio came up to us excitedly. "I think there is something for us outside," he said.

"What is it?" Michael asked.

"Snapper. Red snapper. How about that for dinner?"

He thought for a minute, then whispered, "Yes. Sure."

"Good. Give me twenty dollars." We did and Julio went out into the street and up to a group of men standing next to an ancient automobile.

Michael decided that he would make Red Snapper Française. He was clearly unhappy about it, but he went with the flow. We waited for Julio. He came back with a big burlap sack that obviously held something very big inside. We got in the car, drove away, and after a few blocks Julio stopped and made us get out to look over our purchase.

He pulled the red snapper out of the burlap sack, and I gasped when I saw its pearly pink skin, layer upon layer of scales shimmering in the sunlight.

"Isn't it beautiful?" Julio asked. Michael took a big sniff of the fish.

"Fresh, too," he said, "but who's going to clean it?"

"Don't you worry baby. I'm a *guajiro*. I know how to handle a piece of meat," and he gave Michael a little wink.

Julio informed us that there was going to be an extra guest for the meal, a famous Cuban choreographer named Iván Tenorio. At first he told us Iván was a friend of theirs, then he fessed up and admitted that he was Carlos's lover before Nelson. Iván was lonely and going through a rough time and so Carlos and Julio had been inviting him for lunch every Saturday. In addition to Iván, we had invited the actress Adria Santana and her husband, Pablo. Get ready to sweat, I thought to myself.

We picked Iván up, and he was delighted to meet us. "I've heard so much about your . . . cooking," he said, smiling mischievously. I was struck by Iván's presence. He was small, slender, and quite muscular with short, white hair and a razor-sharp mouth. He carried himself with a dancer's posture and poise, but there was a fire in his eyes, full of passion and creativity, that could only belong to a great choreographer. The trip back to the house, with Michael and me in the back seat, was like watching a Cuban version of the Smothers Brothers, with one insult after another flying between Iván and Julio. They ribbed each other expertly, like family, picking on each others' thinning hair or aging skin. Iván especially liked to tease Julio about being a *guajiro*, although he never used the word. He found other, subtler, ways to condescend.

Suddenly Michael screamed out, "We have to turn around—we forgot about dessert!"

"Carlos is making his specialty," said Julio, *"Arroz con Leche,"* rice with milk.

"So you had rice left over?" Iván asked sarcastically.

"Of course," said Julio.

"It figures you'd serve them leftovers."

I thought to myself how funny it was that the jokes in a classless society were all about class.

When we got back to the house Michael and I watched Julio cut and fillet the fish in five minutes flat. He did know what he was doing.

And then the cooking began. Michael breaded the fish fillets and boiled the pasta. He chopped garlic and made a rich sauce using wine, butter, and parsley. I cleaned up after him, which annoyed Fidel because he thought that was his job.

"Today you are a guest," I told him, "and this time you are going to like the food."

"No vegetables?" he asked.

"Very few," I answered.

"Thank God," he said, and he smiled, satisfied, before pouring himself a rum and taking a seat in his little room at the back of the house to listen to a Whitney Houston CD.

Fidel had already set the large table with all of the house's fine china from the thirties and an embroidered tablecloth. Michael was putting the finishing touches on the meal. He was gently coating the fried snapper fillets in sauce as he monitored a pan that was "burning" the butter to pour over the pasta.

"This cheese we got," he said to me, "I think it's Greek."

"Is that bad?" I asked.

"No! Actually, I think it's what my grandfather used to use. Kasseri," a sharp sheep's milk cheese.

I had helped him shred the whole block earlier, part of which he used to top the fish, and the rest to top the cooked spaghetti. He then poured the nutty brown butter over the pasta. I loved the sizzling sound that rose up as the piping-hot fat melted the cheese over the noodles.

At around one-thirty we all sat down to eat. I was a little put off by the idea of eating cheese on fish, but I must say it was spectacular. Everyone loved it, even Fidel, who accepted our offer to join us at the table. We only got him to eat a few bites of the long beans, which Michael had braised in olive oil and tons of lemon, but this alone was a noteworthy feat. Julio, of course, teased him incessantly.

We all talked loud and laughed hard. Then we took a short break between lunch and dessert. I drank a Havana Club *siéte años* on the rocks and smoked a Romeo y Julieta cigar. Iván and Julio stretched out for a quick nap in the upstairs bedroom, Carlos and Adria talked about a show they were working on, and Michael chatted about America with Adria's husband, Pablo.

Pablo was an American who had decided forty years previously to make his life in Cuba as a musician. His mother had been a famous folk singer and leftist in the United States and had sent him to Cuba as a teenager. It was there that he met Adria and decided never to leave. Their love proved that an embargo can't stop everything. People find their own way.

Julio appeared in the kitchen carrying a big oval bowl.

"I didn't make it," he said, "but I get to carry it!" And he set the dish down on the table.

There is a difference between *Arroz con Leche* and rice pudding. Rice pudding is thickened with eggs, while *Arroz con Leche* only requires patience. A simple combination of rice, milk, and sugar is all that's really needed. Gentle heat and plenty of stirring slowly convince the rice to give off all its starch, bursting into the warm richness of so much boiled milk. The rice the boys used had been cooked with butter, which provided a rich base for the dessert. The milk had been scalded, as it had boiled with the rice for a while, so there was a slightly nutty flavor that complemented the rice. The whole combination was so sensuously creamy that I didn't miss the thickening power of eggs one bit. The rice was soft and fluffy, swimming in a thick bath of sweet milk.

The really exciting part of the dessert was its flavorings. The surface had been sprinkled with a brown powder flecked with bits of green, providing a clue to the deeper flavors that had been cooked into the rice and milk: cinnamon and lime. It's a traditional combination for many Latin desserts, but it surprises me every time I taste it. Earthy sweetness and bright citrus—does it get more Cuban than that? I had one big serving, but Michael ate three bowlfuls, which made Carlos very happy.

The next week Michael and I went out on our own, seeing the now familiar sights of La Habana. No matter where we went, we always seemed to end up at the Hotel Ambos Mundos in Old Havana. Housed in a sixteenth-century building with huge doors that open onto the busy streets, the highlight of the hotel's bar is the woman who plays the piano. She must be well into her sixties, and although her repertoire includes Cuban classics, she prefers to play Cole Porter.

The bar at Ambos Mundos makes a mean mojito. Michael and I would sit, drinking and smoking sugar-laced cigarettes, watching the people passing by on the sidewalk in front of the hotel. We could always spot the German tourists just by looking at their gait or their scrunched mouths. We also liked speculating about which of the macho guys from America were there to visit the

Michael in Regla, across the bay from La Habana, 2004

Cuban señorita they had fallen in love with. They all had the same look on their face, equal parts intoxication and desperation.

And while we loved sitting around people-watching, we took the afternoons to roam freely. We'd walk slowly up and down the narrow streets, taking in that treasure of a city. La Habana. Where every corner is a revelation and a contradiction all at once. Grand architecture and broken-down bicycles. Prostitutes carrying their textbooks on their way to university to study engineering. *Milicianos* with machine guns helping the students in a fourth grade class in their crisp blue uniforms as they cross a busy intersection. Poverty mixed with style. Struggle so full of pride.

On one of our outings we made a new discovery: the Copacabana. Behind this less-than-special tourist hotel is a little slice of paradise—a pool in the ocean. It's really a concrete enclosure with sections cut out to let the water flow through, so you can swim in the salt but never have to face a wave. Michael and I would spend entire days lounging around that little concrete enclave. If you brought *galletas* into the water with you, you could crumble them up and feed them to the tropical fish swimming in the enclosure. They didn't like the waves, either, but they liked Cuban crackers just as much as I did. I wondered how they'd feel about guava paste?

The following Friday preparations began for Saturday's lunch. Julio had bought a leg of pork that Carlos was injecting with a mixture of sour orange, garlic, oregano, and cumin.

After returning from the market Julio called me into the kitchen to show me three different kinds of plantains. I had always thought there was only one kind and told him so.

"That's because you are Cuban-American and ignorant," he said, completely serious. "You've forgotten where you come from. Where's Michael?"

"In the bedroom," I answered.

He yelled down the hallway. "Michael, come in here so I can show you my bananas." He winked at me. "You'll like it, I promise!"

Michael walked into the dining room and Julio began his

demonstration, taking out a small thick plantain and explaining, "This one is smaller and tastes more like flowers. Smell it. You'll see."

I took a whiff, and it did indeed smell like a flower, an exotic mix of chamomile and roses. Then he took out a long, skinny one.

"This one is a *burro*, more bitter and a little tougher." Then he took out a regular looking plantain.

"And this is the one you are used to. Right?"

Michael and I nodded our heads.

"It's called *El Macho*, hard and not very favorable. But big, and that's what you like, right?" He smiled wryly. "Only good for making *mariquitas*!" *Mariquitas* are the thinly sliced banana chips they serve at El Aljibe, and also the Cuban slang word for a homosexual. We all laughed.

The next morning I woke up to the smells that always take me back to my mother's kitchen: oregano, sour orange, and garlic.

In my play *Once Removed* after the Bay of Pigs has failed, the mother, Olga (the part Lucie played) realizes it will be a long time before she gets home. She uses her memories to give her strength in the face of uncertainty. She says, "Christmas Eve . . . Mama . . . The smell of Mama's hands when she had put garlic, bitter oranges and oregano on the pork. Wait for me, Mama. Please wait for me."

There I was smelling it. Just like every Christmas when I was a kid no matter where we were living. I ran into the dining room to find Carlos and Julio hard at work.

"Breakfast?" asked Fidel.

I answered loud enough so Julio could hear me, "No, I am saving myself for lunch."

Carlos yelled back, "You are in for a real Cuban meal."

"But you want café?" asked Fidel, always needing to feel useful.

"Of course," I said, "With milk and sugar."

Fidel ran into the kitchen, happy that he had something to do. I went to sit up on the roof terrace, looking out over the city of La Habana. I felt a new sensation of home. Maybe Judy Garland had it right all along, as she sang it, "Any place I hang my hat is home."

Maybe I didn't need to know exactly where my home was in order to belong. Maybe all I needed was to feel that belonging. Then I would be home no matter where I was.

I lit a Cohiba cigarillo and wondered at my good fortune of being part of so many places. Fidel came upstairs and handed me a cup of café. He poured a long stream of hot milk right in front of me, and I felt like I was waking up all over again. What could be more welcoming? How could I belong here any more than I already did? What did home feel like if not this?

Michael joined me a few minutes later with his own cup of coffee. We sunbathed the morning away after taking a good whiff of the orchid that did indeed smell like chocolate.

When the sun got too hot, we went downstairs to find everyone in a panic. The government had decided that it was a good time to turn the gas off. Carlos informed us that lunch might be late.

"But it could come back on again in a minute," Julio said with a shrug.

"Or it could be two hours from now," snapped Carlos. The air was tense.

Then just as quickly as it went off, the gas came back on. The boys cranked on all the burners to make sure they would finish the meal in time. We offered to help, but they wouldn't hear of it. We were their guests that day, and not because we were paying them to stay in their house.

The same guests from the week before prepared to gather around the table—Adria, Pablo, Iván, Carlos, Julio, Michael, and me, with an extra plate for Fidel if he wanted to join us.

As soon as we sat down, Julio tortured Michael and me with his lessons on Cuban gastronomy. He rapped his finger on the table, demanding attention.

"Three different kinds of fried plantains. Could you ever imagine in your wildest dreams? Now come here Eduardo and Michael. Taste."

He gave us a taste of each plantain, their textures and flavors completely different from one another, just as Julio had described.

"And now my *malanga* fritters, made with pink *malangas*."

"Pink *malangas*? I never heard of that." I was egging him on.

"Of course not. You grew up in Yankeeland. Now taste."

He handed Michael and me each a *malanga* fritter. We tasted and swooned at their earthiness. They were perfectly fried football-shaped pillows of root vegetable. Crispy on the outside and burn-your-mouth hot on the inside, but still creamy and fluffy, and tinted the slightest color of rose.

"What's in these?" Michael asked.

"*Malanga*, lime, eggs, salt, and pepper," Julio replied.

"That's it?" Michael wondered, but he never got an answer because at that moment Carlos came in with the leg of pork.

"Everybody hungry?" he asked.

I certainly was. I spoke very little during the meal but made plenty of grunts and growls to honor the food's primal deliciousness. The pork was tender and moist and delicate, not overly seasoned, so it still actually tasted like pork. The black beans were mysterious, filled with a complex blend of earthy flavors and hearty textures. The plantains and fritters melted in my mouth like honey. We ate until around four, and then we all took a siesta.

I tried to sleep but couldn't. So much more than my hunger had been satisfied. I used the siesta to sit with the knowledge that I had just eaten the most authentic Cuban meal of my life. I wasn't sure what that meant exactly. So many variables had been different from what I had imagined, but I knew the formula had been proven. I had to adjust to the idea that authenticity is not always where you expect to find it.

In the late afternoon we had our dessert, a scrumptious bread pudding with leftover bread and raisins soaked in a custard made with condensed milk and doused in rum syrup. We smoked and drank and joked and laughed. At eight we all had seconds of everything that was left, both dinner and dessert. Then it was time for bed—we couldn't eat or drink or speak anymore.

As they were about to leave, Adria announced grandly that tomorrow was her turn. She had ordered food, because she did not cook, and we were all coming over to her house for a late lunch. Michael and I swore to each other not to eat till then.

And we didn't. In the afternoon we drove to Adria's house in Miramar, a duplex with a large terrace on the roof. She knew Michael and I would love the terrace, so she took us up there immediately to show off her atomic herb garden. She had four huge pots with plants of prehistoric proportions: oregano, basil, and two kinds of mint. Adria had gotten the seeds while doing a play in the United States, and when she'd planted them in Cuba they literally exploded. The oregano leaves were furry and bigger than silver dollars—they reminded me of a 1950s newsreel about the wonders of nuclear mutation. I also appreciated that this was what happened when American plants were allowed into Cuba—obviously, they flourished.

Adria had invited a number of her friends, but she had more than enough food to feed us all. She had ordered several family-style platters of food from a neighbor who ran a catering business to make some extra cash. There were smoked pork chops with roasted pineapple on top—sweet, salty, and sultry, just how I love them. An enormous bowl of rice salad had countless ingredients in it, like something you'd make to clean out your fridge, but in a good way. There were raisins, almonds, shredded chicken, chopped ham, canned peas, hard-boiled eggs, and at least several cups of mayonnaise. And to top it all off, a huge plate of *tamales* that just seemed to keep refilling itself. I would have eaten a dozen, but I could barely finish one. Not because I didn't like it—it was everything a *tamal* should be—but I was still full from our lunch the day before.

I wondered, though, did I really want to eat a dozen? Were the *tamales* that good? If home had a new meaning in my mind, what did that mean about taste? It was while I was staring down that little packet of corn and pork that I realized just how much my standards had changed. The *tamal* was delicious, I knew that much, but how did it compare to the *tamales* of my youth?

And then it hit me. I didn't care. I didn't want to compare them. That was a different home, a different time, with a different family around me. There was no way to get it back. And anyway, I no longer wanted to be the kind of Cuban that let what was lost get in the way of the beauty and joy and life and food that was staring me in the face. Maybe I'd have just one more *tamal*, to make the feeling last.

But Adria had other plans. I had celebrated my birthday a few days earlier without much fanfare. Michael and I went to the Hotel Nacional and drank *guarapo* with Habana Club. We shared a Cuban Sandwich and I smoked a whole Montecristo cigar. Not a No. 5, but a big one.

But Adria wanted to celebrate again. She was not the kind of woman to make a fuss, and she knew I was not the kind of man that enjoyed one. So my cake bore no candles.

But what a cake it was: syrup-soaked sponge so moist and sweet that its texture was as smooth and soft as the Swiss meringue that covered the cake's exterior. In between the layers was an even sweeter compote of flaked coconut, chunky pineapple preserves, and ground toasted walnuts. With its three layers of cake, two layers of fruit and nuts, and stiff, shiny peaks of white meringue on top, the whole thing must have been at least a foot tall.

It was so spectacular that Adria couldn't help herself. She had to sing "Happy Birthday." I didn't mind, though, because everyone sang in Spanish.

I kept thinking about those *tamales*, and then I stopped myself. Do not get stuck in the past, I thought. You have a new Cuba right in front of you. Three whole layers of it. What more do you want?

I helped myself to another piece of cake.

Red Snapper à la Francesa

This dish proves that sometimes fish and cheese go together just fine, especially in a foreign country where you can't find chicken. The only tricky part of this recipe is to keep the olive oil and butter hot enough to fry the fish but not so hot that it scorches. If you're working with big pieces of snapper, use a long fish spatula or two smaller spatulas so the fish doesn't fall apart with all the flipping and saucing. If it does fall apart a little, never fear. This is a very rich dish, so each person is likely to eat less than a whole piece, and anyway, this recipe and the context it was created in are all about sharing.

For the Fish:

1 cup all-purpose flour
½ cup grated Parmesan cheese
1 teaspoon salt
½ teaspoon ground black pepper
2 large eggs
2 tablespoons water
2 pounds red snapper fillets*
⅓ cup olive oil
2 tablespoons salted butter

For the sauce:

6 tablespoons salted butter
12 garlic cloves, peeled and coarsely chopped
2 cups white wine
¼ cup lemon juice
¼ cup water
1 teaspoon salt
½ teaspoon ground black pepper
¼ cup chopped flat-leaf parsley
½ cup grated Parmesan cheese

*We used red snapper in Cuba, but you may substitute any firm fish, like tilapia, roughy, or catfish.

1.   Prepare the fish: Place the flour and Parmesan cheese in a pie plate or dish with raised edges. Season with ½ teaspoon of the salt and ¼ teaspoon of the black pepper. Mix with a fork. Crack the eggs

into a separate pie plate or dish with raised edges and season with the remaining ½ teaspoon salt and ¼ teaspoon black pepper. Add the water and mix with a fork until well blended. Dip both sides of a snapper fillet in the flour mixture. Tap gently to remove any excess. Next, dip both sides in a light coating of egg, then again in the flour mixture. Transfer to a plate until ready to fry. Repeat with remaining fillets.

2. Heat the olive oil and 2 tablespoons of the butter in a large skillet over medium-high heat until hot but not smoking. Fry half the snapper until golden and crispy, turning once, 2 minutes per side. Transfer to a plate and set aside. Repeat with remaining snapper.

3. Prepare the sauce: Add the butter and garlic to the pan. Cook, stirring with a wooden spoon, until the garlic has just begun to brown, 1 minute. Add the wine and cook until the alcohol has evaporated, 4 to 5 minutes. Add the lemon juice and water and season with the salt and pepper. Stir to combine.

4. Return half the snapper fillets to the pan. Cook for 2 minutes to warm through, then carefully transfer the fish to a warm serving platter. Repeat with remaining snapper fillets. Turn off the heat and add half the parsley to the pan, along with ¼ cup of the Parmesan cheese. Stir to combine.

5. To finish, sprinkle the fish with the remaining ¼ cup Parmesan cheese. Spoon a little sauce over each fillet, then garnish with the remaining parsley. Serve immediately.

Makes 4 to 6 servings

[*Pasta with "Burnt" Butter*]

This recipe is a wonderful example of the kind of cultural exchange that can take place over a dining room table. Although the recipe originated from a Greek immigrant's kitchen, it was cooked for Cubans, by an American, coordinated by an exile. It is so simple to prepare, but the care put into browning the butter makes for a unique and complex flavor profile. Michael's Greek grandfather, his *papou*, would be proud to know that this dish was strong enough to cross a ninety-mile stretch of ocean that has held back so much else.

1 pound uncooked spaghetti
6 tablespoons salted butter
½ teaspoon salt
½ teaspoon ground black pepper
¾ cup finely grated kasseri cheese*

*Kasseri is a sharp Greek sheep's milk cheese. If you can't find it, you may substitute pecorino or Parmesan.

1. Cook the pasta according to the package instructions.

2. While the pasta is cooking, melt the butter in a small pan over low heat. When the butter is melted, increase the heat to medium. Cook for about 3 minutes more, swirling the pan occasionally. The butter will bubble loudly, then foam quickly as it begins to brown. As soon as this foam starts to recede, turn off the heat. You don't actually want to burn the butter, but you do want to coax as much flavor as possible out of it by browning it thoroughly.

3. When the pasta is finished cooking, drain it well and transfer it to a big bowl or serving dish. Season with the salt and pepper and toss. Sprinkle the cheese evenly over the surface of the pasta.

4. Pour the butter evenly over the pasta to melt the cheese. The brown bits that leave the pan at the end are the yummiest, so be sure to distribute them around the surface of the dish. Serve immediately, or keep warm in a 200°F oven until you're ready to eat.

Makes 6 servings as a side dish

❚ *Malanga Fritters* ❚

Julio, the *guajiro*, had no problem grating the starchy *malanga* by hand, but this recipe is much easier to make when you use a food processor. Since the batter can sit for a while before you fry it, this dish is wonderful for parties, and a real crowd pleaser. Serve quick *mojo* with them, if you like, but I prefer the fritters on their own. The delicate balance of garlic, salt, lime, and parsley are all fortified by the base of slightly bitter *malanga*. It is truly a taste of Cuba.

2 pounds *malanga*
4 garlic cloves, peeled
¼ cup flat-leaf parsley
2 large eggs
2 teaspoons salt
½ teaspoon ground black pepper
2 tablespoons fresh lime juice
2 cups vegetable oil

1. Peel the *malanga* using a vegetable peeler. Rinse them thoroughly, then cut into 1-inch cubes.

2. In the bowl of a food processor, pulse the garlic and parsley until very finely chopped. Scrape down the sides of the bowl with a spatula and continue pulsing to make sure you don't have any big chunks of garlic.

3. Add the *malanga*, eggs, salt, pepper, and lime juice. Pulse 10 to 15 times, until the mixture is finely chopped, then puree for about 30 seconds. You want the mixture to be smooth, but be careful not to overmix. The *malanga* is very starchy and can definitely overwork the food processor.

4. Transfer the mixture to a bowl. Stir to make sure everything is evenly distributed. Cover with plastic wrap and refrigerate for at least 30 minutes or up to 24 hours.

5. When you're ready to fry, heat the vegetable oil in a 10- to 12-inch skillet with raised edges over medium-high heat until very hot (about 375°F). Drop heaping teaspoons of batter in, 6 at a time. Fry until golden and crispy, 1 to 2 minutes per side. Using a slotted spoon, transfer to a paper towel lined–plate to collect any excess oil. Serve immediately, or keep warm in a low oven until you are finished frying the remaining fritters. Serve alone, or with Quick *Mojo* (see pg 224) as a dipping sauce.

Makes about 32 fritters

[*Arroz con Leche*]

Patience is key here, as is a watchful eye. The precooked rice needs to be treated gently so that it surrenders completely to its delicious bath of cinnamon- and lime-scented milk. This flavor combination is very traditional in Cuba and other Latin American countries, but it surprises me every time I taste it. Again we have a dish full of contrasts, with flavors both musky and bright, spicy and zesty, rich and light. But it is the particular chemistry of rice starch and milk that make this dessert impossibly luxurious.

2 limes
1 cup cooked rice
8 cups whole milk
1 cup granulated sugar
4 tablespoons salted butter
¼ teaspoon salt
2 cinnamon sticks
½ teaspoon vanilla extract
½ teaspoon ground cinnamon

1. Using a vegetable peeler, remove the zest from one of the limes in long pieces. Try to remove only the green zest and not the bitter pith underneath.

2. In a 3½-quart saucepan with a heavy bottom, combine the rice, milk, sugar, butter, salt, cinnamon sticks, and strips of lime zest. Bring to a boil over medium-high heat, stirring occasionally. As soon as the milk comes to a boil, reduce the heat to medium-low and cook, uncovered, until the rice gives off its starch and the mixture thickens, about 1 hour and 30 minutes. The milk should simmer gently throughout, but be sure to stir often and lower the heat if necessary, especially in the last 30 minutes of cooking. If the pan gets too hot and you don't stir enough, the rice will stick to the bottom.

3. Turn off the heat and stir in the vanilla. Remove the cinnamon sticks and lime zest and discard. Pour the mixture into a serving dish. Cool to room temperature, then cover with plastic wrap and refrigerate overnight, or until thickened and chilled completely. Just before serving, sprinkle with the ground cinnamon and the finely grated zest of the other lime. Spoon into individual bowls and serve.

Makes 8 servings

Fourteen

Floating

The day after Adria's party we returned to the United States. As we approached José Martí International Airport in Havana, everything dissolved.

I become the eight-year-old kid in the car on his way to the plane ride that will change everything.

Hindsight's supposed to be twenty-twenty, but if I learned anything from my first trip to the United States, it's that you never really know what's going to happen. I am always preparing myself for a wall to be thrown up between the past and the present, with the possibility that I won't be able to break through it again in the future. It happened before.

I do my best not to think about any of this. I am going home, I think—Manhattan is my home, too. I deal with security, standing in the exit line to pay a fee and get my tourist card stamped. I feel sick.

I board the plane to the Bahamas, a third country, a stopover between Cuba and the United States. The place I go to hide where I've been. The sadness turns to panic because I know that in a few hours I will go through United States customs. I will again feel like a criminal, a traitor.

When we get to United States customs, Michael and I stand in separate lines. I don't want him to be too close to me, but why? I'm not doing anything wrong. I look at the other Cubans, Cuban-Americans, returning from their trips to bring Ivory soap and a little cash to their relatives in La Habana. The look on all our faces is the same. We are scared shitless. We know what we've done. And no matter how right we know it is, someone still says it's wrong. Illegal. We each have a story in our heads, a script we go over and over. Where have we been? What were we doing? How long were we there? We cannot tell the truth. Most of us don't even know what the consequences would be if we did. But still we are afraid. We have gone home. To Cuba. We have broken the law.

In 2001 President Bush declared Cuba off-limits, and not just because of an economic embargo. Cuba, he said, was part of the "axis of evil."

Evil? Those fun-loving, generous people. Evil? That beautiful city in the middle of the Caribbean. Evil? My birthplace. Evil? My Cuban brothers and sisters. No.

No way, President Bush, and all the Florida congressmen, congresswomen, senators, and all the bitter exiles who learned how to vote as a block. They are not evil. They are kinder to me than you have ever been.

Deprived? Yes. But evil, no. Socialist? Some. But evil, no. Proud? Loyal? Passionate? Yes. Patient, persistent, and strong? Absolutely. They refuse to give in to colonization. But does that make them evil? No fucking way.

God, greed, politics, and revenge always have the power to destroy the human values of decency, kindness, and friendship. But most of all they fracture family, in every sense of the word. We, the Cubans of every America: North, South, Central, and the Caribbean; we have been torn apart. And the only place we can see it is standing in line at U.S. customs; there we are all exactly the same.

Our heads hurt. We can't even look at each other. What if someone sees? What if someone knows? Better try to remember the name of the hotel we supposedly stayed at in the Bahamas. We are all waiting to be caught. Our home is a secret. A treasure we will do anything to keep and defend.

We are afraid. But at least we are together.

I wonder why I can't find this kind of connection elsewhere. Why can't I feel this bond without the fear? I'm sweating. I'm tired.

And then I get to customs.

I get a dirty look at my green card.

A leer at the sight of my Cuban passport.

Where were you? What were you doing? How long were you there? I lie because I have to. But I secretly want to get caught. Maybe if I were persecuted enough, the feeling of closeness would last. But my passport is stamped. And I am let through.

And then I'm in a taxi with Michael. Exhausted. But at least I managed to sneak in a box of cigars. The relief temporarily quells my yearning for utopia . . . until the following winter.

The Cook was being produced in Connecticut at the seven hundred seat Hartford Stage, a much larger venue than INTAR's seventy seats. Michael Garcés was directing again, with an entirely new supporting cast, but luckily for me Zabryna was still playing Gladys. She had confessed to me that she was nervous about having to give a less intimate performance in the new space. At the first preview I realized I was nervous, too, but for different reasons. As I watched the all-white audience walk in, I felt like I was standing in line at customs. I worried that my favorite play wouldn't pass inspection.

I wanted the message of *The Cook* to be similar to *Havana Is Waiting:* End the embargo because it's people you're hurting, much more than government. The difference is that *Havana Is Waiting* was all about me, and so my personal narrative always seemed to get more attention than the message of the play. In *The Cook* I wanted the story to belong to Gladys. I wanted the story to belong to someone who stayed after everyone else left.

The big moment for Gladys is when her mistress's daughter returns to see her mother's house in 1997. When Gladys realizes that her former boss harbors hate and resentment toward her for staying in her house, even though Gladys was just keeping her promise, everything changes. She says to the daughter, "Get out of my house . . . Yes my history, my house."

It's the simplest moment, but for Gladys it is everything. In Cuba you're not supposed to claim propriety. "Your" house in fact belongs to the state. For almost forty years Gladys deferred ownership further, all the way back to the woman who left in 1959. When she says, "Yes my history, my house," she's claiming her property, but more than that, she's claiming her life. She's claiming her struggle. She is claiming Cuba for the Cubans that stayed.

We were not in Manhattan anymore, and so I had no idea what the audiences in Hartford would do. How would they deal with such a blatant rejection of American policy? Would they be able to accept socialism as a valid way of life, and even an antidote to a ridiculous embargo? I knew the message would get across, but would they be able to hear it?

I should have given Zabryna, and Gladys, a little more credit. At that first preview, when the moment came and Gladys told the daughter to get out, the all-white audience stopped the show with applause, and I knew we had won them over. I should have learned my own lesson: The moment was not about politics; it was about Gladys.

Félix Solís and Zabryna Guevara
in The Cook *at Hartford Stage, 2005*

That night they gave Zabryna a standing ovation. The same roaring applause, cheers, and whistles that they would give her every night of the production. Every single night.

The critic at the *Hartford Courant* gave me and the production the best review I had ever received in my career. Ticket sales went through the roof. We had a hit, and not off-Broadway. This was a big, respectable, audience-friendly regional theater in the middle of Connecticut.

The last day of *The Cook* in Hartford fell on Easter Sunday. The box office people told me, "Don't expect a sold out house today. It's Easter in Connecticut; they don't go to the theater on Easter."

And at that moment hundreds of people showed up to buy tickets for the last performance. I went to the stage door to smoke. Too much excitement. Just before the show started I took a good look at the audience, and I was humbled.

Hartford Stage had been surprised by how many Latinos and blacks had bought tickets to the show throughout the run. Both groups were difficult demographics for the theater to reach, but we had brought everyone out in full force.

That last night was something else, though. The theater was filled with young people and old people of every race. Every type of person that actually lives in Connecticut. Everyone that actually lives in the United States.

I got on the theater phone from the light booth and called Zabryna in her dressing room.

"Zabryna, it's the crowd we love," I told her. "There are kids who have never been to the theater before. Rock the fucking house, honey!"

And she did. All the actors did. They gave the best performances they had ever given. When it was over, I looked down from the booth. The entire audience was on its feet cheering the same character: a black Cuban woman in her seventies. Maybe we came from different places. Maybe we looked different. But in that theater Gladys was the mother of us all. Her home, her kitchen, her Cuba, was a place we all belonged.

But what about my kitchen? Our trips to Cuba brought out a streak of inventiveness in Michael's and my approach to Cuban cuisine. After eating Julio's fritters, we loved to make our own, using *yuca*, *malanga*, even sweet potatoes (the orange ones). Michael started cooking more meat, especially flank steak. We'd eat it broiled, or marinated, or braised and sauced in Michael's own spicy version of *Ropa Vieja*. His variations on flan were especially tasty, one with pumpkin, one with coconut, and the best with ginger.

I decided that if Fernando's *Arroz con Pollo* gave me a headache, I should stop complaining about it. I stopped listening to the arguments about what my mother or sister or aunt thought should go into the dish. I made up my own recipe using fresh asparagus, white wine, and lots of saffron, instead of *bijol*.

I took the memory and I made it mine.

I mean, why fight it? Tastes change. Memories blur. I don't think any information is ever true for long. If you want to be a part of something, you've got to take it and make it yours.

Throughout my life, whenever I've thought I had it all figured out, something would happen. Something would come along and my whole world would be turned upside down. I'd look for answers from people I respected, people in the theater, people in my life, even people in my family.

I understand now that you can never have all the answers. You can look for home. You can try to figure out what it means. But every meaning is elusive. Every word can escape you just as soon as you've found it.

So you have to take it where it comes. Hang your hat when you find the right hook. Whenever you're lost, you have to ask questions. And whenever you figure something out, you have to share it.

I don't claim to have all the answers, but when I find just one, I want to pass it on.

I have now been teaching for over fifteen years, long enough to have seen all the pitfalls and the joys that come with the profession. I focus on the joy: the students.

If you share, if you teach, you learn, too. When my students leave I let them go out into the world and I never expect to hear from them again. I tell myself that teaching is a job for me, just a way to make money so that I can write. But that's a lie I tell myself to hold it all together.

I care about my students more than I could ever let them know. I do not want the personal to get in the way. The teaching, the learning, the criticism and the rigor have to be first. I put my feelings in a box until the students are gone, but I feel so close to them through it all. I want all of them to find themselves and have full, creative lives. If things do not go perfectly for them, I at least want them to have the tools to express themselves. I wish I could stay with them forever to help them when they need it, but to be a good teacher you have to let them go.

Every year at graduation, I sit in the back row on the stage behind the rest of the faculty watching the students from the School of the Arts get their diplomas. I hide there in the back because I don't want them to see the tears on my cheeks. I don't want any of them to see that in fact I will miss them. I want them to feel free to leave. I do not want their past to have the same power over them as mine did over me.

Most of them leave without looking back, happy to be away from my criticism, I imagine. I would be. Some of them return. Some of them even become friends of mine, but a different kind of friend. Things get complicated when you have been parent, guide, and comrade to a writer.

But I live my life in complication, and I take the joy where it comes.

I am currently working on a million things at INTAR, where I am now Artistic Director. The only peace I get is when Jeff, our bookkeeper, comes up with a brilliant idea that will help keep us afloat for a few more months. In the middle of it all I sometimes wish I could close my eyes and dream the day away. But there's work to be done, so I pick the next best option. I go to lunch.

I excuse myself by telling my right hand, Megan Smith, that I will be back in an hour. I walk down Tenth Avenue just like I did with Irene more then twenty years before. I approach the Dominican lunch counter.

Inside everything is the same. I am surrounded by the same cab drivers, the same waitresses, the same counter, with the colorful sign for fruit drinks: mango, pineapple, mamey. The only thing that's changed is the name. No longer Melys, it's now called Lali. I sit down and the smell of Latin food conquers my senses. I ask what the specials are. The waitress calls back from across the room.

"Pork chops, red beans, split peas, broiled chicken, pigs' feet, and *bacalao.*" I decide on *bacalao* with white rice, red beans, and sweet plantains.

A few minutes later the waitress sets the big plate of food before me. I take a moment to savor the smell. The fish and salt and tomatoes fill my lungs. I grab the fork and scoop up a little bit of rice. A piece of flaky white fish on top. Dip it in some salty tomato sauce.

When I take the first taste, I am overcome by visions of Cuba. Sometimes the past just won't stay put.

I realize there is something I forgot to say about Cuba, about myself.

When you live on an island, everything is the sea. You are surrounded by it and you live for it. You smell it, you eat from it, you breathe it. It is the sea that comes back to you when you are eating a piece of salt cod with tomato sauce.

You close your eyes, you smell the fish, you taste the sea.

If I think about it, I can string my life together in a chain of bodies of water.

My childhood was all about the ocean. I went to the beach every day that was warm, which was ninety percent of the time.

Sometimes we'd swim in the bay of Cojimar, and on those occasions my mother would make us wear tennis shoes because it was rocky and she didn't want us to scar our delicate feet. If we were feeling up to it, we'd drive fifteen minutes from Cojimar to Tarara, the beach right before Mi Callito in Habana del Este. I would swim, holding on to my mother's feet as she floated the day away.

Friend, me, Barbara, Dulce, and Othin on the beach at Tarara, 1960

One summer we went to Varadero. We spent a whole week walking on the white sands and swimming in miles of blue. You can walk well into the ocean and the water will still only come up to your waist. It is so clean and clear and warm. Forget St. Barts, there is no comparison to Varadero.

Later in my life I was stuck in pools. That's Los Angeles for you. There was one summer day after Dad got his license that we crossed Topanga Canyon and went swimming in Malibu. We all ran into the ocean and ran right out. The Pacific with its cold waves was not for us. We were tropical fish that needed the warmth of Varadero.

What I forgot to tell you is that every time I go to Cuba I swim at least once a day. I have to. I still love Mi Callito and the ocean pool behind the Copacabana, but it's Varadero that I long for when I'm gone.

The first time I went back to Varadero since my childhood was after the screening of *Exiles in New York* at the Havana film festival. I drove to the beach with Betty Ann, Annie, and Ed. The perfect beach of my youth.

We parked by the DuPont Mansion and I swam for four hours, unable to pull myself out of the water, Cuba's womb, the center of my soul's tranquility.

But in New York, in October, the same month I left Cuba for the very first time, I can taste the sea as if I am in it. I am sitting at a lunch counter run by Dominicans in the middle of Manhattan. But as I eat the salt cod, my taste buds do not fail me. They take me home to the Caribbean, and I am floating in the still, warm, crystal waters of Cuba.

These are the same waters I have been floating in my entire life.

[*Eduardo's Arroz con Pollo*]

I use chicken thighs for flavor and heartiness, "like Cuban chickens," as Fernando would say. Sour oranges remind me of my youth. There's red onion and bell pepper to be just a little different: like the rebellion of leaving home at sixteen. Fresh asparagus recalls my days surrounded by hippies, who never would have touched a can of cream of asparagus soup. There is plenty of saffron to meet the high-minded demands of my father, and *pimientos* and white wine to bring all the flavor and delicacy of my mother. I use Valencia rice, from Spain, to honor my family's origin, even before Oscar and Manuela and Cuca and Fernando. I am proud to say that even with all these influences, there is still one voice that comes through. This is my dish. My way. My *Arroz con Pollo*.

4 pounds bone-in chicken thighs, skin removed
½ cup sour orange juice (or ¼ cup orange juice mixed with ¼ cup lime juice)
5 teaspoons salt
1 teaspoon ground black pepper
¼ cup vegetable oil
¼ cup olive oil
2 red onions, peeled and cut into ¼-inch dice (about 1½ cups)
1 red pepper, stem and seeds removed, cut into ¼-inch dice
4 garlic cloves, peeled and finely chopped
1 cup diced tomatoes
1 gram saffron (about 4 big pinches)
1 cup white wine
2 cups Valencia (short-grain) rice
6 cups chicken broth
1 pound asparagus, stems removed, cut into 1-inch pieces, with the tips reserved
2 cups frozen peas, thawed
One 4- to 5-ounce jar *pimientos*, drained and sliced into ¼-inch strips

1. Season the chicken thighs with the sour orange juice, 2 teaspoons of the salt, and ½ teaspoon of the black pepper. Toss to coat. Cover and marinate in the refrigerator for at least 1 hour or overnight.

2. Heat the vegetable oil in a large pot or Dutch oven over high heat. Remove the chicken from the marinade and pat dry with paper towels. Fry half the chicken until golden brown, turning once, 5 minutes per side. Transfer the cooked chicken to a plate and set aside. Repeat with remaining chicken.

3. Add the olive oil to the pot along with the onions and red pepper. Season with 1 teaspoon of the remaining salt and the remaining ½ teaspoon black pepper. Cook until softened slightly, 3 minutes. Add the garlic, tomatoes, and saffron and cook, stirring, 1 minute more. Add the wine and cook until the alcohol has evaporated, scraping any caramelized bits off the bottom of the pot with a wooden spoon, 3 minutes.

Me in the ocean behind the Copacabana, Miramar, 2005

4. Add the rice, chicken broth, asparagus stalks (not the tips), and remaining 2 teaspoons of salt. Stir gently. Return the chicken parts to the pot. Bring the whole thing to a boil, then transfer to the lower third of the oven and bake, uncovered, 25 minutes. If the liquid evaporates too quickly, add a little more wine or broth.

5. Remove the pot from the oven and scatter the peas and reserved asparagus tips evenly over the surface of the rice. Garnish with *pimientos*. Return to the oven to warm through, 10 minutes more. Serve immediately.

Makes 6 servings

Acknowledgments

Thanks to our editors, Erin Moore and Jessica Sindler; our publisher, Bill Shinker; and our agents, Gillian MacKenzie and Patricia McLaughlin; for making this book happen.

Thanks to our families: Gilda Machado, Gilda Elisabeth Zimmerling, Jeanette Machado, Michelle Zimmer, Mirta Gavilan, Yolanda Sarraff, Maria Perez, Paul, Kathy, and Celene Domitrovich, George and Athena Hanzakos.

Thanks to Mark and Nancy Sertich, Sandi and Andrew Farkas, George King and Marianne King-Buschmann, and Roseann Lambros for opening their homes and kitchens to our creative processes.

Thanks to all the people who ate the food, and to our greatest supporters, Megan Smith, Nicole LaLiberté, and Connie Ramirez.

Y muchisimas gracias a nuestros amigos en Cuba: Lizette Vila, Adria Santana, Carlos Repilado, Julio Gomez, Iván Tenorio, Helmo Hernandez, y Wilfredo Benitez.

Photo Credits